CONCISE
DICTIONARY OF
ECONOMICS

A Perfect Reference for Aspirants of Civil Services,
all Competitive Examinations, and Intersted Reders

I0084667

Editorial Board

V&S PUBLISHERS

Published by:

V&S PUBLISHERS

F-2/16, Ansari road, Daryaganj, New Delhi-110002
☎ 23240026, 23240027 • Fax: 011-23240028
Email: info@vspublishers.com

Regional Office : Hyderabad
5-1-707/1, Brij Bhawan (Beside Central Bank of India Lane)
Bank Street, Koti, Hyderabad - 500 095
☎ 040-24737290
E-mail: vspublishershyd@gmail.com

Branch Office : Mumbai
Godown # 34 at The Model Co-Operative Housing, Society Ltd.,
"Sahakar Niwas", Ground Floor, Next to Sobo Central, Mumbai - 400 034
☎ 022-23510736
E-mail: vspublishersmum@gmail.com

Follow us on:

All books available at **www.vspublishers.com**

© Copyright: **V&S PUBLISHERS**
ISBN 978-93-505703-2-6
Edition: 2015

Printed at: Param Offsetters, Okhla, New Delhi

Contents

Publisher's Note

Innumerable books are available in the market on economics and allied sciences, both as a textbook and reference manual. Written for different age-groups and class, quite a number of these books come replete with jargon-filled terms; and just fail to connect with readers' inclination and curiosity level. On top of that, new words keep finding their way into the books every other day. Every new addition contributes to difficulty in comprehending the matter.

An average reader is interested only in knowing what a specific word means without getting lost with heavy sounding inputs.

Following an open-ended discussion with a cross-section of students and average readers we realized that many currently available books on economic subjects take readers' understanding for granted; and make short passing references while alluding to the term in the text. Presentations of this nature just don't assist students and other readers in understanding the subject properly. This is the principal reason why V&S Publishers thought of bringing out a dictionary in economics to give readers an idea of the essential terms needed to understand this all important vibrant subject that keeps changing with the times.

V&S Publishers has so far come out with five dictionaries of terms; in science, physics, chemistry, biology and mathematics. Dictionaries of other sought-after subjects are in the works awaiting completion and publication. All these books have been written to help readers grasp the meaning of popular terms, notations and applications. And so is this dictionary of economic terms. For easy reference terms have been arranged alphabetically. Terms that have come into the reckoning even in the late 2012 have been incorporated; and suitably explained such that an average school and college student can grasp them easily. Clear images, illustrations and examples, where appropriate, have been added. For all readers, who have not made a special study of economics as a subject, terms have been suitably explained for ease in comprehension along with appropriate appendices at the end of the book.

Economics is undergoing a 'revolution, albeit one that is difficult to get clear perspective on. The author has been selective in choosing entries so that the balance of the book is maintained at the target audience.

Some may think, the book has omitted some important entries while others may see it as having included a number of frivolous ones. To this end, all criticism and suggestions for improvement are welcome.

Introduction

Economics is the prime mover of human welfare. One way or the other, directly or indirectly every satisfaction originates out of some quantifiable activity. Read any newspaper. You would find a surfeit of topics related to material welfare occupying prominent place among news covered. New news broadcasting channels are coming up on TV exclusively devoted to economics. This growth in channels appears surprising in the face of the fact that many readers, including students consider it a dry and one of the difficult-to-understand subjects. Despite this, there is a growing tribe of interested readers trying to fathom the intricacies of 'what in essence constitutes the study of economics'. Have you noticed the clamour for 'economics' as a subject among students during the time of college and university admissions? Demand keeps increasing each passing year. Articles in newspapers and magazines these days include a good number of economic terms and if you are not at least perfunctorily aware, so to say, with them you would feel ashamed inside yourself. You would literally be forced to remain 'statue' with mouth shut. Quite an embarrassing situation! Wouldn't that be if you are the one at the receiving end? This is the principal reason why V&S Publishers thought of bringing out a dictionary in economics to prevent you from getting caught on the wrong foot.

Economics, in essence, is the science that deals with the production, distribution and consumption of wealth. It studies the various problems of land, labour, capital, interest, taxation, etc. and tries to find a solution or the best possible way to tackle these problems on the ground. The subject not only deals with the present and future growth of a country's economy at the micro level, like the consumption of a household or an individual but also studies the same at a bigger and more complex level or the macro level, like the national income or the production of an industry. GDP is one of the most important components of macroeconomics. It reflects the health of the nation and its citizens. International lending institutions sanction loans and grants according to the per capita GDP. What all factors are taken into account while calculating gross domestic product or gross national product? Where does foreign national's contribution included? Different types of employment and influence of inflation are core elements in the study of economics. The general budget shows the income and expenditure of the nation. The manner in which direct and indirect taxes are collected and distributed are major constituents of budgetary policy. International trade rules and agreements influence nations' policies. The job of the economists is to identify the economic problems of a country's economy and find solutions for the same, thereby promoting a healthy and smooth economic growth.

There are two schools of thoughts in economics, viz. the Classical and the Modern. The economists belonging to these two schools have contributed a lot in the field of economics through a number of theories. But, as the human wants are endless, so are the economic problems and therefore, economists are continuously working towards finding solutions for these new problems.

While economists explain economic activities in a language ordinarily understood by students and practitioners, there are many students who fail to comprehend as well as other interested readers who have not studied the subject are also left behind. This group needs help. And such help is made through this dictionary of economics.

The dictionary covers all that the traditional study aims at. It is made with the intent of providing the readers with a handy referral for the terminology used in the subject. The dictionary covers almost all the terms that form a part and parcel of economics in simple and easily comprehensible language. In order to enhance the readers' knowledge and bring about more relevance, many examples and graphs have been used along with the definitions of the terms.

The dictionary has been arranged alphabetically A-Z. Attempt has been made to include terms that have come into frequent use. A number of entries contain cross reference except where the word or phrase is self contained and complete in itself. To simplify understanding, graphs accompany the entry wherever considered necessary.

While every attempt has been made to keep the dictionary simple and straight forward, we go by the understanding that even the best of the books have scope for improvement. If you feel that some matter needs modification or addition to text or even deletion, please inform us of the action to be taken. We would be grateful for your contribution.

A

Ability-To-Pay Principle

A principle of taxation in which taxes are based on the income or resource-ownership of people to pay the tax. The income tax is one of the most common taxes that seeks to abide by the ability-to-pay principle. In theory, the income tax system is set up such that people with greater income pay more taxes. Proportional and progressive taxes follow this ability-to-pay principle, while regressive taxes, such as sales taxes and social security taxes, don't. The logic behind the ability-to-pay principle is that taxes are collected by the government to finance public goods that provide benefits to all members of society. And because taxes are a diversion of resources from the household to the government sector, it makes sense to tax, or divert income away from, the people who actually have the income.

Above The Line

In balance of payments accounting, this refers to those transactions that are included in calculating the balance of payments whether surplus or deficit. Transactions below the line, typically are official reserve transactions and sometimes short term capital flows, are not included.

Absolute Cost Advantage

The ability to produce a good at lower cost, in terms of real resources, than another country. In a Ricardian model, cost is in terms of only labour. Absolute advantage is neither necessary nor sufficient for a country to export a good. See comparative advantage.

Absolute Advantage Trade Policy

The idea, advocated by opponents of globalization, that a country should import only goods in which other countries have an absolute advantage, particularly goods that the importing country cannot (or cannot "reasonably") produce itself.

Absorption

1. Total demand for final goods and services by all residents (consumers, producers, and government) of a country (as opposed to total demand for that country's output). The term was introduced as part of the Absorption Approach.
2. Roll-up.

Absorption Approach

A way of understanding the determinants of the balance of trade, noting that it is equal to income minus absorption.

Abundance

A term that applies when individuals can obtain all the goods they want without cost. If a good is abundant, it is free.

Abundant

Available in large supply. Usually meaningful only in relative terms, compared to demand and/or to supply at another place or time.

Abundant Factor

The factor in a country's endowment with which it is best endowed, relative to other factors, compared to other countries. May be defined by quantity or by price.

Academic Consortium On International Trade

A group of academic economists and lawyers who are specialized in international trade policy and international economic law. ACIT's purpose is to prepare and circulate policy statements and papers that deal with important, current issues of international trade policy.

Accelerator

The causal relationship between changes in consumption and changes in investment.

Accelerator Principle

In macroeconomic models the accelerator principle relates to changes in the rate of real output growth to the level of desired investment spending (investment demand) in the economy. A decline in the rate of real GDP growth, for example, will cause the amount of investment demand to decrease (the investment demand curve will shift to the left).

Accession

The process of adding a country to an international agreement, such as the GATT, WTO, EU, or NAFTA.

Accession Country

A country that is waiting to become a member of any international agreement.

Accommodating Transaction

In the balance of payments, a transaction that is a result of actions taken officially to manage international payments; in contrast with autonomous transaction. Thus official reserve transactions are accommodating, as may be short-term capital flows that respond to expectations of intervention.

Accumulation

The acquisition of an increasing quantity of something. The accumulation of factors, especially capital, is a primary mechanism for economic growth.

Acid Rain

The precipitation of dilute solutions of strong mineral acids, formed by the mixing in the atmosphere of various industrial pollutants primarily sulphur dioxide and nitrogen oxides with naturally occurring oxygen and water vapour.

ACP Countries

A group of African, Caribbean, and Pacific less developed countries that were included in the Lomé Convention and now the Cotonou Agreement. As of June 2011, the group included 79 countries.

Acquired Endowments

Resources a country builds for itself, like a network of roads or an educated population.

Actionable Subsidy

A subsidy that is not prohibited by the WTO but that member countries are permitted to levy countervailing duties.

ACTPN
Advisory Committee on Trade Policy and Negotiations

Ad Valorem
Per unit of value (i.e., divided by the price).

Ad Valorem Duties
Defined as those duties that are established as a certain percentage of the price of the product.

Ad Valorem Equivalent
The ad valorem tariff that would be equivalent, in terms of its effects on trade, price, or some other measure, to a non tariff barrier.

Ad Valorem Tariff
Tariff defined as a percentage of the value of an imported good.

Ad Valorem Tax
A tax based on the value (or assessed value) of property. Ad valorem tax can also be levied on imported items.

Adaptive Expectations
Adaptive expectations means that people form their expectations about what will happen in the future based on what has happened in the past. For example, if inflation has been higher than expected in the past, people would revise expectations for the future.

ADB
1. African Development Bank Group.
2. Asian Development Bank

ADD
Anti-dumping duty.

Adding-Up Problem
The concern that if several developing countries expand their exports of the same good simultaneously, then the price of that good in world markets will fall worsening their terms of trade, perhaps lowering their export revenues and real incomes as a result.

Adjustable Peg
An exchange rate that is pegged, but for which it is understood that the par value will be changed occasionally. This system can be subject to extreme speculative attack and financial crisis, since speculators may easily anticipate these changes.

Adjusted For Inflation
Corrected for price changes to yield an equivalent in terms of goods and services. The adjustment divides nominal amounts for different years by price indices for those years e.g. the CPI or the implicit price deflator and multiplies by 100. This converts to real values, i.e. valued at the prices of the base year for the price index.

Adjusted R-Squared
A goodness-of-fit measure in multiple regression analysis that penalises additional explanatory variables by using a degrees of freedom adjustment in estimating the error variance.

Adjustment Assistance
Government programme to assist those workers and/or firms whose industry has declined, either due to competition from imports (trade adjustment assistance) or from other causes. Such programmes usually have two (conflicting) goals: to lessen hardship for those affected, and to help them change their behaviour — what, how, or where they produce.

Adjustment Cost
The cost — temporary but sometimes severe — incurred by a person or firm in moving from one equilibrium

to another. Many of the costs associated with trade liberalization are adjustment costs and are not accounted for in the usual measures of gains from trade.

Adjustment Mechanism

The theoretical process by which a market changes in disequilibrium, moving toward equilibrium if the process is stable. .

Administered Price

A price for a good or service that is set and maintained by government, usually requiring accompanying restrictions on trade if the administered price differs from the world price.

Administered Protection

Protection (tariff or NTB) resulting from the application of any one of several statutes that respond to specified market circumstances or events, usually determined by an administrative agency. Several such statutes are permitted under the GATT, including anti-dumping duties, countervailing duties, and safeguards protection.

Administrative Agency

A unit of government charged with the administration of particular laws. In the United States, those most important for administering laws related to international trade are the ITC and ITA.

Administrative Entry Procedure

Formalities required to bring a product into a country. If these are unnecessarily difficult or time consuming, they constitute a nontariff barrier.

Administrative Guidance

In the context of trade policy, this usually refers to an informal system of Japanese industrial policy, called gyosei-shido, where official pronouncements serve as guidelines for domestic businesses.

Advance Deposit Requirement

A requirement that some proportion of the value of imports, or of import duties, be deposited prior to payment, without competitive interest being paid.

Advanced Country

A developed country or "more developed country" (MDC), is a sovereign state that has a highly developed economy and advanced technological infrastructure relative to other less developed nations. Most commonly the criteria for evaluating the degree of economic development is gross domestic product (GDP), the per capita income, level of industrialization, amount of widespread infrastructure and general standard of living. Which criteria are to be used and which countries can be classified as being developed are subjects of debate.

Advantage

Usually refers to a cost advantage, though it could refer to a strategic advantage (such as first mover advantage) or to a superiority of technology or quality.

Adverse Selection

principle that says that those who most want to buy insurance tend to be those most at risk, but charging a high price for insurance (to cover the high risk) will discourage those at less risk from buying insurance at all. Adverse selection arises when a negotiation between two people with asymmetric information restricts the quality of the good traded. This typically happens because the person with more information can negotiate a favourable exchange. This is frequently referred to as the "market for lemons.".

Adverse Terms Of Trade

A terms of trade that is considered unfavourable relative to some benchmark or to past experience. Developing countries specialized in primary products are sometimes said to suffer from adverse or declining terms of trade.

Advisory Committee On Trade Policy and Negotiations

The highest-level of several committees that advise USTR on trade policy and trade negotiations. This one includes representatives of private-sector businesses, trade associations, unions, state and local governments, and other organizations.

AEC

1. African Economic Community.
2. ASEAN Economic Community

African Development Bank Group

A multinational development bank for Africa.

African Economic Community

An organization of African countries that aims to promote economic, cultural and social development among the African economies. Among other things, it intends to promote the formation of FTAs and customs unions among regional groups within Africa that will eventually merge into an African Common Market.

African Growth And Opportunity Act

It is a U.S. legislation enacted May 2000 providing tariff preferences, as well as trade facilitation and technical assistance to African producers, to

African countries that qualify. As of August 2012, 41 countries had been declared eligible.

AG

Comparable to "Inc" in the U.S. and Ltd in the U.K., this abbreviation for the German*Aktiengesellschaft* indicates a limited-liability corporation.

Agenda 21

A plan of action adopted at the Rio Summit to promote sustainable development.

Agent

1. An entity within the economy that makes economic decisions and engages on economic activity. Used to refer to individual consumers, households, and firms.
2. One who acts on behalf of someone else.
3. In Principal-Agent Theory, the person whose job it is to act to the benefit of someone else (the principal), but who may require some incentive to do so.

Agglomeration

The phenomenon of economic activity congregating in or close to a single location, rather than being spread out uniformly over space.

Agglomeration Economy

Any benefit that accrues to economic agents as a result of having large numbers of other agents geographically close to them, thus tending to lead to agglomeration. This is a basic feature of the New Economic Geography.

Aggregate

As an adjective or noun (with stress on the first syllable), this refers to the sum or total of multiple items. As a verb (with stress on the last syllable), this means to combine such items or add them up.

Aggregate Demand

Aggregate demand is the total spending on goods and services in the economy.
AD = C + I + G + (X - M).

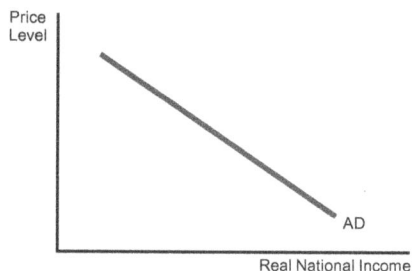

The aggregate demand curve is made up of a series of separate curves giving the level of consumption, investment, government expenditure and the net level of exports. This Keynesian aggregate demand curve is upward sloping as the level of expenditure will tend to increase as income increases. How much this happens depends on the marginal propensity to consume.

Aggregate Demand Curve

In macroeconomic theory the aggregate demand curve relates to the level of real national income (GDP) demanded (the total quantity of goods and services demanded) to the price level (as measured by the GDP deflator).

Aggregate Expenditure

In macroeconomic theory aggregate expenditure is the total amount of desired spending by consumers, governments, private investors and foreign buyers (net of spending on imports) at each level of real national income (GDP).

Aggregate Expenditures Schedule

A curve that traces out the relationship between expenditures—the sum of consumption, investment, government expenditures, and net exports—and the national income, at a fixed price level.

Aggregate Measure Of Support

The measurement of subsidy to agriculture used by the WTO as the basis for commitments to reduce the subsidization of agricultural products. It includes the value of price supports and direct subsidies to specific products, as well as payments that are not product specific.

Aggregate Production Possibility Frontier

The production possibility frontier, or curve obtained by adding the production possibilities of two or more countries or regions.

Aggregate Supply

The total supply of a country's output, usually assumed to be an increasing function of its price level in the short run but independent of the price level in the long run.

Aggregate Supply Curve

In macroeconomic theory the short run aggregate supply curve relates to the total quantity of goods and services supplied and the price level (as measured by the GDP deflator). The long run aggregate supply curve is a vertical line at the full employment (capacity output) level of real national income (GDP).

Aggregate Transformation Curve

Aggregate production possibility frontier.

Aggregation

The combining of two or more kinds of an economic entity into a single category. Data on international trade necessarily aggregate goods and services into manageable groups. For macroeconomic purposes, all goods and services are usually aggregated into just one.

Agrarian Reform

Change in the policies affecting agriculture, usually including redistribution of land and sometimes also changes in other policies related to the inputs and outputs of agriculture. Agreement On Textiles And Clothing is a 10-year transitional programme of the WTO to phase out the quotas on textiles and apparel of the MFA.

Agreement On Trade In Civil Aircraft

A plurilateral agreement within the WTO eliminating duties on aircraft (except military) and aircraft parts. It includes disciplines on government procurement and inducements to purchase. As of August 2012 it had 31 signatories.

Agricultural Good

A good that is produced by agriculture.

Agricultural Terms of Trade

The prices of agricultural outputs relative to the prices of agricultural inputs. If agricultural output prices rise relative to input prices, we say that there is a positive agricultural terms of trade effect.

Agriculture

Production that relies essentially on the growth and nurturing of plants and animals, especially for food, usually with land as an important input; farming.

Agriculture Agreement

The agreement within the WTO that commits member governments to improve market accessand reduce trade-distorting subsidies in agriculture, starting with the process of tariffication.

Aid

Assistance provided by countries and by international institutions such as the World Bank todeveloping countries in the form of monetary grants, loans at low interest rates, in kind, or a combination of these.

Aid For Trade

The strategy of promoting economic development by helping countries to create or improve infrastructure needed to facilitate international trade. This was one of the intended components of the Doha Round negotiations, and was institutionalized in a WTO work programme on Aid-for-Trade in the Hong Kong Ministerial Conclave.

Airbus

Airbus, a subsidiary of EADS, is a company producing aircraft in Europe. It was originally backed by a consortium of four companies from four countries (France, Germany, Spain, and the U.K.) and their governments. That backing has been one of the subjects of the Boeing-Airbus Dispute.

Alchian-Allen Theorem

The proposition, due to Alchian and Allen (1964), that when the same absolute cost (as for transportation) is added to the prices of a low-price, low-quality good and a high-price, high-quality good, the relative demand for the latter will increase, since it's relative price falls. Summarized as "shipping the good apples out," the result has been confirmed in international trade by Hummels and Skiba (2004).

Allocation

An assignment of economic resources to uses. Thus, in general equilibrium, an assignment off actors to industries producing goods and services, together with the assignment of resulting final goods and services to consumers, within a country or throughout the world economy.

Allocative Efficiency

Refers to whether or not an allocation is efficient. A change from an allocation that is not efficient, to one that is, may be termed an "increase" in allocative efficiency.

Alternative Cost

The value of the product that particular resources could have produced had they been used in the best alternative way; also called opportunity cost.

Alternative Hypothesis

The hypothesis against which the null hypothesis is tested.

Alternative Minimum Tax

An IRS mechanism created to ensure that high-income individuals, corporations, trusts, and estates pay at least some minimum amount of tax, regardless of deductions, credits or exemptions. Alternative minimum tax operates by adding certain tax-preference items back into adjusted gross income. While it was once only important for a small number of high-income individuals who made extensive use of tax shelters and deductions, more and more people are being affected by it. The AMT is triggered when there are large numbers of personal exemptions on state and local taxes paid, large numbers of miscellaneous itemized deductions or medical expenses, or by Incentive Stock Option (ISO) plans.

Alternative Trade Adjustment Assistance

An addition to the US programme of trade adjustment assistance, enacted in 2002, that provides wage insurance for a limited group of older workers.

Alternatives

Options among which to make choices.

Amber Box

The category of subsidies in the WTO the total value of which is to be reduced. The term is used primarily in the Agriculture Agreement and includes most domestic support measures that distort production and trade. Also called orange box.

Ambient Charge

A form of tax on non uniformly mixed pollutants. It is calculated to be the same in terms of the emission's impact on ambient environmental quality at some receptor site. As a result, an ambient charge to a firm closer to the receptor site will normally be higher per kg than that charged to firms further away.

American Enterprise Institute

American Enterprise Institute for Public Policy Research is a think tank doing research and writing on "issues of government, politics, economics, and social welfare," including international economics. Politically, it is somewhat right-of-centre, providing a home for US Republicans when not in government. Contrasts with the Brookings Institution.

Amicus Brief

A document filed in a legal proceeding by an interested party who is not directly part of the case. In the WTO an issue has been whether to permit dispute settlement panels to accept such submissions, especially from NGOs.

Amortization

The deduction of an expense in installments over a period of time, rather than all at once.

Amplitude

The extent of the up and down movements of a fluctuating economic variable; that is, the difference between the highest and lowest values of the variable.

AMS

Aggregate measure of support.

Ancerta

Australia-New Zealand Closer Economic Relations Trade Agreement. Also ANZCERTA and just CER.

Andean Community

An organization currently of four Andean countries — Bolivia, Colombia, Ecuador, and Peru, — formed in 1997 out of the Andean Pact (Venezuela ceased membership in 2006). It provides for economic and social integration, including regional trade liberalization and a common external tariff, as well as harmonization of other policies.

Andean Pact

The Cartagena Agreement of 1969, which provided for economic cooperation among a group of five Andean countries; predecessor to the Andean Community.

Andean Trade Promotion And Drug Eradication Act

US legislation enacted in 2002 authorizing the U.S. president to provide tariff preferences to countries in the Andean region in connection with the effort to curtail production of illegal drugs.

Annecy Round

The second (1949) of the trade rounds conducted under the auspices of the GATT.

Annuity

A fixed amount paid once a year or at interval of a stipulated period.

Ante Date

To give a date prior to that on which it is written, to any cheque, bill or any other document.

Anti-Competitive

Contributing to market power and associated behaviour, especially including prices above those that would occur with perfect competition. Anti-Counterfeiting Trade Agreement is a plurilateral agreement signed October 1, 2011, to combat the "proliferation of commercial-scale counterfeiting and piracy" in the realm of intellectual property.

Anti-Dumping Duty

Tariff levied on dumped imports. The threat of an anti-dumping duty can deter imports, even when it has not been used, and anti-dumping law is therefore a form of nontariff barrier.

Anti-Dumping Suit

A complaint by a domestic producer that imports are being dumped, and the resulting investigation if dumping and injury are found, the country can impose anti-dumping duty.

Anti-Trust Laws

Designed to promote open markets by limiting practices that reduce competition.

Anti-Trust Policy

U.S. term for competition policy, motivated by it's initial purpose of breaking up trusts.

Apparel

Clothing. The apparel sector is important for trade because, as a very labour intensive sector, it is a likely source of comparative advantage for developing countries. See textiles and apparel.

Apparent Consumption

Production plus imports minus exports, sometimes also adjusted for changes in inventories. The intention here is not to distinguish different uses for a good within the country, but only to infer the total that is used there for any purpose.

Appellate Body

The standing committee of the WTO that reviews decisions of dispute settlement panels.

Appellation Of Origin

A geographical indication.

Applied Tariff Rate

The actual tariff rate in effect at a country's border.

Appreciation

A rise in the value of a country's currency on the exchange market, relative either to a particular currency or to a weighted average of other currencies. The currency is said to appreciate. Opposite of "depreciation."

Appreciation Of Money

It is a rise in the value of money caused by a fall in the general price fall.

Appropriate Level Of Protection

In the SPS Agreement of the WTO, the acceptable level of risk to health that WTO members are entitled to pursue through SPS measures.

Appropriation Bill

It is a bill that authorizes payment and appropriation of expenses from the Consolidated Fund. This bill is introduced only after the general discussion on budget proposals and the completion of voting on grants. The procedure to pass the bill in parliament is like other money bills.

Aquifer

An aquifer is an underground layer of water-bearing permeable rock or unconsolidated materials (gravel, sand, or silt) from which groundwater can be extracted using a water well. The study of water flow in aquifers and the characterization of aquifers is called hydrogeology. Related terms include aquitard, which is a bed of low permeability along an aquifer, and aquiclude (or aquifuge), which is a solid, impermeable area underlying or overlying an aquifer. If the impermeable area overlies the aquifer, pressure could cause it to become a confined aquifer.

AR(L) Serial Correlation

The errors in a time series regression model follow an AR(L) model.

Arab League

Informal name of the League of Arab States.

Arbitrage

A combination of transactions designed to profit from an existing discrepancy among prices, exchange rates, and/or interest rates on different markets without risk of these changing. Simplest is simultaneous purchase and sale of the same thing in different markets, but more complex forms include triangular arbitrage and covered interest arbitrage.

Arbitration
A method for solving disputes, generally of an industrial nature, between the employer and his employees.

Arc Elasticity Of Demand
If P_i and Q_i are the first values of price and quantity demanded, and P_z and Q_z are the second values, then arc elasticity equals - $[(Q_1 - Q_2)/(Q_i + Q_{.z})]/[(P_1 - P_2)|(P_1 + P_2)]$.

Argument For Protection
A reason given (not necessarily a good one) for restricting imports by tariffs and/or NTBs.

Armington Assumption
The assumption that internationally traded products are differentiated by country of origin. Due to Armington (1969) in an international macroeconomic context, but now a standard assumption of international CGE models, used to generate smaller and more realistic responses of trade to price changes than implied by homogeneous products.

Armington Elasticity
The elasticity of substitution between products of different countries.

Arm's Length Price
The of a product in a transaction between unrelated buyer and seller. Contrasts with transfer price.

Arrangement On Export Credits
A "gentlemen's agreement" among governments of the OECD to limit the generosity of the terms and conditions of export credits that they provide.

Article
A specific section of a negotiated agreement.

Article XIX
The Safeguards Clause of the GATT.

Article XXIV
The article of the GATT that permits countries to form free trade areas and customs unions as exceptions to the MFN principle.

As-Ad
The model and/or diagram that determines the level of aggregate economic activity through the interaction of aggregate supply and aggregate demand.

Asean Economic Community
The goal of ASEAN to become fully integrated economically by 2015, achieving a single market and other objectives.

Asean Free Trade Area
A free trade area announced in 1992 among the ASEAN countries that is in the process of being implemented. It does not quite meet the the normal definition of an FTA, however, in that tariffs on imports from members are not necessarily zero, but rather given by the common effective preferential tariff.

Asean Plus Six
The group of countries included in ASEAN include China, Japan, South Korea, India, Australia, and New Zealand. This group has met occasionally to pursue cooperation.

Asean Plus Three
The group of countries included in ASEAN include China, Japan, and South Korea. Since 1997, this group has met periodically to pursue many areas of cooperation.

Asian Crisis

A major financial crisis that began in Thailand in July 1997 and quickly spread to other East Asian countries.

Asian Development Bank

A multilateral institution based in Manila, Philippines, that provides financing for development needs in countries of the Asia-Pacific region. As of August 2012, ADB reported having 67 member countries, of which 48 were within Asia.

Asia-Pacific Economic Cooperation

An organization of countries in the Asia-Pacific region, launched in 1989 and devoted to promoting open trade and practical economic cooperation. As of August 2012, APEC had 21 member countries.

Asset

Anything of monetary value that is owned by a person. Assets include real property, personal property, and enforceable claims against others (including bank accounts, stocks, mutual funds, and so on).

Asset Approach

A theory of determination of the exchange rate that focuses on its role as the price of an asset. With high capital mobility, equilibrium requires that expected returns on comparable domestic and foreign assets be the same.

Assets

Assets are economic resources. Anything tangible or intangible that is capable of being owned or controlled to produce value and that is held to have positive economic value is considered an asset. Simply stated, assets represent value of ownership that can be converted into cash

(although cash itself is also considered an asset).

Assimilative Capacity

The extent to which the environment can accommodate or tolerate pollutants.

Assist

A service or other input to production provided by an importer to the foreign exporter, the value of which must be added to the invoice price in calculating its value for customs purposes.

Assistance In Kind

public assistance that provides particular goods and services, like food or medical care, rather than cash.

Association Agreement

Early predecessor to the Europe Agreements but excluding provision for political dialogue.

Association Of Caribbean States

A group of 25 countries of the Caribbean that signed a convention in 1994 to foster "consultation, cooperation and concerted action."

Association Of Natural Rubber Producing Countries

An inter-governmental organization, formed by natural rubber producing countries to promote the overall interests of the commodity.

Association Of Southeast Asian Nations

An organization of countries in southeast Asia, the purpose of which is to promote economic, social, and cultural development as well as peace and stability in the region. Starting with five member countries in 1967, it had expanded to ten members as of August 2012.

ASWP

Any safe world port. Meaning that the product offered with this designation will be delivered to essentially anywhere in the world.

Asymmetric Information

a situation in which the parties to a transaction have different information, as when the seller or a used car has more information about its quality then the buyer. The economics of information search tells us that everyone falls short of having perfect information. It suggests that everyone will have different information about different things. For example, if you aren't a plumber (nor have any desire to become one), then you aren't likely to seek information about the wages paid to plumbers in Boise, Idaho. In contrast, this information could be quite beneficial to plumbers in Pocatello, Idaho. Asymmetric Information for the market occurs when buyers and sellers have different information about a good. Sellers often have better information about a good than buyers because they are more familiar with it. They know more about it's quality, durability, and other features. Buyers, in contrast, have limited contact with the commodity and thus have less information. For example, if you sell a car that you've owned for several years, you know how well it's been maintained, whether or not it needs frequent repairs, and what causes that strange "clanking" sound. A buyer who test drives the car for only a few miles is likely to be unaware of these facts. Another common example of asymmetric Information is in the labour market. Workers are knowledgeable about their skills, industriousness, and productivity. Employers, in contrast, have limited information about the quality of prospective workers.

Asymmetric Shock

An exogenous change in macroeconomic conditions affecting differently the different parts of a country, or different countries of a region. Often mentioned as a source of difficulty for countries sharing a common currency, such as the Euro Zone.

At Par

At equality. Two currencies are said to be "at par" if they are trading one-for-one. The significance is more psychological then economic, but the long decline of the Canadian dollar "below par" with the U.S. dollar, and the more recent variation of the euro between above and below par, also with the U.S. dollar, has been cause for concern.

Atlantic Council

An organization based in Washington, DC, that seeks to promote leadership and engagement in international affairs.

Atlas Method

The method used by the World Bank for comparison of national incomes (GNI or GNP) across countries. It essentially uses nominal exchange rates averaged over three years with adjustment for inflation at home and abroad.

Attenuation Bias

Bias in an estimator that is always toward zero; thus, the expected value of an estimator with attenuation bias is less in magnitude than the absolute value of the parameter.

Attrition

The decline in employment in a firm or industry that occurs naturally due to workers' quitting or retiring. The pain of shrinking an industry due, say, to trade liberalization is minimized if it can be accomplished through attrition. In the UK, attrition is called natural wastage.

Auction Quota

An import quota that is allocated by selling the rights to the highest bidder. The auction pricethen provides a market-determined measure of the quota's ad valorem equivalent.

Australia-New Zealand Closer Economic Relations Trade Agreement

A free trade agreement formed in 1983 between Australia and New Zealand. Said to be one of the most comprehensive bilateral free trade agreements in the world, it was also the first to include trade in services. Identified as ANCERTA, ANZCERTA, and CER.

Autarky

The situation of not engaging in international trade; self-sufficiency. (Not to be confused with "autarchy," which in at least some dictionaries is a political term rather than an economic one, and means absolute rule or power.)

Autarky Equilibrium

In a model of an economy, the configuration of prices and quantities at which quantities supplied and demanded within the economy are equal, so that no trade would take place even if it were permitted.

Autarky Price

Price in autarky; that is, the price of something within a country when it is not traded by that country. Relative autarky prices turn out to be the most theoretically robust (but empirically elusive) measures of comparative advantage.

Automated Commercial Environment

ACE is an online system developed by U.S. Customs and Border Protection to process international trade.

Automatic Licensing

The licensing of imports or exports for which licenses are assured, for gathering information, or as a holdover from when licenses were not automatic. Depending on how the licensing is administered, automatic licensing can add to the bureaucratic and/or time cost of trade.

Automatic Stabilizer

Government spending programmes which respond to changes in the level of national income in such a way as to offset those changes. For example, unemployment insurance benefits typically rise when the economy enters a recession, and decline when prosperity returns.

Automaticity

The feature of the WTO dispute settlement mechanism whereby panel reports are adopted (subject to review by the Appellate Body) automatically unless blocked by a unanimous vote of the membership. Under the prior GATT, unanimity was required to adopt, rather than reject, panel reports.

Autonomous

Refers to an economic variable, magnitude, or entity that is caused independently of other variables that it may in turn influence; exogenous.

Autonomous Consumption

That portion of consumption that is autonomous. For example, if the consumption function has the form $C=C_0+cY$, where C_0 and c are parameters and Y is income, then C_0 may be called autonomous consumption. An increase in autonomous consumption then represents an upward shift in the consumption function.

Autonomous Transaction

In the balance of payments, a transaction that is not itself a result of actions taken officially to manage international payments; in contrast with accommodating transaction.

Autoregressive Process Of Order One [AR(L)]

A time series model whose current value depends linearly on its most recent value plus an unpredictable disturbance.

Auxiliary Regression

A regression used to compute a test statistic-such as the test statistics for heteroskedasticity and serial correlation or any other regression that does not estimate the model of primary interest.

Availability Theory

A theory of the determinants of international trade, due to Kravis (1956), that says that countries import what they do not have available domestically and export what they do. The theory can be said to encompass explanations of trade that stress factor endowments, technological differences, and product differentiation.

Average Cost

The average cost is computed by dividing the total cost of goods available for sale by the total units available for sale. This gives a weighted-average unit cost that is applied to the units in the ending inventory. There are two commonly used average cost methods: Simple Weighted-average cost method and moving-average cost method.

Average Fixed Cost

In the theory of the firm fixed costs are costs of production which are constant whatever the level of output. Average fixed costs are total fixed costs divided by the number of units of output, that is, fixed cost per unit of output.

Average Product

The average product of a factor in a firm or industry is its output divided by the amount of the factor employed.

Average Productivity

Total quantity divided by the total quantity of input.

Average Propensity

The fraction of total income spent on an activity, such as consumption or imports.

Average Propensity To Consume

The fraction of total (or perhaps disposable) income spent on consumption. Contrasts with marginal propensity to consume.

Average Propensity To Import

The fraction of total income spent on imports; thus the ratio of imports to GDP. Contrasts withmarginal propensity to import.

Average Propensity To Save

The average propensity to save (APS), also known as the savings ratio, is an economics term that refers to the proportion of income which is saved, usually expressed for household savings as a percentage of total household disposable income. The ratio differs considerably over time and between countries. The savings ratio can be affected by (for example): the proportion of older people, as they have less motivation and capability to save; the rate of inflation, as expectations of rising prices can encourage people to spend now rather than later (monetary base/mass depreciation).

Average Revenue And Marginal Revenue

Average revenue is the level of total revenue divided by output. Marginal revenue is the revenue that the firm receives for the next unit of output.

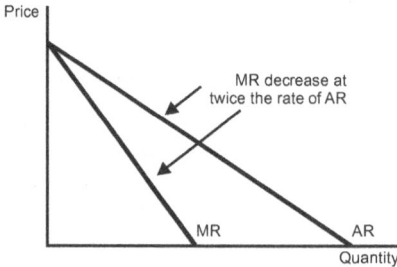

The average revenue curve is the demand curve that the firm faces. It shows the quantity that will be demanded at each price level. The marginal revenue curve shows how much extra revenue the firm will get from selling one more unit. The MR curve will always slope downwards at twice the rate of the AR curve.

Average Revenue Product

In the theory of factor pricing, average revenue product is total revenue divided by the number of units of the factor employed.

Average Tariff

An average of a country's tariff rates. This can be calculated in several ways, none of which are ideal for representing how protective the country's tariffs are. Most common is the trade-weighted average tariff, which under-represents prohibitive tariffs, since they get zero weight.

Average Tax Rate

The amount paid as tax as a fraction of the amount being taxed. In the case of an income tax, the total amount of tax as a fraction of total income.

Average Total Cost

is the sum of all the production costs divided by the number of units produced.

Average Variable Cost

Total variable cost divided by the quantity of output. (MY) (AVC) = variable (short-run) cost per unit output. In the LR, all factor costs are variable (HHC).

Axes

The fixed lines on a graph which carry the scales against which the coordinates are plotted.

B

Backward Bending

Refers to a curve that reverses direction, usually if, after moving out away from an origin or axis, it then turns back toward it. The term is used most frequently to describe supply curves for which the quantity supplied declines as price rises above some point, as may happen in a labour supply curve, the supply curve for foreign exchange, or an offer curve.

Backward Indexation

The setting of wages based, in part, on past performance of prices.

Backward Integration

Acquisition by a firm of its suppliers.

Backward Linkage

The use by one firm or industry of produced inputs from another firm or industry.

Backward-Bending Supply Of Labour

In some circumstances it may be possible for the labour supply curve to become backward-bending as people become less willing to work at higher wage levels. As wages increase above a certain point less work will actually be done as work is an inferior good and leisure becomes more highly valued at the margins. The income effect has gradually become opposite to the substitution effect and starts to outweigh it at a wage level of W2.

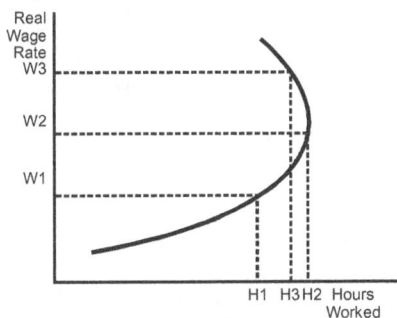

Baffling Pigs And Duks

Acronyms for the 12 original members and non-members of the Euro Zone. BAFFLING PIGS = Belgium, Austria, Finland, France, Luxembourg, Ireland, Netherlands, Germany, Portugal, Italy, Greece, and Spain. DUKS = Denmark, United Kingdom, and Sweden.

Bailout

The provision, usually by a government, of funds to a firm or to another government in danger of insolvency so as to prevent them from defaulting on their debt.

Balance Of Agricultural Trade

The value of agricultural exports less the value of agricultural imports. If agricultural export value is higher than agricultural import value, there is a positive agricultural balance of trade. This concept is the counterpart of a general balance of trade specific to agriculture.

Balance Of Merchandise Trade

The value of a country's merchandise exports minus the value of its merchandise imports.

Balance Of Payments

1. A list, or accounting, of all of a country's international transactions for a given time period, usually one year. Payments into the country (receipts) are entered as positive numbers, called credits; payments out of the country (payments) are entered as negative numbers called debits.

2. A single number summarizing all of a country's international transactions: the balance of payments surplus.

Balance Of Payments Accounts

A record of all transactions involving a country's exports and imports of goods and services, borrowing and lending.

Balance Of Payments Adjustment Mechanism

Any process, especially any automatic one, by which a country with a payments imbalance moves toward balance of payments equilibrium. Under the gold standard, this was the specie flow mechanism.

Balance Oof Payments Argument For Protection

A common reason for restricting imports, especially under fixed exchange rates, when a country is losing international reserves due to a trade deficit. It can be said that this is a second best argument, since a devaluation could solve the problem

without distorting the economy and therefore at smaller economic cost.

Balance Of Payments Deficit

A negative balance of payments surplus.

Balance Of Payments Equilibrium

Meaningful only under a pegged exchange rate, this referred to equality of credits and debits in the balance of payments using a traditional definition of the capital account. A surplus or deficiti mplied changing official reserves, so that something might ultimately have to change.

Balance Of Payments Surplus

A number summarizing the state of a country's international transactions, usually equal to the balance on current account plus the balance on financial account, but excluding official reserve transactions, or omitting also other volatile short-term financial-account transactions. It indicates the stress on a regime of pegged exchange rates.

Balance Of Trade

The value of a country's exports minus the value of its imports. Unless specified as the balance of merchandise trade, it normally incorporates trade in services, including earnings (interest, dividends, etc.) on financial assets.

Balance Of Trade (Or Payment)

The difference between the visible exports and visible imports of two countries in trade with each other is called balance of payment. If the difference is positive the balance of payment (BOP) is called favourable and if negative it is called unfavourable.

Balance On Capital Account

A country's receipts minus payments for capital account transactions.

Balance On Current Account

A country's receipts minus payments for current account transactions. Equals The balance of trade plus net inflows of transfer payments.

Balance Sheet

It is a statement of accounts, generally of a business concern, prepared at the end of a year, showing debits and credits under broad heads, to find out the profit and loss position.

Balanced Budget

1. A government budget surplus that is zero, thus with net tax revenue equaling expenditure.
2. A balanced budget change in policy or behaviour is one in which a component of the government budget, usually taxes, is adjusted as necessary to maintain a balanced budget.

Balanced Growth

Growth of an economy in which all aspects of it, especially factors of production, grow at the same rate.

Balanced Trade

1. A balance of trade equal to zero.
2. The assumption that the balance of trade must be zero in equilibrium, as would be the case with a floating exchange rate and no capital flows. This is a standard assumption in real models of international trade, which exclude financial assets.

Balassa-Samuelson Effect

The hypothesis that increase in productivity of tradables relative to nontradables, if more than abroad, will cause appreciation of the real exchange rate and thus the Penn Effect. Due toBalassa (1964) and Samuelson (1964); also Harrod (1933), and thus called the Harrod-Balassa-Samuelson Effect.

Baldwin Envelope

The consumption possibility frontier for a large country, constructed as the envelope formed by moving the foreign offer curve along the country's transformation curve.

Baltic Dry Index

An index of the rates charged for chartering large ships that transport coal, iron ore, and grain. It is regarded as a useful indicator of the current level of world trade.

Banana War

A trade dispute between the EU and the U.S. over EU preferences for bananas from former colonies. On behalf of U.S.-owned companies exporting bananas from South America and the Caribbean, the U.S. complained to the WTO, which ruled in favour of the U.S.

Bancor

The international currency proposed by Keynes for use as the basis for the international monetary system that was being constructed at the end of World War II. Instead, the Bretton Woods System that emerged was based on the U.S. dollar.

Bank For International Settlements

An international organization that acts as a bank for central banks, fostering cooperation among them and with other agencies.

Bank Rate

Bank rate, also referred to as the discount rate, is the rate of interest which a central bank charges on the loans and advances to a commercial bank. Whenever a bank has a shortage of funds they can typically borrow it from the central bank based on the monetary policy of the country.

Bank, Commercial

A financial institution accepts cheque deposits, holds savings, sells traveller's cheques and performs other financial services.

Banker's Cheque

A cheque by one bank on another.

Bankruptcy

The legal process that a person or firm goes through if they are unable to pay their debts. The process seeks an orderly sharing of the losses by creditors and a chance to start fresh, usually after some delay, for the debtor. No such process exists for national governments or countries, exacerbating the problems of debt crisis and financial crisis.

Banque Ouest Africaine De Developpement

The West African Development Bank, BOAD serves as a development bank for Bénin, Burkina, Côte d'Ivoire, Guinée Bissau, Mali, Niger, Sénégal, and Togo.

Barrier

1. Any impediment to the international movement of goods, services, capital, or other factors of production. Most commonly a trade barrier.
2. An entry barrier.

Barriers To Entry

Factors that prevent firms from entering a market, such as government rules or patents.

Barriers To Entry

Factors that prevent firms from entering a market, such as government rules or patents.

Barter

Barter is a system of exchange by which goods or services are directly exchanged for other goods or services without using a medium of exchange, such as money. It is usually bilateral, but may be multilateral, and usually exists parallel to monetary systems in most developed countries, though to a very limited extent. Barter usually replaces money as the method of exchange in times of monetary crisis, such as when the currency may be either unstable (e.g., hyperinflation or deflationary spiral) or simply unavailable for conducting commerce.

Barter Economy

An economic model of international trade in which goods are exchanged for goods without the existence of money. Most theoretical trade models take this form in order to abstract from macroeconomic and monetary considerations.

Barter System

System where there is an exchange of goods without involving money.

Barter Terms Of Trade

Can refer to either the net barter terms of trade or the gross barter terms of trade, which are equal under balanced trade. Term was introduced by Taussing (1927).

Base Group

The group represented by the overall intercept in a multiple regression model that includes dummy explanatory variables.

Base Year

The year used as the basis for comparison by a price index such as the CPI. The index for any year is the average of prices for that year compared to the base year; e.g., 110 means that prices are 10% higher than in the base year. The base year is also the year whose prices are used to value something in real terms or after adjusting for inflation.

Basel Capital Accord

Also known at Basel I, this was an agreement in 1988 by the Basel Committee of central bankers to measure the credit risk of commercial banks and set minimum standards for bank capital in order to reduce the likelihood of international repercussions due to bank failures.

Basel II

A substantially revised set of standards for capital adequacy of banks, with an agreed text first issued in June 2004.

Basic Balance

One of the more frequently used measures of the balance of payments surplus or deficit underpegged exchange rates, the basic balance was equal to the current account balance plus the balance of long-term capital flows.

Basic Competitive Model

The model of the economy that pulls together the assumptions of self-interested consumers, profit maximizing firms, and perfectly competitive markets.

Basis Point

One one-hundredth of a percentage point. Small changes in interest rates are commonly measured in basis points.

Bastable's Test

One of two conditions needed for infant industry protection to be welfare-improving, this requires that the protected industry be able to pay back an amount equal to the national losses during the period of protection.

BEA

Bureau of Economic Analysis

Beachhead Effect

The idea that if costs of entering a market, such as through exports, become sunk costs, then a temporary change in market conditions such as an exchange rate can cause a lasting change in trade patterns. As one explanation for hysteresis in international trade, this was named by Baldwin (1988).

Bear

An investor with a pessimistic market outlook; an investor who expects prices to fall and so sells now in order to buy later at a lower price. A Bear Market is one which is trending downwards or losing value.

Bearer

This term on cheques and bills denotes that any person holding the same has the same right in respect of it, as the person who issued it.

Beef Hormone Case

A trade dispute that began in 1989 when the EC banned imports of beef from cows that had been injected with growth hormones, arguing that the health effects of these hormones were suspect. The U.S. eventually complained under the WTO in 1996, arguing the absence of scientific evidence of any harm, and in 1997 the WTO panel agreed with the U.S.

Beggar Thy Neighbour

For a country to use a policy for its own benefit that harms other countries. Examples are optimal tariffs and, in a recession, tariffs and/or devaluation to create employment.

Behind The Border Barriers

This refers to a variety of nontariff barriers that operate inside countries rather than at the border, but that nonetheless can restrict trade. Examples include technical barriers to trade, labeling requirements, and sanitary & phytosanitary regulations.

Bell Trade Act

Enacted by the US Congress in 1946, this specified economic conditions for Philippine independence from the US, including the exchange rate, access to resources, and trade barriers. Some of this was revised in the Laurel-Langley Agreement.

Benefit

The gain received from voluntary exchange.

Benefit-Cost Analysis

An economically based tool designed to inform decision makers who try to achieve the highest level (or at least higher levels) of total surplus. Calculating total benefits net of total costs is equivalent to calculating the sum of producer and consumer surplus. Benefits net of costs are maximized where marginal benefits equal marginal costs-a condition that is satisfied by equilibrium in a perfectly competitive market.

Benefits

A cardinal measure of economic well-being expressed in currency units. Geometrically, benefits can be computed as the area under a demand curve in the absence of external economies or diseconomies of consumption.

Benefits In Kind

Noncash forms of pay or assistance.

Benelux

1. A word referring to a grouping of the three countries, Belgium, Netherlands, and Luxembourg. Claimed by *The Economist* (May 3, 2008) to have been coined in August 1946 by its Belgian correspondent.

2. The economic union of the three Benelux countries, initially a customs union, later an economic union, and now part of the European Union.

Benign Neglect

Refers to doing nothing about a problem, in the hope that it will not be serious or will be solved by others. Said to be U.S. policy toward its balance of payments deficit in the late 1960s, based on other countries' need for dollar reserves.

Bentham, Jeremy (1748-1832)

Founder of the school of utilitarian philosophy, Bentham accepted much of Adam Smith's work on economics but believed Smith wrong in assuming that there was a necessary identity of private and social interests. Bentham spent much of his life designing social institutions which he thought would bring all such interests into harmony with one another. He developed the concepts of utility, pain and pleasure into what he called a "felicific calculus" by which it was possible to establish, for example, that the evil of a crime is proportionate to the number of people harmed by it and that the punishment should be based not on motive, but the amount of social pain, or disutility, caused by the offense. His life was remarkable not only for his intellectual achievements in the fields of law, economics and social reform, but for his eccentricity which carried over even into death. In return for leaving his considerable estate to the University of London, Bentham induced the University to keep his embalmed remains on hand to attend meetings when utilitarian philosophy would be discussed.

Bequest Savings Motive
People save so that they can leave an inheritance to their children.

Bequest Values
Willingness to pay to preserve the environment for the benefit of our children and grandchildren.

Bergsonian Social Welfare Function
A social welfare function that takes as arguments only the levels of utility of the individuals in society. Due to Bergson (1938) as interpreted by Samuelson (1981). Also called a Bergson-Samuelson social welfare function.

Berne Convention
The Berne Convention for the Protection of Literary and Artistic Works requires that signatory countries provide national treatment in the protection of copyrights.

Bernoulli Random Variable
A random variable that takes on the values zero or one.

Bertrand Competition
The assumption, sometimes assumed to be made by firms in an oligopoly, that other firms hold their prices constant as they themselves change behaviour. Contrasts with Cournot competition. Both are used in models of international oligopoly, but Cournot competition is used more often.

Best Linear Unbiased Estimator (Blue)
Among all linear unbiased estimators, the estimator with the smallest variance. OLS is BLUE, conditional on the sample values of the explanatory variables, under the Gauss-Markov assumptions.

Beta
A measure of the nondiversifiable risk attached to an investment.

Better Factories Cambodia
A programme of the International Labour Organization initiated in 2001 to improve working conditions in the garment factories of Cambodia producing for export. It grew out of a trade agreement between Cambodia and the United States, in which the US promised to permit greater imports from Cambodia in return for improved working conditions.

Bias
1. Bias of technology, either change or difference, refers to a shift towards or away from use of a factor. The exact meaning depends on the definition of neutral used to define absence of bias. Factor bias matters for the effects of technological progress on trade and welfare.
2. Bias of a trade regime refers to whether the structure of protection favours importables or exportables,

based on comparing their effective rates of protection. If these are equal, the trade regime is said to be neutral.

3. Bias of growth refers to economic growth through factor accumulation and/or technological progress and whether if favours one sector or another. Growth is said to be export biased if the export sector expands faster than the rest of the economy, import biased if the import-competing sector does so.

Biased Estimator

An estimator whose expectation, or sampling mean, is different from the population value it is supposed to be estimating.

Biased Towards Zero

A description of an estimator whose expectation in absolute value is less than the absolute value of the population parameter.

Bicycle Theory

With regard to the process of multilateral trade liberalization, the theory that if it ceases to move forward (i.e., achieve further liberalization), then it will collapse (i.e., past liberalization will be reversed). The idea was suggested by Bergsten (1975) and named by him in Bergsten and Cline (1982, p. 71).

Bid Price

The highest price an investor is willing to pay for a stock.

Bid/Ask Spread

The difference between the price that a buyer must pay on a market and the price that a seller will receive for the same thing. The difference covers the cost of, and provides profit for, the broker or other intermediary, such as a bank on the foreign exchange market.

Big Mac Index

An index of PPP exchange rates based solely on the prices of the Big Mac sandwich in McDonald's restaurants around the world, published each spring by the *Economist*.

Bilateral

Between two countries, in contrast to plurilateral and multilateral.

Bilateral Agreement

An agreement between two countries, as opposed to a multilateral agreement.

Bilateral Aid

Aid from a single donor country to a single recipient country, in contrast to multilateral aid.

Bilateral Exchange Rate

The exchange rate between two countries' currencies, defined as the number of units of either currency needed to purchase one unit of the other.

Bilateral Investment Treaty

An agreement between two countries on how their countries will deal with foreign direct investment between them. BITs typically give investors in the host country certain rights, so as to encourage investment.

Bilateral Quota

An import (or export) quota applied to trade with a single trading partner, specifying the amount of a good that can be imported from (exported to) that single country only.

Bilateral Trade

The trade between two countries; that is, the value or quantity of one country's exports to the other, or the sum of exports and imports between them.

Bilateral Trade Balance

The value of a country's exports to a single other country, minus the value of its imports from that country. While data on bilateral trade imbalances are often reported, economists discount them as essentially meaningless, due to the potential for triangular trade.

Bilateral Transfer

A transfer payment from one country to another.

Bill

It is a well drafted legislative proposal that later becomes an Act on being approved by both the Lok Sabha and Rajya Sabha.

Bill Of Exchange

A written, dated, and signed three-party instrument containing an unconditional order by a drawer that directs a drawee to pay a definite sum of money to a payee on demand or at a specified future date. Also known as a draft. It is the most commonly used financial instrument in international trade.

Bill Of Lading

The receipt given by a transportation company to an exporter when the former accepts goods for transport. It includes the contract specifying what transport service will be provided and the limits of liability.

Billion Prices Project

A project at the Massachusetts Institute of Technology to collect prices from online retailers around the world so as to monitor inflation across countries and time.

Bimetallism

The definition of the value of a currency in terms of two different metals usually gold and silver at the same time. That is, the issuer of the currency promises to exchange it for either a certain fixed amount of one metal or for a certain (different) amount of the other metal. System was used by most countries (except the U.K.) through most of the 19th century.

Binary Response Model

A model for a binary (dummy) dependent variable.

Binding

As an adjective, this refers to a restriction that is met exactly, and is therefore having an effect on behaviour, in contrast to nonbinding.

Binding Overhang

The extent to which a country's tariff binding exceeds its applied rate.

Binomial Distribution

The probability distribution of the number of successes out of n independent Bernoulli trials, where each trial has the same probability of success.

Birth Rate

The number of births in a year per 1,000 population.

Black Market

An illegal market, in which something is bought and sold outside of official government-sanctioned channels. Black markets tend to arise when a government tries to fix a price without itself providing all of the necessary supply or demand. Black markets in foreign exchange almost always exist when there are exchange controls.

Black Money

It means unaccounted money, concealed income and undisclosed wealth. In order to evade taxes some people falsify their account and do not record all transactions in their books. The money which thus remains unaccounted for is called Black Money.

Black Sea Economic Cooperation

A group of eleven countries, formed in 1992, with the objective of fostering "interaction and harmony" among the members through political and economic cooperation.

Black Wednesday

The day, September 16 1992, that the Bank of England was forced to withdraw from the Exchange Rate Mechanism because of speculation against the pound that drained its reserves. It is said that financier George Soros profited 1 billion pounds from the episode.

Blair House Accord

An agreement on agricultural subsidies between US and EC negotiators in November 1992 that broke an impasse in the Uruguay Round negotiations.

Blockade

A militarily enforced interference with a country's trade, usually by naval forces preventing access to its ports.

Blood Diamonds

Also called conflict diamonds these are diamonds the mining and marketing of which have been used to finance, or have otherwise contributed to, civil war. In an effort to undermine this market, the Kimberly Process requires participants to certify that shipments of diamonds are conflict free.

Blue Box

A special category of subsidies permitted under the WTO Agriculture Agreement, it includes payments that are linked to production but with provisions to limit production through production quotas or requirements to set aside land from production.

Board of Directors

Individuals chosen by shareholders in a corporation to administer the affairs of the business.

Boeing-Airbus Dispute

A trade dispute between the US and EU, concerning subsidies that each alleges the other provides to its large aircraft manufacturer.

Bogor Goals

The objectives agreed upon at a 1994 meeting of APEC leaders in Bogor, Indonesia. These included "free and open trade and investment by 2010 for industrialized economies and by 2020 for developing economies."

Bond

A debt instrument, issued by a borrower and promising a specified stream of payments to the purchaser, usually regular interest payments plus a final repayment of principal. Bonds are exchanged on open markets including, in the absence of capital controls, internationally, providing a mechanism for international capital mobility.

Bond Market

The market for bonds, in which the prices of the bonds, and therefore the correspondin ginterest rates, are determined by the interaction of buyers and sellers.

Bond Yield

The return earned on a bond.

Bonus

It is in addition to normal payment of dividend to shareholders by a company, or an extra gratuity paid to workers by the employer.

Boom

A state of economic prosperity, as in boom times.

Boom-Bust Cycle

A pattern of performance over time in an economy or an industry that alternates between extremes of rapid growth (booms) and extremes of slow growth or decline (busts), as opposed to sustained steady growth.

BOP

Balance of payments.

Border Effect

A discontinuity that exists in prices or in quantities of trade at the border between countries. If the price of a good is higher on one side of a border than the other, this is a border effect. If agravity equation includes a dummy for trade across a border and that dummy is significant, that also indicates a border effect.

Border Price

The price of a good at a country's border.

Border Protection

1. In the context of trade policy, this refers to policies such as tariffs and quotas that enhance profits and employment in a domestic industry, as opposed to other policies such as production subsidies that might have similar effects without restricting trade.
2. Measures to prevent unwanted entry across a nation's border of illegal or harmful goods or people.

Border Tax Adjustment

Rebate of indirect taxes (taxes on other than direct income, such as a sales tax or VAT) on exported goods, and levying of them on imported goods. May distort trade when tax rates differ or when adjustment does not match the tax paid.

Borderless World

The concept that national borders no longer matter, perhaps for some specified purpose.

Borrowing

The amount that an entity, usually a country or its government, has borrowed. Thus often the (negative of) the net foreign asset position or the national debt.

Boulding, Kenneth Ewart (1910-1993)

An American economist whose work covers both mainstream and radical forms of economic theory. Boulding was born in Liverpool, England in 1910. He taught at the University of Michigan from 1949 to 1967,and subsequently at the University of Colorado, retiring in 1980. His publications reflect the broad range of his academic interests and contain frequent criticisms of orthodox economics. Boulding advocated the integration of economic with biological concepts and he had urged that economic policy should be evaluated on the basis of a larger normative theory of evaluative judgement rather than on economic criteria alone.

Bowed

Curved. "Bowed out" is used to describe a typical transformation curve, which is concave to the origin. In contrast, a transformation curve reflecting increasing returns to scale might be "bowed in" toward the origin.

Box

Used with a colour, a category of subsidies based on status in WTO:

red = forbidden, amber or orange=go slow (i.e., reduce the subsidy), green = permitted, blue = subsidies tied to production limits. Terminology seems only to be used in agriculture, where in fact there is no red box.

Boycott

To protest by refusing to purchase from someone, or otherwise do business with them. In international trade, a boycott most often takes the form of refusal to import a country's goods. A primary boycott limits trade with the target; a secondary boycott limits trade with those that trade with the target.

BP-Curve

In the Mundell-Fleming model, the curve representing balance of payments equilibrium. It is normally upward sloping because an increase in income increases imports while an increase in the interest rate increases capital inflows. The curve is used under pegged exchange rates for effects on the balance of payments and under floating rates for effects on the exchange rate.

BPO

Business process outsourcing

Brain Drain

The migration of skilled workers out of a country. First applied to the migration of British-trained scientists, physicians, and university teachers in the early 1960's, mostly to the United States.

Branch Plant Economy

An economy that relies heavily on branch plants, i.e., production subsidiaries, of foreign companies, and therefore on foreign-owned capital and technology.

Break-Even

Break-even occurs where total cost is equal to total revenue. Anywhere below break-even the firm is making a loss and anywhere above a profit.

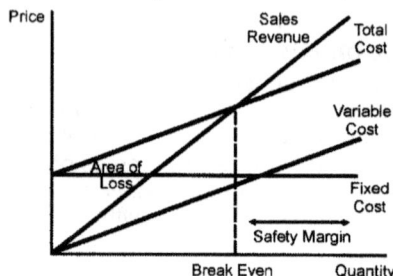

The break-even level of output depends on the level of fixed and variable costs. High fixed costs may raise the level of break-even output. One way to calculate break-even is to look at the "contribution" each unit sold makes to the fixed costs. If a good is sold for Rs.5 and the variable costs are Rs.3, then each unit makes a contribution of Rs.2 to fixed costs. If the fixed costs are Rs. 200, then the break-even level of output will be at 100 units of output.

Break-Even Chart

A chart showing how both total revenue and total cost vary with changes in the total number of units of a product that is sold. The break-even point is the minimum number that must be sold to avoid loss.

Brecher-Alejandro Proposition

The proposition, proved in Brecher and Alejandro (1977), that foreign capital inflows with full repatriation must be immizerizing.

Bretton Woods

An international monetary system operating from 1946-1971. The value of the dollar was fixed in terms of gold, and every other country held its currency at a fixed exchange rate against the dollar; when trade deficits occurred, the central bank of the deficit country financed the deficit with its reserves of international currencies. The Bretton Woods system collapsed in 1971 when the US abandoned the gold standard.

Bribe

A payment made to person, often a government official such as a customs officer, to induce favourable treatment.

BRIC

Acronym for four large low-income countries, Brazil, Russia, India, and China, that were growing rapidly in the early years of the 21st century. Term was coined by O'Neill (2001). Sometimes expanded to BRICIs to include Indonesia or BRICS to include South Africa.

Brixit

Term used in the British press starting in June 2012 for the possible exit of Britain from the European Union. The term was devised as analogous to the term grexit.

Broker's Fee

The fee for a transaction charged by an intermediary in a market, such as a bank in a foreign-exchange transaction.

Brookings Institution

A nonprofit, public-policy think tank located in Washington, D.C., Brookings resident and nonresident fellows do research and writing on a variety of public policy issues, including international economics. Politically, it is somewhat left-of-centre, providing a home for US Democrats when not in government.

Brownfields

Brownfield sites are abandoned or underused industrial and commercial facilities available for re-use. Expansion or redevelopment of such a facility may be complicated by real or perceived environmental contaminations.

Brown Field Investment

FDI that involves the purchase of an existing plant or firm, rather then construction of a new plant.

Brussels Tariff Nomenclature

An international system of classification for goods that was once widely used for specifying tariffs. It was changed, in name only, to the CCCN in 1976 and later superseded by the Harmonized System of Tariff Nomenclature.

BTT

Barter terms of trade

Bubble

A rise in the price of an asset based not on the current or prospective income that it provides but solely on expectations by market participants that the price will rise in the future. When those expectations cease, the bubble bursts and the price falls rapidly.

Bubble Economy

Term for an economy in which the presence of one or more bubbles in its asset markets is a dominant feature of its performance. Japan was said to be a bubble economy in the late 1980s.

Budget

A summary of intended expenditures along with proposals for how to meet them. A budget can provide guidelines for managing future investments and expenses. The budget deficit is the amount by which government spending exceeds government revenues during a specified period of time usually a year.

Budget

An estimate of expected revenues and expenditure for a given period, usually a year, item by item.

Budget Constraint

1. For an individual or household, the condition that income equals expenditure (in a static model), or that income minus expenditure equals the value of increased asset holdings (in a dynamic model).
2. For a country, the condition that the value of exports equals the value of imports or, if capital flows are permitted, that exports minus imports equals the net capital outflow. It is equivalent to income from production equaling expenditure on goods plus net acquisition of foreign assets.
3. The curve, usually a straight line, representing either of these conditions.

Budget Deficit

When the expenditure becomes more than revenues, then the budgetary exercise is considered a failure as there is shortage of funds. Such a situation is said to be a 'Budget Deficit'.

Budget Estimates

These are assessment of expenditure by the government for a year. This also includes the estimate of Revenue Deficit and Fiscal Deficit for the year.

Budget Line

1. A line showing all combinations of quantities of good X and good Y the consumer can buy given a specific income. Its slope equals -1 times the price of good X divided by the price of good Y when X is measured along the horizontal axis and Y is measured along the vertical axis. The Y intercept in this case equals income divided by the price of Y.
2. Given a specific level of income (I) and assuming there are only two goods (x & y) and further assuming prices are Px and Py respectively, then a budget line can be plotted showing all commodity combinations of x and and y that a consumer can afford.

Budget Surplus

Refers in general to an excess of income over expenditure, but usually refers specifically to the government budget, where it is the excess of tax revenue over expenditure (including transfer and interest payments).

Budget/Annual Financial Statement

According to the section – 112 of the Indian Constitution, the government presents a statement of estimated receipts, expenditure and a detailed plan that is presented for every financial that is for 1st of April to 31st of March of each year. There are usually three divisions of budget and for each of them a statement of expenditure & receipts are presented. These three divisions include – Contingency Fund, Consolidated Fund and Public Account.

Buffer Stock

A large quantity of a commodity held in storage to be used to stabilize the commodity's price. This is done by buying when the price is low and adding to the buffer stock, selling out of the buffer stock when the price is high, hoping to reduce the size of price fluctuations. See international commodity agreement.

Built-In Agenda

Issues that were scheduled for continued negotiations within the WTO in the Uruguay Round agreement. In addition to reviewing the implementation of various agreements, these included negotiations for further liberalization in agriculture and services.

Bull

An investor with an optimistic market outlook; an investor who expects prices to rise and so buys now for resale later. A Bull Market is one in which prices are rising. c.i.f., abbrev: Cost, Insurance and Freight: Export term in which the price quoted by the exporter includes the costs of ocean transportation to the port of destination and insurance coverage.

Bundling

A marketing technique whereby a firm that sells two products requires customers who buy one of them to buy the other as well.

Burst

In the case of a price bubble, the usually sudden reversal of a price from rising over time to falling.

Business

A business (also known as enterprise or firm) is an organization involved in the trade of goods, services, or both to consumers. Businesses are predominant in capitalist economies, where most of them are privately owned and administered to earn profit to increase the wealth of their owners. Businesses may also be not-for-profit or state-owned. A business owned by multiple individuals may be referred to as a company, although that term also has a more precise meaning.

Business (Firm)

Private profit-seeking organizations that use resources to produce goods and services.

Business Cycle

The pattern followed by macroeconomic variables, such as GDP and unemployment that rise and fall irregularly over time, relative to trend. Cyclical movements of large countries cause similar movements in their trading partners, inexplicably under real business cycle theory and thus called the trade comovement puzzle.

Business Process Outsourcing

The outsourcing and/or offshoring of business processes, such as the back office functions such as accounting, human resource management, etc.

Business Roundtable

An organization of CEOs of major US corporations. It pursues a number of initiatives, including facilitating international trade and investment agreements and enforcing US rights under existing agreements.

Buy American Act

U.S. legislation, from 1933, requiring that government purchases give preference to domestic producers unless imports are at least a specified percentage cheaper. This is an example of a government procurement NTB that was partially given up under the Tokyo Round.

Buyback Arrangement

A form of countertrade in which a foreign seller of plant, equipment, or technology is required to purchase part of the resulting production.

Buyer

A "buyer" or merchandiser is a person who purchases finished goods, typically for resale, for a firm, government, or organization. (A person who purchases material used to make goods is sometimes called a purchasing agent.)

Buyer's Market

An area in which the supply of certain goods exceeds the demands so that purchasers can drive hard bargains.

Byrd Amendment

A US law enacted in 2000 requiring that revenues from anti-dumping duties and countervailing duties be given to the US domestic producers who had filed the cases. This was subject of a trade dispute in the WTO and ruled to be not compatible with WTO rules.

C

Call Money
Price paid by an investor for a call option. There is no fixed rate for call money. It depends on the type of stock, its performance prior to the purchase of the call option, and the period of the contract. It is an interest bearing band deposits that can be withdrawn on 24 hours notice.

Capital
Wealth in the form of money or property owned by a person or business and human resources of economic value. Capital is the contribution to productive activity made by investment is physical capital (machinery, factories, tools and equipments) and human capital (eg general education, health). Capital is one of the three main factors of production other two are labour and natural resources.

Capital Abundant
A country is capital abundant if its endowment of capital is large compared to other countries. Relative capital abundance can be defined by either the quantity definition or the price definition.

Capital Account
1. (Current definition) Since sometime in the 1990s, "capital account" refers to a minor component of international transactions, involving unilateral transfers of ownership of property. The common definition, below, describes what is now called the financial account.
2. (Common definition) A country's international transactions arising from changes in holdings of real and financial capital assets (but not income on them, which is in the current account). Includes FDI, plus changes in private and official holdings of stocks, bonds, loans, bank accounts, and currencies.
3. (Bretton-Woods definition) Same as common definition except excluding official reserve transactions. This definition was used under the Bretton Woods System of pegged exchange rates, but is less meaningful under floating exchange rates.

Capital Account Balance
Balance on capital account

Capital Account Deficit
Debits minus credits on capital account.

Capital Account Surplus
Credits minus debits on capital account. Same as balance on capital account.

Capital Accumulation
Addition to the stock of capital.

Capital Adequacy Ratio

The ratio of a bank's capital to its risk-weighted credit exposure (liabilities). International standards recommend a minimum for this ratio, intended to permit banks to absorb losses without becoming insolvent, in order to protect depositors.

Capital Asset Pricing Model

A way to show the prices of securities and other risk-free assets.

Capital Augmenting

Said of a technological change or technological difference if one production function produces the same as if it were the other, but with a larger quantity of capital. Same as factor augmentingwith capital the augmented factor. Also called Solow neutral.

Capital Budget

A plan of proposed capital outlays and the means of financing them for the current fiscal period. It is usually a part of the current budget. If a Capital Programme is in operation, it will be the first year thereof. A Capital Programme is sometimes referred to as a Capital Budget.

Capital Budgeting

Capital budgeting (or investment appraisal) is the planning process used to determine whether an organization's long term investments such as new machinery, replacement machinery, new plants, new products, and research development projects are worth pursuing. It is budget for major capital, or investment, expenditures.

Capital Consumption

The using up of real capital by not maintaining or replacing it as it wears out.

Capital Consumption Allowance

In national income accounting the capital consumption allowance records the amount by which the capital stock has been used up or depreciated during the accounting period. May also be called simply "depreciation."

Capital Consumption Allowance

The name used in the National Income and Product Accounts for depreciation of capital.

Capital Control

Any policy intended to restrict the free movement of capital, especially financial capital, into or out of a country.

Capital Density

The amount of capital per unit land area in a country. Sometimes used for just particular types of capital, such as housing capital or human capital.

Capital Duty

A tax on the value of a newly formed company, or one that has newly been transfered to a different taxing jurisdiction.

Capital Expenditure

The total expenditure by the government on acquiring any asset that may include investment in shares, machinery, building or land. The scope of capital expenditure extends to payments, advancements or loans that are approved or sanctioned to the State governments, union territories, public sector undertakings by the Central government.

Capital Flight

The movement of savings and liquid financial assets from one country to another and from one currency to another. Often during financial crises, residents of the crisis country will transfer savings and other liquid assets into U.S. dollar-denominated assets, often in the United States. This has the effect of putting pressure on the exchange rate and often leads to devaluation and the draining of liquidity out of the crisis country's banking and financial system.

Capital Flow

International capital movement.

Capital Formation

Capital formation is a concept used in macroeconomics, national accounts and financial economics. Occasionally it is also used in corporate accounts. It can be defined in three ways:

1. It is a specific statistical concept used in national accounts statistics, econometrics and macroeconomics. In that sense, it refers to a measure of the net additions to the (physical) capital stock of a country (or an economic sector) in an accounting interval, or, a measure of the amount by which the total physical capital stock increased during an accounting period. To arrive at this measure, standard valuation principles are used.

2. It is used also in economic theory, as a modern general term for capital accumulation, referring to the total "stock of capital" that has been formed, or to the growth of this total capital stock.

3. In a much broader or vaguer sense, the term "capital formation" has in more recent times been used in financial economics to refer to savings drives, setting up financial institutions, fiscal measures, public borrowing, development of capital markets, privatization of financial institutions, development of secondary markets. In this usage, it refers to any method for increasing the amount of capital owned or under one's control, or any method in utilising or mobilizing capital resources for investment purposes. Thus, capital could be "formed" in the sense of "being brought together for investment purposes" in many different ways. This broadened meaning is not related to the statistical measurement concept nor to the classical understanding of the concept in economic theory. Instead, it originated in credit-based economic growth during the 1990s and 2000s, which was accompanied by the rapid growth of the financial sector, and consequently the increased use of finance terminology in economic discussions.

Capital Gain

The increase in value that the owner of an asset experiences when the price of the asset rises, including when the currency in which the asset is denominated appreciates.

Capital Gains Tax

Tax paid on the gain realized upon the sale of an asset. It is a tax on profits from the sale of capital assets, such as shares. A capital loss can be used to offset a capital gain, reducing any tax you would otherwise have to pay.

Capital Good

A capital good, or simply capital in economics, is a manufactured means of production. Capital goods are acquired by a society by saving wealth which can be invested in the means of production.
Individuals, organizations and governments use capital goods in the production of other goods or

commodities. Capital goods include factories, machinery, tools, equipment, and various buildings which are used to produce other products for consumption. Capital goods, then, are products which are not produced for immediate consumption; rather, they are objects that are used to produce other goods and services. These types of goods are important economic factors because they are the key to developing a positive return from manufacturing other products and commodities. Manufacturing companies also use capital goods. Capital goods help their company make functional goods to sell individuals valuable services. As a result, capital goods are sometimes referred to as producers' goods or means of production. An important distinction should also be made between capital goods and consumer goods, which are products directly purchased by consumers for personal or household use.

Capital Inflow

A net flow of capital, real and/or financial, into a country, in the form of increased purchases of domestic assets by foreigners and/or reduced holdings of foreign assets by domestic residents. Recorded as positive, or a credit, in the balance on capital account.

Capital Infusion

An increase in financial capital provided from outside a bank, corporation, or other entity.

Capital Intensity

A measure of the relative use of capital, compared to other factors such as labour, in a production process. Often measured by the ratio of capital to labour, or by the share of capital in factor payments.

Capital Intensive

Describing an industry or sector of the economy that relies relatively heavily on inputs of capital, usually relative to labour, compared to other industries or sectors.

Capital Loss

The decrease in value that the owner of an asset experiences when the price of the asset falls, including when the currency in which the asset is denominated depreciates. Contrasts with capital gain.

Capital Market

A broad term, encompassing all the many mechanisms by which savings can be conveyed to those who wish to use it for investment. Most obviously, it includes the markets for stocks and bonds.

Capital Market Imperfection

Anything that interferes with the ability of economic agents to borrow and lend as much as they wish at a fixed rate of interest that truly reflects probability of repayment. A common source of imperfection is asymmetric information.

Capital Mobility

The ability of capital to move internationally. The degree of capital mobility depends on government policies restricting or taxing capital inflows and/or outflows, plus the risk that investors in one country associate with assets in another.

Capital Movement

Capital inflow and/or outflow.

Capital Outflow

A net flow of capital, real and/or financial, out of a country, in the form of reduced holdings of domestic assets by foreigners and/or increased holdings of foreign assets by domestic residents. Recorded as negative, or a debit, in the balance on capital account.

Capital Output Ratio

The ratio of the quantity of capital to the quantity of output, usually in the one-sector economy of a simple growth model.

Capital Resources

Goods made by people and used to produce other goods and services. Examples include buildings, equipment, and machinery.

Capital Scarce

A country is capital scarce if its endowment of capital is small compared to other countries. Relative capital scarcity can be defined by either the quantity definition or the price definition.

Capital Stock

The total amount of physical capital that has been accumulated, usually in a country.

Capitalism

A system of economic organization characterized by the private ownership of the means of production, private property, and largely market-based control over the production and distribution of goods and services.

Capitalist

1. An owner (or sometimes only a manager) of capital.
2. Associated or identified with capitalism.

Capitalist Class

Those members of society who own the capital stock, often used in a pejorative sense by Marxists and other socialist critics of capitalism.

Capitalist Economies

Economies which use market-determined prices to guide peoples choices about the production and distribution of goods; these economies generally have productive resource which are privately owned.

Capital-Labour Ratio

The ratio of the quantity of capital (usually only physical) to the quantity of labour, usually as employed in a particular industry, but sometimes referring to the entire factor endowment of a country.

Capital-Saving

A technological change or technological difference that is biased in favour of using less capital, compared to some definition of neutrality.

Capital-Using

A technological change or technological difference that is biased in favour of using more capital, compared to some definition of neutrality.

Carat

Measure or weight of precious stones. 24 carat gold is the purest gold, thus 22 carat gold means a piece of gold in which 22 parts are pure gold and 2 parts of an alloy, usually copper.

Carbon Tariff

A tariff levied on the basis of carbon dioxide that an import's production emits into the atmosphere. The purpose is to treat imports equally with domestic goods that are subject to costly environmental regulation or tax, and also to motivate other countries to use such environmental policies.

Carbon Tax

a charge on fossil fuels (coal, oil, natural gas) based on their carbon content.

When burned, the carbon in these fuels becomes carbon dioxide in the atmosphere, the chief greenhouse gas.

Carcinogens
Substances that cause cancer.

Cardinal Utility
Utility that is measurable in a cardinal sense, like a person's weight or height (which means that the difference between two utilities-i.e., marginal utility-is meaningful).

Caribbean Basin Initiative
A non-reciprocal preferential trading arrangement originally enacted in 1983 by the United States, providing duty-free access to a group of Caribbean countries for selected products. It was renewed and extended in 2000 and currently has 17 beneficiary countries.

Caribbean Community
The Caribbean Community and Common Market was formed among four Caribbean countries in 1973 and had 15 members as of August 2012. Its purpose is the promotion of economic integration among the member countries and coordination of foreign policies.

Caribbean Development Bank
A financial institution whose members are primarily the countries of the Caribbean region and whose purpose is to foster economic development in the region.

Caribcan
A non-reciprocal commitment by Canada to provide duty free access to exports of most products from 18 Commonwealth Caribbean countries and territories.

CARICOM Single Market And Economy
The economic objectives of the CARICOM group, which include becoming a common market.

Cariforum
A grouping consisting of the CARICOM countries plus the Dominican Republic.

Cariforum-Ec Epa
An economic partnership agreement between the European Community and the CARIFORUM countries, signed in 2008.

Carriage Of Goods By Sea Act
U.S. legislation governing ocean transport of cargo.

Carrier
A firm that provides transportation of persons or goods.

Carry Trade
The practice of borrowing in the currency of a country where interest rates are low and lending the proceeds in the currency of a country where interest rates are higher, in hopes of profiting from the difference. Success depends on exchange rates remaining relatively constant. Also known as uncovered interest arbitrage.

Cartel
A group of producers with an agreement to collude in setting prices and output. An organization of producers seeking to limit or eliminate competition among its members, most often by agreeing to restrict output to keep prices higher than would occur under competitive conditions. Cartels are inherently unstable because of the potential for producers to defect from the agreement and

capture larger markets by selling at lower prices.

Categorical Assistance

public assistance aimed at a particular category of people, like the elderly or the disabled.

Causal Effect

A ceteris paribus change in one variable has an effect on another variable.

Causation

Relationship that results when an change in one variable is not only correlated with but actually causes the change in another one.

Caution Money

It is the money deposited as security for the fulfilment of a contract or obligation.

Cecchini Report

A 1988 report by a group of experts, chaired by Paolo Cecchini, examining the benefits and costs of creating a single market in Europe, in accordance with provisions of the Treaty of Rome.

Celtic Tiger

Name for Ireland during its period of very rapid economic growth, which ended with the financial crisis of 2008. Name was prompted by analogy with the Asian Tigers.

Census

Official gathering of information about the population in a particular area. Government departments use the data collected in planning for the future in such areas as health education, transport, and housing.

Centre For Economic and Policy Research

An Washington DC-based organization established in 1999 that conducts and disseminates research on economic policy issues, both US domestic and international.

Central American Bank For Economic Integration

"The leading source of multilateral financing for the integration and development of Central America," CABEI acts as a development bank for the region.

Central American Common Market

A group of Central American countries — El Salvador, Guatemala, Honduras, and Nicaragua — that formed a common market in 1960, with Costa Rica added in 1962. It largely disintegrated in the 1970s and 80s due to military conflicts, but reformed as the Central American Free Trade Zone (but without Costa Rica) starting in 1993.

Central And Eastern European Countries

Refers, informally, usually to the former Communist countries of Europe.

Central Bank

An agency empowered by a government to manage a country's monetary and financial institutions, issue and maintain the domestic currency, and handle the official reserves of foreign exchange. Primarily a "bank for banks."

Central European Free Trade Agreement

1. A free trade agreement initiated 2006 among Albania, Bosnia and Herzegovina, Croatia, the former Yugoslav Republic of Macedonia, Moldova, Montenegro, Serbia and the United Nations Interim Administration Mission in Kosovo.
2. A free trade agreement initiated 1993 among the Czech Republic, Hungary, Poland, Slovakia, and Slovenia, later also including Bulgaria and Romania. Its purpose was in part to reverse the bias against trade among these neighbouring countries that had developed during the process of transition. This was superseded by the accession of these countries to the Europeann Union.

Central Planning

The system in which central government bureaucrats (as opposed to private entrepreneurs or even local government bureaucrats) determine what will be produced and how it will be produced.

Centralization

Organizational structure in which decision making is concentrated at the top.

Centrally Planned Economy

A planned economic system in which the production, pricing, and distribution of goods and services are determined by the government rather than market forces. Also referred to as a "non market economy." Former Soviet Union, China, and most other communist nations are examples of centrally planed economy.

Centre For Economic Policy Research

A European network for economic research, in many fields of economics including international trade and international macroeconomics. Its affiliated researchers issue working papers and conduct academic conferences.

Centre William Rappard

The building in Geneva, Switzerland, that houses the World Trade Organization.

Cenvat

This scheme is implied for most of the goods and reduce the cascading effect of indirect taxes on finished products.

Cepal

Comision Economica para America Latina y el Caribe (Spanish for Economic Commission for Latin America and the Caribbean.

Cepii

"The CEPII is France's leading institute for research on the international economy." Known particularly for the economic data that it makes available.

CEPR

Centre for Economic Policy Research

Certainty

Precise knowledge of an economic variable, as opposed to belief that it could take on multiple values. Contrasts with uncertainty. One aspect of complete information.

CES Function

A function with constant elasticity of substitution. CES is popular for both production and utility functions. Used extensively in New Trade Theory as the Dixit-Stiglitz utility function fordifferentiated products under monopolistic competition.

CET Function
Constant elasticity of transformation function.

Ceteris Paribus
The Latin for "other things being equal."

Ceteris Paribus
Latin phrase meaning, approximately, "holding other things constant." Used as shorthand for indicating the effect of one economic variable on another, holding constant all other variables that may affect the second variable.

CFA Franc
Currency of the Communaute Financiere Africaine.

Chaebol
A form of large business in South Korea, a conglomerate consisting of many companies centred around a parent company. They are family controlled and have strong ties to government. They are similar to the keiretsu of Japan, except that the chaebol do not own banks.

Chain Of Comparative Advantage
A ranking of goods or countries in order of comparative advantage. With two countries and many goods, goods can be ranked by comparative advantage (e.g., by relative unit labour requirements in the Ricardian model). A country's exports will then lie nearer one end of the chain than its imports. With two goods, many countries can be ordered similarly.

Chamberlin, Edward (1899-1967)
An American economist who studied at Iowa and Michigan before graduating with a doctorate from Harvard in 1927, Chamberlin subsequently spent his academic career teaching at the latter university. His major interest was in the interaction of monopoly and competition, which he saw not as opposites, but as always-present elements in business situations which interact with one another. He is best known for his theory of monopolistic competition in which equilibrium is influenced by product differentiation and selling costs as well as by optimum output. Chamberlin's major book, *Monopolistic Competition,* was published in 1933, only a matter of months before a similar analysis was published in Britain by Joan Robinson of Cambridge University. The language used in the two treatments of the subject was different, but the analysis and the conclusions reached are so similar that only specialists need worry about the difference between imperfect competition and monopolistic competition.

Change In Consumer Surplus
The change in consumer surplus due to a change in market conditions, usually a price change. For a price change, it is measured by the area to the left of the demand curve between the two prices, indicating a gain if price falls and a loss if it rises.

Change In Demand
A shift in the entire demand curve so that at any given price, people will want to buy a different amount. A change in demand is caused by some change other than a change in the goods price.

Change In Producer Surplus
The change in producer surplus due to a change in market conditions, usually

a price change. For a price change, it is measured by the area to the left of the (upward sloping part of the) supply curve between the two prices, indicating a gain if price rises and a loss if it falls.

Change In Quantity Demanded
Movement up or down a given demand curve caused by a change in the goods price with no shift in the curve itself.

Change In Quantity Supplied
A price change causing movement along the supply curve but no shift in the position of the curve itself.

Change In Supply
A change in one of the cost determinants of supply causing a shift in the position of the supply curve. Choice : The act of selecting among alternatives, a concept crucial to economics.

Chapeau
In the context of GATT articles, this means an introductory paragraph.

Chapter 11
1. In NAFTA, this portion deals with foreign direct investment. Most controversially, it includes a provision for a firm from one member country that has invested in another to bring action against a unit of government in that country if it has acted to reduce the value of its investment.
2. A portion of U.S. bankruptcy law under which a firm can file for protection while it reorganizes.

CHF
Acronym for the currency of Switzerland, the Swiss franc, standing for Confœderatio Helvetica Franc.

Chiang Mai Initiative
An agreement in 2000 among the "ASEAN+3" countries (ASEAN plus China, Japan, and S. Korea) to cooperate in four main areas: monitoring capital flows, regional surveillance, swap networks, and training personnel.

Chicken War
A trade dispute between the U.S. and the EEC that began in 1962 when the EEC extended thevariable levy of the CAP to poultry, tripling German tariffs on U.S. chickens. A GATT panel quantified the damage and led to U.S. retaliatory tariffs on cognac, trucks, and other goods. The U.S. 25% tariff on trucks today is a remnant of the chicken war.

Child Labour
1. Employment of children under a specified minimum age.
2. Work that is harmful to a child's physical or mental health, development, or education, and that is therefore targeted for elimination by labour standards.

Child Labour Deterrence Act
A bill introduced into the US Congress by Tom Harkin, but never passed, that would have prohibited imports of products produced by child labour.

Chindia
A collective name for China and India, sometimes used in discussing the increasing role that these two countries play in the international economy.

Chinese Economic Area
Unofficial name for the area comprising Hong Kong, Taiwan, and either China as a whole or just its Special Economic Zones.

Chi-Square Distribution

A probability distribution obtained by adding the squares of independent standard normal random variables. The number of terms in the sum equals the degrees of freedom in the distribution.

Chlorinated Chicken Dispute

The issue of whether Europe should be able to restrict, or require labelling of, US exports of chicken that has been bathed in a chlorine solution to kill bacteria.

Chlorofluorocarbon

A chemical once used in refrigerators, air conditioners, and as aerosol propellants that, when released high into the atmosphere, destroyed the ozone. This environmental danger was resolved by banning these chemicals as well as banning trade in products that included them, through the Montreal Protocol.

Choice

Because wants are unlimited and resources are limited, all economies must choose which goods and services should be produced and in what quantities.

CIA

1. Cash in advance
2. Central Intelligence Agency

CIF

The price of a traded good including transport cost. It stands for "cost, insurance, and freight," but is used only as these initials (usually lower case: c.i.f.). It means that a price includes the various costs, such as transportation and insurance, needed to get a good from one country to another. Contrasts with FOB.

Circular Flow

The "circular flow of income and expenditure" refers to the fact that income earned in production is spent on goods that were produced, providing the funds to pay that income. In an open economy, expenditure leaks out of that circle as imports, but re-enters as exports or as capital inflows.

Circular Flow Of Goods And Services (Or Circular Flow Of Economic Activity)

A model of an economy showing the interactions between households and business firms as they exchange goods and services and resources in markets.

Circular Migration

The movement of a country's people first out of the country and then back in.

Circumvention

Actions taken by traders to avoid paying duties.

Cites

Convention on International Trade in Endangered Species of Wild Fauna and Flora

Civil Society

The name used to encompass a wide and self-selected variety of interest groups, worldwide. It does not include for-profit businesses, government, and government organizations, whereas it does include most NGOs.

Civilian Labour Force

All persons over the age of sixteen who are not in the armed forces nor institutionalized and who are either employed or unemployed.

Classical

Referring to the writings, models, and economic assumptions of the first century of economics, including Adam Smith, David Ricardo, and John Stuart Mill.

Classical Economics

The economics of Adam Smith, David Ricardo, Thomas Malthus, and later followers such as John Stuart Mill. The theory concentrated on the functioning of a market economy, spelling out a rudimentary explanation of consumer and producer behaviour in particular markets and postulating that in the long term the economy would tend to operate at full employment because increases in supply would create corresponding increases in demand.

Classical Economists

Economists prevalent before the Great Depression who believed that the basic competitive model provided a good description of the economy and that if short periods of unemployment did occur, market forces would quickly restore the economy to full employment.

Classical Errors-In-Variables (CEV)

A measurement error model where the observed measure equals the actual variable plus an independent, or at least an uncorrelated, measurement error.

Classical Linear Model

The multiple linear regression model under the full set of classical linear model assumptions.

Classical Linear Model (CLM) Assumptions

The ideal set of assumptions for multiple regression analysis. The assumptions include linearity in the parameters, no perfect collinearity, the zero conditional mean assumption, homoskedasticity, no serial correlation, and normality of the errors.

Classical Unemployment

unemployment that results from too-high real wages; it occurs in the supply constrained equilibrium, so that rightwards shifts in aggregate supply reduce the level of unemployment.

Classification Of Products By Activity

Statistical Classification of Products by Activity is the classification system used for bothgoods and services in the European Union. Its structure is parallel to that of NACE.

Classification System

A system for organizing, recording, and reporting data of a particular kind, such as international trade, industrial output, etc. Typical systems divide data into categories, each assigned numbers. These may be subdivided, using an additional digits, so that more digits mean a finer, or more disaggregated, classification.

Clean Fuel

Fuels which have lower emissions than conventional gasoline and diesel. Refers to alternative fuels as well as to reformulated gasoline and diesel.

Cleanup

treatment, remediation, or destruction of contaminated material.

Clear

A market is said to clear if supply is equal to demand. Market clearing can be brought about by adjustment of the price (or the exchange rate, in the case of the exchange market), or by some form of government (or central bank) intervention in or regulation of the market.

Clearcutting

a logging technique in which all trees are removed from an area, typically 20 acres or larger, with little regard for long-term forest health.

Clearing Agreement

A reciprocal trade agreement between two countries to buy a specified minimum amount of each other's products over a certain time, using a specified clearing currency.

Clearing System

An arrangement among financial institutions for carrying out the transactions among them, including canceling out offsetting credits and debits on the same account.

Climate Change

a regional change in temperature and weather patterns. Current science indicates a discernible link between climate change over the last century and human activity, specifically the burning of fossil fuels.

Closed Currency Position

A commitment to take or make delivery of a currency in the future that is covered by a contract in the forward market; opposite of an open position.

Closed Economy

A closed economy is one in which there are no foreign trade transactions or any other form of economic contacts with the rest of the world.

Coase Theorem

The proposition that the allocation of property rights does not matter for economic efficiency, so long as they are well defined and a free market exists for the exchange of rights between those who have them and those who do not. the assertion that if property rights are properly defined, then people will be forced to pay for any negative externalities they impose on others, and market transactions will produced efficient outcomes.

Cobb-Douglas Function

The Cobb–Douglas functional form of production functions is widely used to represent the relationship of output and two inputs. The Cobb-Douglas form was developed and tested against statistical evidence by Charles Cobb and Paul Douglas during 1900–1947.

Cobb-Douglas Production Function

A production function of the form $Q = AL^{a1}K^{a2}M^{a3}$, where Q is the output rate, L is the quantity of labour, K is the quantity of capital, M is the quantity of raw materials, and A, a_1, a_2, and a_3 are constants that are greater than 0 and less than 1.

Cobden-Chevalier Treaty

A preferential trade agreement between Britain and France that went into effect in 1860. It was followed by a flurry of other such agreements among European countries.

CoCom

CoCom is an acronym for Coordinating Committee for Multilateral Export Controls. CoCom was established by Western bloc powers in the first five years after the end of World War II, during the Cold War, to put an arms embargo on COMECON (Warsaw Pact) countries.

Codex Alimentarius

This is the international "food code," consisting of standards, codes of practice, guidelines, and recommendations for producing and processing food. It is administered by the Codex Alimentarius Commission.

Coefficient

1. A number or symbol multiplied by a variable.
2. In a regression analysis, the estimated numerical association between one variable and another, usually taken to represent the sign and size of the causal effect of one on the other.

Collateral

In lending agreements, collateral is a borrower's pledge of specific property to a lender, to secure repayment of a loan. The collateral serves as protection for a lender against a borrower's default - that is, any borrower failing to pay the principal and interest under the terms of a loan obligation. If a borrower does default on a loan (due to insolvency or other event), that borrower forfeits (gives up) the property pledged as collateral - and the lender then becomes the owner of the collateral. In a typical mortgage loan transaction, for instance, the real estate being acquired with the help of the loan serves as collateral.

Collateral Security

Additional security a borrower supplies to obtain a loan.

Collective Action Problem

The difficulty of getting a group to act when members benefit if others act, but incur a net cost if they act themselves.

Collusion

Cooperation among firms to raise price and otherwise increase their profits.

Columbian Exchange

The exchange of goods, but also populations, diseases, and ideas that took place between the Eastern Hemisphere and the Western Hemisphere, across the Atlantic Ocean, in the centuries following the voyage of Christopher Columbus in 1492.

Column 1 Rates

In the United States, this refers to the MFN tariff rates that are applied to countries with whom the US has normal trade relations.

Column 2 Rates

In the United States, this refers to the usually higher-than-MFN tariff rates that are applied to countries with whom the US does not have normal trade relations. Currently (August 2012), only Cuba and Cambodia are subject to Column 2 tariffs. (Trade with several other countries is simply prohibited.)

Comecon

The Council for Mutual Economic Assistance 1949–1991, was an economic organization under the leadership of the Soviet Union that comprised the countries of the Eastern Bloc along with a number of socialist states elsewhere in the world. The Comecon was the Eastern Bloc's reply to the formation of the Organization for European Economic Co-operation in non-communist Europe.

Command Economy

A mode of economic organization in which the key economic functions—what, how, and for whom—are principally determined by government directive. Sometimes called a "centrally planned economy."

Commercial Bank
An institution that accepts and manages deposits from households, firms and governments and uses of those deposits to earn interest by making loans and holding securities.

Commercial Paper
Short-term, negotiable debt of a firm; thus a bond of short maturity issued by a company.

Commercial Policy
Encompassing instruments of trade protection employed by countries to foster industrial promotion, export diversification, employment creation, and other desired development-oriented strategies. They include tariffs, quotas, and subsidies.

Commercial Risk
The risk for an exporter that the buyer will not pay. Contrasts with political risk.

Commercial Service
Any service provided by a firm, as opposed to a government agency or an individual worker.

Committee On Foreign Investment In the United States
An inter-agency committee of the US government that reviews foreign direct investment into the United States to determine if it might endanger US national security and, if so, stop it.

Commodity
Could refer to any good, but in a trade context a commodity is usually a raw material orprimary product that enters into international trade, such as metals (tin, manganese) or basic agricultural products (coffee, cocoa).

Commodity Markets
Commodity markets are markets where raw or primary products are exchanged. These raw commodities are traded on regulated commodities exchanges, in which they are bought and sold in standardized contracts.

Commodity Pattern Of Trade
The trade pattern of a country or the world, focusing on goods and services traded as opposed to the factor content of that trade.

Commodity Prices
Usually means the prices of raw materials and primary products.

Commodity Terms Of Trade
1. Real price of commodities relative to manufactures. This would be the same as the most familiar terms of trade the net barter terms of trade for many developing countries that export primary commodities and import manufactures.
2. This terms is also used more broadly as a synonym for the net barter terms of trade for any country.

Common Agricultural Policy
The regulations of the European Union that seek to merge their individual agricultural programmes, primarily by stabilizing and elevating the prices of agricultural commodities. The principle tools of the CAP are variable levies and export subsidies.

Common Currency
A currency union (also known as monetary union) is where two or more states share the same currency, though without there necessarily having any further integration such as an Economic and Monetary Union, which has, in addition, a customs union and a single market.

Common Effective Preferential Tariff

The CEPT tariff is the tariff that a member of the ASEAN Free Trade Area applies to imports that originate in another AFTA country. Unlike conventional free trade areas, the CEPT tariff is not required to be zero, but only between zero and 5%. In addition, countries are permitted to designate products as excluded from the CEPT for several reasons.

Common External Tariff

The single tariff rate agreed to by all members of a customs union on imports of a product from outside the union.

Common Market

A group of countries that eliminate all barriers to movement of both goods and factors among themselves, and that also, on each product, agree to levy the same tariff on imports from outside the group. Equivalent to a customs union plus free mobility of factors.

Common Market Of Eastern And Southern Africa

A trade agreement involving 20 nations (as of 2011) of Eastern and Southern Africa. It went into effect in 1994, replacing a Preferential Trade Area that had begun in 1982, with the aim of forming a free trade area by 2000 and achieving other trade liberalization and transport facilitation over a period of 16 years.

Common Property Resources

Resources for which there are no clearly defined property rights; property owned in common by a society.

Common Tangent

A straight line that is tangent to two or more curves. Used in the Lerner diagram.

Common Trade Policy

In addition to the common external tariff required by a customs union, the European Union has a common trade policy that encompasses rules for exports and imports, export credit insurance, and the administration of anti-dumping and countervailing duties.

Commonwealth Of Independent States

An organization formed in 1991 of the nations that had been part of the USSR. Current membership (2013) includes 12 countries.

Communaute Financiere Africaine

Communaute Financiere Africaine = African Financial Community is a group of Central and West African countries, formerly ruled by France, who share two versions of a common currency, the CFA franc, that is guaranteed by the French treasury.

Communism

An economic system in which capital is owned by government.

Community Indifference Curve

One of a family of indifference curves intended to represent the preferences, and sometimes the well-being, of a country as a whole. This is a handy tool for deriving quantities of trade in a two-good model, although its legitimacy depends on the existence of community preferences, which in turn requires very restrictive assumptions.

Community Preferences

A set of consumer preferences, analogous to those of an individual as might be represented by autility function, but representing the preferences of a group of consumers. The existence of well-behaved community preferences requires restrictive assumptions about individual preferences and/or incomes.

Community Right-To-Know
Public accessibility to information about toxic pollution.

Compact Fluorescent
Flourescent light bulbs small enough to fit into standard light sockets, which are much more energy-efficient than standard incandescent bulbs.

Company
This word has many meanings, but in economics it is usually a synonym for firm.

Comparative Advantage
A country has a comparative advantage in the production of a good or service that it produces at a lower opportunity cost than its trading partners.

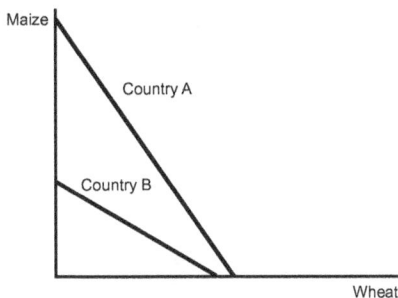

Comparative advantage can be shown by production possibility curves. Here country A has an absolute advantage in both goods, but country B can produce wheat at a relatively lower opportunity cost and therefore has a comparative advantage in wheat production.

Comparative Static
Refers to a comparison of two equilibria from a static model, usually differing by the effects of a single small change in an exogenous variable.

Compensated Demand Curve
A demand curve constructed under the assumption that demander's income is not held constant, but rather is varied to hold level of utility at a constant level. The change in consumer surpluscalculated from particular compensated demand curves measures compensating variation and equivalent variation.

Compensating Variation
The amount of money one would pay to gain a benefit such as a price decrease or the amount of income one would accept to agree upon the imposition of a harm such as a price increase. Money required to leave an individual as well off as before the economic change. Amount an individual would be willing to pay for the change, or willing to accept as compensation for a change.

Compensating Wage Differentials
the additional amount paid for a job that has certain unattractive features, such as risk of injury, as compared with a job that requires similar skills but lacks these negative features.

Compensation
1. The GATT principle that members who violate GATT rules must compensate other countries by lowering tariffs or making other concessions, or be subject to retaliation.
2. The actual or potential payment by the winners from a change in trade or other policy to the losers, intended to undo the harm to the

latter. Actual compensation is rare, but the potential for compensation is used as the basis for most evaluations of the gains from trade.

Compensation Principle

As a basis for welfare comparisons, the idea that if a policy change (such as a tariff reduction) could be Pareto improving if it were accompanied by appropriate lump-sum transfers from winners to losers, then it is viewed as beneficial even when those transfers do not occur.

Compensation Trade

Countertrade, including especially payment for foreign direct investment out of the proceeds from that investment.

Competition

The interactions between two or more sellers or buyers in a single market, each attempting to get or pay the most favourable price. Economists usually interpret and model these interactions as among individual economic agents — firms or consumers. Popular terminology extends also to competition among nations, especially competing exporters.

Competition Policy

Policies intended to prevent collusion among firms and to prevent individual firms from having excessive market power. Major forms include oversight of mergers and prevention of price fixing and market sharing. Called "anti-trust policy" in the U.S.

Competitive

1. Applied to a market or industry, this usually means perfectly competitive. Contrasts with imperfectly competitive.
2. Applied to a firm or a country's products, this means having low price, high quality, or other attractive characteristics compared to other firms or countries. Applied to a firm, this may also include the effectiveness and aggressiveness of its marketing.

Competitive Equilibrium Price

The price at which the quantity supplied and the quantity demanded are equal to each other.

Competitive Factor Market

A market for a factor in which both suppliers and demanders are perfectly competitive, taking the factor price as given.

Competitive Firm

A firm operating under conditions of perfect competition, a market condition in which no individual buyer or seller has any significant influence over price. A competitive firm is a price taker, responding to whatever price is established in the market for its output.

Competitiveness

Usually refers to characteristics that permit a firm to compete effectively with other firms due to low cost, superior technology, or aggressive marketing, perhaps internationally.

Competitiveness Index

A measure of an economy's international competitiveness, such as the Global Competitiveness Index.

Complement

One good is a complement for another if an increase in demand for one (or a fall in its price) causes an increase in the demand for the other.

Complementary Exporting

The export of one firm's products through the distribution channels of another firm.

Complementation Agreement

1. Free trade agreement.
2. An agreement between a firm and governments of two or more countries to eliminate dutieson its output, in order to attract it to locate in one of the countries.

Complements

A price change for one product leads to a shift in the opposite direction in the demand for another product.

Complete Information

The assumption that economic agents (buyers and sellers, consumers and firms) know everything that they need to know in order to make optimal decisions. Types of incomplete information are uncertainty and asymmetric information.

Complete Specialization

1. Non-production of some of the goods that a country consumes, as in definition 2 of specialization.
2. Production only of goods that are exported or nontraded, but none that compete with imports.
3. Production of only one good.
4. Being the only country in the world to produce a good.

Compliance Costs

Expenditures associated with fulfiling requirements of environmental regulations.

Composite Currency

A currency defined as a specified combination of two or more currencies, normally existing only as a unit of account rather than as a physical currency. Examples include the SDR and the ECU.

Composite Good

A fictional good that is used in economic analysis to stand in for a large number of goods, usually all other goods than the one that is the focus of attention.

Compost

Process whereby organic wastes, including food wastes, paper, and yard wastes, decompose naturally, resulting in a product rich in minerals and ideal for gardening and farming as a soil conditioners, mulch, resurfacing material, or landfill cover.

Compound Interest

Compound interest arises when interest is added to the principal, so that, from that moment on, the interest that has been added also earns interest. This addition of interest to the principal is called compounding. A bank account, for example, may have its interest compounded every year: in this case, an account with ₹1000 initial principal and 20% interest per year would have a balance of ₹1200 at the end of the first year, ₹1440 at the end of the second year, and so on.

Compound Tariff

A tariff that combines both a specific and an ad valorem component. Thus, on an import with quantity q and price p, a compound tariff collects a revenue equal to $t_s q + t_a pq$, where t_s is the specific tariff and t_a is the ad valorem tariff.

Compulsory Licensing

A requirement for a patent holder to let others produce its product, under specified terms. Countries may require this of foreign patent holders so as to access a product at lower cost. This is permitted by the TRIPs Agreement for certain purposes, such as protecting public health.

Computable General Equilibrium

Refers to economic models of microeconomic behaviour in multiple markets of one or more economies, solved computationally for equilibrium values or changes due to specified policies. The equations are anchored with data from the countries being modeled, while behavioural parameters are either assumed or adapted from estimates elsewhere.

Computed Value

A method of customs valuation when neither transaction value nor deductive value are available: sum the costs of production and preparing goods for export, then include imputed profit and overhead.

Concave

Said of a curve that bulges away from some reference point, usually the horizontal axis or the origin of a diagram. More formally, a curve is concave from below (or concave to something below it) if all straight lines connecting points on it lie on or below it.

Concentration Ratio

A common measure of industry concentration, defined as the percent of sales in the industry accounted for by the largest n firms. n is some small number such as 4 or 6, and the result is called the "n-firm concentration ratio."

Concertina Tariff Reduction

The reduction of a country's highest tariff to the level of the next highest, followed by the reduction of both to the level of the next highest after that, and so forth. Also called the concertina rule. This is known to raise welfare if all goods are net substitutes.

Concession

The term used in GATT negotiations for a country's agreement to bind a tariff or otherwise reduce import restrictions, usually in return for comparable "concessions" by other countries. Use of this term, with its connotation of loss, for what economic theory suggests is often a source of gain, is part of what has been called GATT-Speak.

Concessional Financing

Loans made by a government at an interest rate below the market rate as an indirect method of providing a subsidy.

Concessional Sale

Sale of a product at a price lower than the market would indicate. Often part of a package of foreign aid.

Conditional Cash Transfer

A programme in a developing country to encourage pro-growth and poverty-reducing activities by households, especially education, by paying them cash conditional on behaviour, especially sending children to school.

Conditional Distribution

The probability distribution of one random variable, given the values of one or more other random variables.

Conditional Expectation

The expected or average value of one random variable, called the dependent or explained variable, that depends on the values of one or more other variables, called the independent or explanatory variables.

Conditional Forecast
A forecast that assumes the future values of some explanatory variables are known with certainty.

Conditional MFN
The levying of most favoured nation tariffs on exports of a country only if it has satisfied certain conditions. Members of the WTO can apply conditional MFN only to non-members.

Conditional Variance
The variance of one random variable, given one or more other random variables.

Conditionality
The requirement imposed by the International Monetary Fund that a borrowing country undertake fiscal, monetary, and international commercial reforms as a condition to receiving a loan for balance of payments difficulties.

Conference Board
A "global, independent business membership and research association working in the public interest," founded in 1916. It provides data and analysis intended to improve performance of businesses.

Confidence Fairy
A term used frequently in New York Times opinion pieces by Paul Krugman during and after the global recession that began in 2007, referring to the views of those who believe that the economy can be stimulated by balancing government budgets so as to reassure potential investors.

Confidence Interval (Ci)
A rule used to construct a random interval so that a certain percentage of all data sets, determined by the confidence level, yields an interval that contains the population value.

Confidence Level
The percentage of samples in which we want our confidence interval to contain the population value; 95% is the most common confidence level, but 90% and 99% are also used.

Congestion
The costs and inefficiencies that result when a space becomes crowded. For example, costs of international trade may rise due to congestion of ports, if these facilities are not expanded along with trade.

Consensus
Essentially, this means unanimous agreement, and it is the basis for decision making in the WTO. Formal voting is avoided, and a decision will be blocked if any member formally objects.

Conservative Social Welfare Function
A social welfare function that takes special account of the costs to individuals of losing relative to the status quo, and that therefore seeks to avoid large losses to significant groups within the population.

Consignment
1. Something that is put into the care of another, as when a batch of traded goods is consigned to a shipper for transport to another location.
2. A method of marketing in which the seller entrusts a product to an agent, who then attempts to sell it on the seller's behalf, or "on consignment."

Consistent Estimator

An estimator that converges in probability to the population parameter as the sample size grows without bound.

Consistent Test

A test where, under the alternative hypothesis, the probability of rejecting the null hypothesis converges to one as the sample size grows without bound.

Console

A bond with no maturity date, which instead pays a fixed amount per year forever. Its simplicity makes it a convenient example in textbooks, where it appears much more frequently than in the real world.

Consolidated Fund

This fund is made of the revenues that is received by Government plus the loans that is raised by this revenue as well as the receipts from recoveries of loans granted by it.

Constant Cost

This could have many meanings, but when stated as an assumption of an economic model, it means that cost of producing a good, per unit, is the same for all units.

Constant Dollars

Dollars of constant purchasing power. That is, corrected for inflation. More precisely includes reference to a base year for comparison, e.g. "in constant 1992 dollars."

Constant Elasticity Model

A model where the elasticity of the dependent variable. with respect to an explanatory variable, is constant; in multiple regression, both variables appear in logarithmic form.

Constant Elasticity Of Transformation Function

A function representing an economy's transformation curve along which the elasticity of transformation is constant.

Constant Market Share Analysis

A technique for decomposing the change in a country's trade into components that correspond to holding its market shares constant in various markets. Introduced to international trade by Tyszynski (1951), it is an application of shift and share analysis of Creamer (1943).

Constant Returns To Scale

A property of a production function such that scaling all inputs by any positive constant also scales output by the same constant. Such a function is also called homogeneous of degree one or linearly homogeneous. CRTS is a critical assumption of the H-O Model of international trade. Contrasts with increasing returns and decreasing returns.

Constant-Cost Industry

An industry with a horizontal long-run supply curve and a linear cost function; its expansion does not result in an increase or decrease in input prices.

Constraint Set

The set of options among which a decision-maker is able to choose, given its resources and the market conditions that it faces.

Constrict

While this word generally means to make something narrower, in economics it is commonly used for making something, especially the money supply, smaller (or perhaps to allow it to grow more slowly).

Consular Fees And Formalities

Charges and procedures required of importers. May constitute nontariff barriers.

Consultation

The first step in the WTO dispute settlement process, whereby countries are expected to consult directly regarding any objection or disagreement and seek to resolve it without further steps.

Consultative Group To Assist The Poor

A consortium of public and private funding organizations working to expand access to financial services in poor countries.

Consumer Income

Often, the term "consumer income" is used synonymously with a country's gross domestic product (GDP). In technical national income account terms, consumer income should more specifically refer to disposable income or household income, which would be approximately 70 percent of GDP.

Consumer Movement

Mode 2 of four modes of supply of traded services, this one entails the buyer moving (temporarily) to the foreign location of the seller, as in the case of tourism.

Consumer Price Index

A measure of the average amount (price) paid for a market basket of goods and services by a typical U.S. consumer in comparison to the average paid for the same basket in an earlier base year. A price index in which the basket of goods is defined by what a typical consumer purchases.

Consumer Protection Legislation

laws aimed at protecting consumers, for instance by assuring that consumers have more complete information about items they are considering buying.

Consumer Sovereignty

Consumer sovereignty is the economic principle that consumers determine the production of goods. The term can prescribe what consumers should be permitted, or describe what consumers are permitted. The term was coined by William Harold Hutt in his book Economists and the Public (1936).

Consumer Spending

Consumer spending or consumer demand or consumption is also known as personal consumption expenditure. It is the largest part of aggregate demand or effective demand at the macroeconomic level. There are two variants of consumption in the aggregate demand model, including induced consumption and autonomous consumption.

Consumer Subsidy Equivalent

Same as consumer support estimate

Consumer Support Estimate

Introduced by the OECD to quantify agricultural policies, this measures transfers to or from consumers that are implicit in these policies. Since industrialized-country's agricultural producers are routinely supported by raising prices, CSE estimates are usually negative.

Consumer Surplus

The net benefit realized by consumers when they are able to buy a good at the prevailing market price. It is equivalent to the difference between the maximum amount consumers would be willing to pay and the amount they actually do pay for the units of the good purchased. Graphically it is the triangle above the market price and below the demand curve.

Consumers

A consumer is a person or group of people who are the final users of products and or services generated within a social system. A consumer may be a person or group, such as a household. The concept of a consumer may vary significantly by context or an individual who buys products or services for personal use and not for manufacture or resale.

Consumption

In macroeconomics, the total spending, by individuals or a nation, on consumer goods during a given period. Strictly speaking, consumption should apply only to those goods totally used, enjoyed, or "eaten up" within that period. In practice, consumption expenditures include all consumer goods bought, many of which last well beyond the period in question —e.g., furniture, clothing, and automobiles.

Consumption Expenditures

The total dollar value of all goods and services purchased by the household sector for current use.

Consumption Externality

An externality arising from consumption.

Consumption Function

Generally, the relationship between consumer expenditures and all the influences that determine them. More specifically, the relationship between consumers' disposable incomes (personal income less taxes) and the amount they wish to spend on consumer goods and services.

Consumption Possibility Frontier

A graph of the maximum quantities of goods (usually two) that an economy can consume in a specified situation, such as autarky and free trade. Used to illustrate the potential benefits from trade by showing that it can expand consumption possibilities.

Consumption Spending

Spending on consumer goods and services.

Contagion

The phenomenon of a financial crisis in one country spilling over to another, which then suffers many of the same problems.

Contestable Market

The theory of contestable markets, associated primarily with its 1982 proponent William J. Baumol, holds that there exist markets served by a small number of firms, which are nevertheless characterized by competitive equilibria (and therefore desirable welfare outcomes) because of the existence of potential short-term entrants.

Contingency Clauses

Statements within a contract that make the level of payment or the work to be performed conditional upon various factors.

Contingency Fund

The fund that is used by the government in order to meet the unforeseen expenditure or incase to meet emergencies. The contingency fund is generally used when the government cannot wait for long for the parliament to authorise the expenses on the expenditure.

Contingent Valuation Method

Directly asks people what they are willing to pay for a benefit an/or willing to receive in compensation for tolerating a cost through a survey or questionnaire. Personal valuations for increases or decreases in the quantity of some good are obtained contingent upon a hypothetical market. The aim is to elicit valuations or bids which are close to what would be revealed if an actual market existed. Several biases, including strategic, design, (starting point, vehicle, and informational), hypothetical, and operational are discussed above and below.

Continuous Random Variable

A random variable that takes on any particular value with probability zero.

Continuous Time

The use of a continuous variable to represent time, as in an economic model.

Continuum Model

A model in which some entities that are normally discrete and exist in finite numbers are modeled instead by a continuous variable. This can sometimes simplify the treatment of large numbers of entities. In trade theory, the most notable example is the continuum-of-goods model.

Continuum-of-Goods Model

A class of trade models in which goods are indexed by a continuous variable, approximating the case of very large numbers of goods. The classic, original examples are Dornbusch, Fischer, and Samuelson (1977, 1980).

Contract Curve

1. In an Edgeworth Box for consumption, the allocations of 2 goods to 2 consumers that are Pareto efficient. Starting with an allocation that may not be on the contract curve, it shows the ways that the consumers might contract to exchange the goods with each other.

2. In an Edgeworth Box for production, this name is sometimes also used for the efficiency locus.

3. The locus of points where the marginal rates of substitution are the same for both consumers (in exchange between consumers) or the locus of points where the marginal rates of technical substitution are the same for both producers (in exchange between producers).

4. Using a separate indifference map (or 2-variable isoquant production function) for each of two individuals (firms) with respect to the same two commodities (inputs), the contract curve is traced by the points of tangency of the two sets of indifference (isoquant) curves when the inverted map of one individual (firm) is superimposed on the map of the other individual (firm) forming an 'Edgeworth box'. The curve traces all possible points of final equilibrium between the two individuals (firms). The opposite sides of the box are the axes for the same good (input) of the two individuals (firms).

Contracting Party

A country that has signed the GATT. The term Contracting Parties with both words capitalized means all Contracting Parties acting jointly.

Contractionary

Tending to cause aggregate output (GDP) and/or the price level to fall. Term is typically applied to monetary policy (a decrease in the money supply or an increase in interest rates) and to fiscal policy (a decrease in government spending or a tax increase), but may also apply to other macroeconomic shocks. Contrasts with expansionary.

Convention

A statement of principle as to acceptable behaviour. For example, members of the International Labour Organization have agreed to a long list of conventions regarding the acceptable treatment of workers.

Convention On International Trade In Endangered Species

Convention on International Trade in Endangered Species of Wild Fauna and Flora is an agreement among originally 80 governments effective in 1975 to prevent trade in wild animals and plants from threatening their survival. It works by requiring licensing of trade in covered species.

Conventional International Law

The portion of international law that results from formal agreements among nations, such as the GATT.

Convergence

The process of becoming quantitatively more alike. In an international context, it often refers to countries becoming more alike in terms of their factor prices or in terms of their per capita incomes, perhaps as a result of trade or other forms of economic integration.

Convertible Currency

A currency that can legally be exchanged for another or for gold. In times of crisis, governments sometimes restrict such exchange, giving rise to black market exchange rates.

Convex

1. Said of a curve that bulges toward some reference point, usually the horizontal axis or the origin of a diagram. More formally, a curve is convex from below (or convex to something below it) if all straight lines connecting points on it lie on or above it.

2. Said of a set that contains all straight line segments joining points within it.

Convex Combination

A convex combination is a linear combination of points (which can be vectors, scalars, or more generally points in an affine space) where all coefficients are non-negative and sum up to 1. All convex combinations are within the convex hull of the given points. In fact, the collection of all such convex combinations of points in the set constitutes the convex hull of the set.

Convex Hull

The boundary of the set of points that are either members of, or convex combinations of, points from two or more other sets. The convex hull of two or more isoquants consists of the innermost of the isoquants themselves plus the points between them on their common tangents.

Convexity

This is just the state of being convex. More generally in economics it refers to the sets (production possibilities, preferences, and constraints which, if they are convex, may yield well behaved economic equilibria. In contrast, models that are nonconvex tend to have multiple equilibria and display discontinuous behaviour (jumps).

Coordinates

A coordinate system is a system which uses one or more numbers, or coordinates, to uniquely determine the position of a point or other geometric element on a manifold such as Euclidean space. The order of the coordinates is significant and they are sometimes identified by their position in an ordered tuple and sometimes by a letter, as in 'the x-coordinate'. The coordinates are taken to be real numbers in elementary mathematics, but may be complex numbers or elements of a more abstract system such as a commutative ring. The use of a coordinate system allows problems in geometry to be translated into problems about numbers and vice versa; this is the basis of analytic geometry.

Coordination

Cooperation in setting economic policy, especially across countries, so that policies of different governments reinforce each other rather than cancelling each other out.

Copyright

A legal right (usually of the author or composer or publisher of a work) to exclusive publication, production, sale, distribution of some work. What is protected by the copyright is the "expression," not the idea. Notice that taking another's idea is plagiarism, so copyrights are not the equivalent of legal prohibition of plagiarism.

Core

The set of allocations that cannot be improved upon by a subset of consumers trading among themselves. In an pure exchange economy, the core is the contract curves.

Core Inflation

The rate of inflation excluding certain sectors whose prices are most volatile, specifically food and energy.

Core Labour Standard

Several labour standards that are considered the most basic and fundamental. The ILO identifies eight conventions as "fundamental," covering the topics: freedom of association and collective bargaining, forced labour, child labour, and discrimination.

Core Propositions

The core propositions of the HO Model are the factor price equalization theorem, theHeckscher-Ohlin Theorem, the Stolper-Samuelson Theorem, and the Rybczynski Theorem, according to Ethier (1974).

Corn Laws

British regulations on the import and export of grain, mainly wheat, intended to control its price. The laws were repealed in 1846, signaling a shift toward free trade.

Corner Solution

Case in which the budget line reaches the highest achievable indifference curve at a point along an axis (analogous cases occur in the theory of production).

Corporacion Andina De Fomento

A financial institution created to "promote and foster the integration of the Andean region." It acts as a development bank for Latin America.

Corporate Income Tax

A tax based on the income, or profit, received by a corporation; A tax on the profits of corporations. Differences in corporate tax rates across countries can be a cause of foreign direct investment as well as transfer pricing.

Corporation

A legal entity formed to conduct business and possessing certain privileges not available to single proprietorships or partnerships, notably limited liability which confines the shareholder's possible losses to the amount paid to purchase shares in the business.

Correlation

A measure of the extent to which two economic or statistical variables move together, normalized so that its values range from -1 to +1. It is defined as the covariance of the two variables divided by the square root of the product of their variances. The correlation is used in trade theory to express weak relationships among economic variables.

Correlation Coefficient

Denoted as "r", a measure of the linear relationship between two variables. The absolute value of "r" provides an indication of the strength of the relationship. The value of "r" varies between positive 1 and negative 1, with -1 or 1 indicating a perfect linear relationship, and r = 0 indicating no relationship. The sign of the correlation coefficient indicates whether the slope of the line is positive or negative when the two variables are plotted in a scatter plot.

Correlation Result

A theoretical property of models with arbitrary numbers of goods or other variables that takes the form of a correlation among variables rather than a strict prediction for each one. Thus represents a weaker average relationship among the variables.

Used for comparative advantageand other properties of trade models in higher dimensions.

Corruption

Dishonest or partial behaviour on the part of a government official or employee, such as a customs or procurement officer. Also actions by others intended to induce such behaviour, such as bribery or blackmail.

Cost

Cost is the price of a factor of production used in producing final output. Cost, together with the final price and quantity of output, is a key factor in economic decision-making. Thus profit equals price per unit multiplied by the quantity of output (or revenue) minus the total cost of all factors of production. (HHC).

Cost Advantage

Possession of a lower cost of production or operation than a competing firm or country. In the case of countries, this could refer to an absolute advantage, although it is more likeliy a comparative advantage.

Cost Benefit Analysis

A technique that assesses projects through a comparison between their costs and benefits, including social costs and benefits for an entire region or country. Depending on the project objectives and its the expected outputs, three types of CBA are generally recognised: financial; economic; and social. Generally cost-benefit analyses are comparative, i.e. they are used to compare alternative proposals. Cost-benefit analysis compares the costs and benefits of the situation with and without the project; the costs and benefits are considered over the life of the project.

Cost Function

A function relating the minimized total cost in a firm or industry to output and factor prices.

Cost Of Capital

The cost incurred by a firm to raise additional funds. Depends on the interest rate and taxes that it faces, as well as its ability to raise funds through equity.

Cost Of Living

The cost of a representative bundle of goods and services in consumption, usually as measured by the consumer price index.

Cost Push Inflation

Cost push inflation occurs where costs of production rise independently of demand factors. Costs may increase for a number of reasons - it may be wage increases or perhaps an increase in raw material prices (oil prices in this diagram).

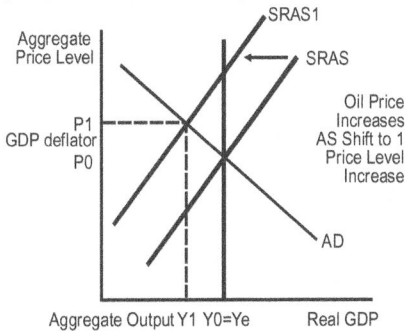

Cost push inflation can be shown using the aggregate demand and aggregate supply curves. In this case it is not the aggregate demand that increases, it is the aggregate supply curve that shifts to the left, as in the diagram.

Cost-Effectiveness Analysis

Least expensive way of achieving a given environmental quality target, or the way of achieving the greatest improvement in some environmental target for a given expenditure of resources.

Cost-of-Living Adjustments

Automatic adjustments in incomes paid to individual recipients which are tied to the inflation rate, usually measured by the Consumer Price Index.

Costs Of Production

All resources used in producing goods and services, for which owners receive payments.

Cotonou Agreement

A partnership agreement between the EU and the ACP Countries signed in June 2000 in Cotonou, Benin, replacing the Lomé Convention. Its main objective is poverty reduction, "to be achieved through political dialogue, development aid and closer economic and trade cooperation."

Council For Mutual Economic Assistance

An international organization formed in 1956 among the Soviet Union and other Communist countries to coordinate economic development and trade. It was disbanded in 1991.

Count Data

Count data is a statistical data type, a type of data in which the observations can take only the non-negative integer values {0, 1, 2, 3, ...}, and where these integers arise from counting rather than ranking. The statistical treatment of count data is distinct from that of binary data, in which the observations can take only two values, usually represented by 0 and 1, and from ordinal data, which may also consist of integers but where the individual values fall on an arbitrary scale and only the relative ranking is important.

Count Variable

An individual piece of count data is often termed a count variable. When such a variable is treated as a random variable, the Poisson, binomial and negative binomial distributions are commonly used to represent its distribution.

Counter-Cyclical

Designed to offset or counteract the effects of fluctuations of an economic variable that rises and falls over time. Examples are increased payments to unemployed workers when GDP falls below full employment, and increased payments to farmers when crop prices fall below some target level.

Counterfeit Goods

Products that appear to duplicate branded goods without the permission of the brand owner. If they are in fact duplicates, then buyers benefit from a low price, while brand owners may lose. Often, however, they are inferior copies, useless or even dangerous.

Counterpurchase Contract

A form of countertrade in which the foreign seller is required to purchase something from the buyer, usually unrelated goods or services.

Countertrade

Countertrade means exchanging goods or services which are paid for, in whole or part, with other goods

or services, rather than with money. A monetary valuation can however be used in counter trade for accounting purposes. In dealings between sovereign states, the term bilateral trade is used. Or "Any transaction involving exchange of goods or service for something of equal value."

Countervailing Duties

Duties (tariffs) that are imposed by a country to counteract subsidies provided to a foreign producer.

Country Of Origin

The country in which a good was produced, or sometimes, in the case of a traded service, the home country of the service provider. With production processes spread across many countries (fragmentation), origin is often ambiguous. In practice, is it subject to rules of origin.

Country Risk

The risk associated with operating in, trading with, or especially holding the assets issued by, a particular country. In the case of assets, country risk helps to explain why borrowers in some country must pay higher interest rates than borrowers from other countries, thus paying a country risk premium.

Country Size

Any of many measures of the size of a country. For most economic comparisons, however, country size refers to GDP.

Country Terms Of Trade

The relative value of a country's export prices divided by the relative value of a country's import prices, measured as an index. We say a country's terms of trade are improving if export prices are rising relative to import prices.

Coupon

The interest payment on a bond, so-named because bonds originally were pieces of paper with small sections, called coupons, that were cut off and exchanged for the interest payments.

Cournot Competition

The assumption, often assumed to be made by firms in an oligopoly, that other firms hold their outputs constant as they themselves change behaviour. Contrasts with Bertrand competition. Both are used in models of international oligopoly, but Cournot competition is used more often.

Cournot's Law

That the sum of the balances of payments or of trade across all countries must be zero. Term seems to have been coined by, and perhaps only used by, Mundell (1960, p. 102), who credited it to Cournot (1897).

Covariance

A measure of linear dependence between two random variables.

Cover

To use the forward market to protect against exchange risk. Typically, an importer with a future commitment to pay in foreign currency would buy it forward, and exporter with a future receipt would sell it forward, and a purchaser of a foreign bond would sell forward the expected proceeds at maturity. See hedge.

Coverage Ratio

A measure of the presence of nontariff barriers, defined as the value of imports subject to one or a group of NTBs, divided by the total value of imports. Contrasts with frequency ratio and tariff equivalent.

Covered Interest Arbitrage

A combination of transactions on two countries' securities and exchange markets designed to profit from failure of covered interest parity. A typical set of transactions would include selling bonds in one market, using the proceeds to buy spot foreign currency and foreign bonds, and selling forward the return at a future date.

Covered Interest Parity

Equality of returns on otherwise comparable financial assets denominated in two currencies, assuming that the forward market is used to cover against exchange risk. As an approximation, covered interest parity requires that $i = i* + p$ where i is the domestic interest rate, $i*$ is the foreign interest rate, and p is the forward premium.

Covered Interest Rate

The covered interest rate, in a currency other than your own, is the nominal interest rate plus the forward premium on the currency; thus the percent you will earn holding the foreign asset while protecting against exchange-rate change by selling the foreign currency forward.

CPI

A consumer price index (CPI) measures changes in the price level of consumer goods and services purchased by households. The CPI in the United States is defined by the Bureau of Labour Statistics as "a measure of the average change over time in the prices paid by urban consumers for a market basket of consumer goods and services." The CPI is a statistical estimate constructed using the prices of a sample of representative items whose prices are collected periodically. Sub-indexes and sub-sub-indexes are computed for different categories and sub-categories of goods and services, being combined to produce the overall index with weights reflecting their shares in the total of the consumer expenditures covered by the index. It is one of several price indices calculated by most national statistical agencies. The annual percentage change in a CPI is used as a measure of inflation. A CPI can be used to index (i.e., adjust for the effect of inflation) the real value of wages, salaries, pensions, for regulating prices and for deflating monetary magnitudes to show changes in real values. In most countries, the CPI is, along with the population census and the USA National Income and Product Accounts, one of the most closely watched national economic statistics.

Craftsperson
A worker who completes all steps in the production of a good or service.

Crawling Peg
An exchange rate that is pegged, but for which the par value is changed frequently by small amounts and in a preannounced fashion in response to signals from the exchange market.

Credibility
The condition of being believed. Particularly relevant when a government or central bank tries to influence an economic variable, such as the exchange rate or the rate of inflation, since belief that it will fail induces market responses that hasten that failure.

Credit
(1) In monetary theory, the use of someone else's funds in exchange for a promise to pay (usually with interest) at a later date. The major examples are short-term loans from a bank, credit extended by suppliers, and commercial paper.
(2) In balance-of-payments accounting, an item such as exports that earns a country foreign currency.

Credit Crunch
A shortage of available loans. In well-functioning markets, this would simply mean a rise in interest rates, but in practice it often means that some borrowers cannot get loans at all, a situation of credit rationing.

Credit Rationing
Credit is rationed when no lender is willing to make a loan to a borrower or the amount lenders are willing to lend to borrowers is limited, even if the borrower is willing to pay more than other borrowers of comparable risk who are getting loans.

Credit, Letter Of
A letter from a bank or a firm authorizing payment to a third person of a specific sum for which the sender assumes full responsibility.

Creditor
A creditor is a party (e.g. person, organization, company, or government) that has a claim on the services of a second party. It is a person or institution to whom money is owed. The first party, in general, has provided some property or service to the second party under the assumption (usually enforced by contract) that the second party will return an equivalent property and service. The second party is frequently called a debtor or borrower. The first party is the creditor, which is the lender of property, service or money. The term creditor is frequently used in the financial world, especially in

reference to short term loans, long term bonds, and mortgage loans. In law, a person who has a money judgment entered in their favour by a court is called a judgement creditor. The term creditor derives from the notion of credit. In modern America, credit also refers to a rating which indicates the likelihood a borrower will pay back his or her loan. In earlier times, credit also referred to reputation or trustworthiness.

Creditor Nation

A country whose assets owned abroad are worth more than the assets within the country that are owned by foreigners.

Creeping Inflation

This term seems to be used both for a rate of inflation that is low but nonetheless high enough to cause problems, and for a rate of inflation that itself gradually moves higher over time.

Criteria

Standards or measures of value that people use to evaluate what is most important.

Critical Value

In hypothesis testing, the value against which a test statistic is compared to deter mine whether or not the null hypothesis is rejected.

Crony Capitalism

Used to describe a capitalist economy in which government or corporate officials and insiders provide lucrative opportunities for their friends and relatives. Term became popular during the Asian Crisis to describe some of the victim countries, but is now often used elsewhere as well.

Cross Elasticity

1. An elasticity that has been ignored by a student in a problem set.
2. The elasticity of supply or demand for one good or service with respect to the price of another.

Cross Elasticity Of Demand

The change in the quantity demanded of one product or service impacting the change in demand for another product or service. For example, percentage change in the quantity demanded of a good divided by the percentage change in the price of another good (a substitute or complement)

Cross Rate

1. The exchange rate between two currencies as implied by their values with respect to a third currency.
2. Thus, since most currencies are commonly quoted in U.S. dollars, the exchange rate between any two currencies other than the dollar.

Cross Retaliation

Retaliation in which the response is in a different sector or under a different WTO agreement than the action that prompted it. For example, a country suspends intellectual property protection in response to a violation of anti-dumping in manufacturing; or restricts service imports in response to a subsidy in agriculture.

Cross Sectional Variation

The differences in an economic variable that exist at a point in time comparing different economic units, such as consumers, firms, industries, or countries. Often used to seek evidence of causes of trade, growth, and other behaviours.

Cross Subsidization

The practice of charging higher prices to one group of consumers in order to subsidize lower prices for another group.

Cross Subsidy

The use of profits from one activity to cover losses from another. Thus the use of high prices for some of a firm's products, for example, to permit it to price below cost for others. In international trade, this could be one explanation for dumping.

Cross-Border Supply

The provision of an internationally traded service across national borders without requiring physical movement of buyer or seller, as when the service can be provided by long-distance communication.

Cross-Country Regression

The use of regression analysis on data from multiple countries, the purpose being to describe and perhaps explain their differences. For example, regressions of country GDP growth rates on their levels of trade or openness show a strong positive relationship between trade and growth, though without establishing causation.

Cross-Elasticity Of Demand

The (percentage) change in the quantity demanded of a good consequent upon a (one percent) change in the price of an associated good.

Cross-Hauling

The simultaneous shipment of the same product in opposite directions over the same route. The export of the same good by two countries to each other would be cross-hauling, if it occurs at the same time.

Cross-Licensing

The permission by two firms to use each other's intellectual property rights.

Cross-Sectional Data Set

A data set collected from a population at a given point in time.

Crowding Out

The tendency for federal government, by deficit financing to compete with firms or persons for borrowed funds; that is, firms and households unable to borrow at a low rate of interest curtail their investment and consumption spending.

Cryptosporidium

A protozoan (single-celled organism) that can infect humans, usually as a result of exposure to contaminated drinking water.

Cultural Argument For Protection

The view that imports undermine a country's culture and identity — for example by changing consumption patterns to ones more similar to those abroad, or by reducing demands for domestically produced art and music — and therefore that imports should be restricted.

Cum

Latin for "with," as in tax cum subsidy.

Cumulation

1. In an anti-dumping case against imports from more than one country, the summation of these imports for the purpose of determining injury. That is, the imports are deemed to have caused injury if all of them together could have done so, even if individually they would not.

2. In overlapping free trade areas, a provision that allows inputs from one FTA to qualify as originating under another FTA's rules of origin.

Cumulative Distribution Function (CDF)

A function that gives the probability of a random variable being less than or equal to any specified real number.

Currency

1. The money used by a country; e.g., the national currency of Japan is the yen.
2. The physical embodiment of money, in the forms of paper bills or notes, and metal coins.

Currency Appreciation

An increase in the value of one currency relative to another currency. Appreciation occurs when, because of a change in exchange rates; a unit of one currency buys more units of another currency. Opposite is the case with currency depreciation.

Currency Area

A group of countries that share a common currency. Originally defined by Mundell (1961) as a group that have fixed exchange rates among their national currencies.

Currency Basket

A group of two or more currencies that may be used as a unit of account, or to which another currency may be pegged.

Currency Bloc

1. A group of countries that share a common currency; a currency area.
2. A group of countries that peg their different national currencies to a single currency.

Currency Board

An extreme form of pegged exchange rate in which management of both the exchange rate and the money supply are taken away from the central bank and given to an agency with instructions to back every unit of circulating domestic currency with a specified amount of foreign currency. Operates similarly to the gold standard.

Currency Crisis

The crisis that occurs when particpants in an exchange market come to perceive that an attempt to maintain a pegged exchange rate is about to fail, causing speculation against the peg that hastens the failure and forces a devaluation.

Currency Factor

The portion of a rate of return that is due to the currency in which the asset is denominated. The currency factor can be nonzero either because of currency risk or because of expected appreciation or depreciation.

Currency In Circulation

The amount of a country's currency that is in the hands of the public (households, firms, banks, etc), as opposed to sitting in the vaults of the central bank.

Currency Intervention

Exchange market intervention.

Currency Manipulation

The use of exchange market intervention to keep the exchange rate above or below theequilibrium exchange rate. The term is most likely to be applied to a country that keeps its currency undervalued for the purpose of making its good more competitive.

Currency Misalignment

An exchange rate that is above or below the equilibrium exchange rate, perhaps but not necessarily due to currency manipulation.

Currency Mismatch

Having assets that are denominated in a different currency than liabilities, so that a change in exchange rate between those currencies can have a large positive or negative effect on net wealth.

Currency Realignment

A change in the par value of a pegged exchange rate.

Currency Reserves

This usually means international reserves.

Currency Risk

Uncertainty about the future value of a currency.

Currency Risk Premium

The extent to which the interest rate in on bonds denominated in a currency exceeds what can be explained by default risk and expected changes in the exchange rate. What remains is presumed to be compensation for currency risk.

Currency Speculation

To buy or sell a currency in anticipation of its appreciation or depreciation respectively, the intent being to make a profit or avoid a loss.

Currency Substitution

The use of foreign currency (e.g., U.S. dollars) as a medium of exchange in place of or along with the local currency (e.g., Rupees).

Currency Union

A group of countries that agree to peg their exchange rates and to coordinate their monetary policies so as to avoid the need for currency realignments.

Currency War

Efforts by multiple countries to influence exchange rates to their own perceived advantage, at the expense of others. Term used in September 2010 by Guido Mantega, Brazil's finance minister, referring to actions by China, and then by other countries in response, to prevent their currencies from appreciating.

Current Account

Part of a nation's balance of payments which includes the value of all goods and services imported and exported, as well as the payment and receipt of dividends and interest. A nation has a current account surplus if exports exceed imports plus net transfers to foreigners. The sum of the current and capital accounts is the overall balance of payments.

Current Account Balance

The current account balance is one of two major measures of the nature of a country's foreign trade (the other being the net capital outflow). A current account surplus increases a country's net foreign assets by the corresponding amount, and a current account deficit does the reverse. Both government and private payments are included in the calculation. It is called the current account because goods and services are generally consumed in the current period.

Current Account Deficit

This deficit is determined on finding the difference between the nation's exports and imports.

Current Account Surplus

Credits minus debits on current account. Same as balance on current account.

Current Dollar

Values which have not been adjusted to remove the influence of changes in the general price level.

Current Dollars

The phrase, "in current dollars" means "not adjusted for inflation."

Current Prices

Refers to prices in the present, rather than in some base year; e.g., "GDP at current prices" means GDP as measured, in contrast to real GDP, or "GDP at XXXX prices," where the latter is measured in the prices of year XXXX.

Custom Duties

These are levies that are incurred from the goods exported from or imported to the country.

Customary International Law

The portion of international law that has developed over time through custom and usage, rather than formal agreement. Contrasts with conventional international law.

Customs

The process that through which imported goods must pass in crossing the border of a country or other customs area.

Customs Area

A geographic area that is responsible for levying its own customs duties at its border.

Customs Brokerage

A firm that facilitates the clearance of goods through customs by handling the paperwork.

Customs Classification

1. The category defining the tariff to be applied to an imported good.
2. The act of determining this category, which may be subject to various rules and/or to the discretion of the customs officer.

Customs Clearance

The processing of imported goods through a country's border procedures for inspection and taxation.

Customs Cooperation Council Nomenclature

An international system of classification of goods for specifying tariffs, called the Brussels Tariff Nomenclature prior to 1976, and later superseded by the Harmonized System of Tariff Nomenclature

Customs Declaration

A written statement by an importer or traveler of the dutiable imports that they are bringing into a country.

Customs Duty

Duty levied on the imports of certain goods. Includes excise equivalents. Unlike tariffs customs duties are used mainly as a means to raise revenue for the government rather than protecting domestic producers from foreign competition.

Customs Harmonization

Efforts to adopt common procedures across countries for identifying and valuing imported goods for the purpose of levying customs duties. One such effort was the adoption of the harmonized system of customs classification.

Customs Officer

The government official who monitors goods moving across a national border and levies tariffs.

Customs Procedure

The practices used by customs officers to clear goods into a country and levy tariffs. Includes clearance procedures such as documentation and inspection, methods of determining a good's classification, and methods of assigning its value as the base for an ad valorem tariff. Any of these can impede trade and constitute a NTB.

Customs Station

An office through which imported goods must pass in order to be monitored and taxed by customs officers.

Customs Territory

A geographical area the borders of which are managed, imposing duties and controls on goods entering the area. A customs territory may not be an internationally recognized country, and the customs territory of a country may be larger or smaller than the country.

Customs Union

A group of countries that adopt free trade (zero tariffs and no other restrictions on trade) on trade among themselves, and that also, on each product, agree to levy the same tariff on imports from outside the group. Equivalent to an FTA plus a common external tariff.

Customs User Fee

A charge levied on traders for the service of passing through customs.

Customs Valuation Agreement

The Customs Valuation Agreement of the WTO replaced the Customs Valuation Code, but specified similar rules: Use a transaction value when available; if not, use deductive value orcomputed value.

Customs Valuation Code

A plurilateral agreement of the Tokyo Round specifying rules for customs valuation.

Customs Valuation Procedure

The method by which a customs officer determines the customs value. When this method is biased against importing, it becomes an NTB.

Customs Value

The value of an imported good for the purpose of levying an ad valorem tariff.

Cyclical Fluctuations

Short term variations in the level of national income such as those which occur from year to year. Contrast with "secular" changes which occur over longer periods of time.

Cyclical Unemployment

The portion of unemployment that is due to the business cycle and thus rises in recessions but then disappears eventually after the recession ends.

D

Damage Function

Relationship that shows how pollution damage varies with the level of pollution emitted, and what the monetary value of that damage is.

Data Frequency

The interval at which time series data are collected. Yearly, quarterly, and monthly are the most common data frequencies.

Deadweight Loss From Monopoly

If a perfectly competitive market is transformed into a monopoly, the deadweight loss is the reduction in total surplus resulting from this transformation.

Deadweight Loss From Monopsony

If a perfectly competitive market is transformed into a monopsony, the deadweight loss is the reduction in total surplus resulting from this transformation.

Death Rate

Numbers of people dying per thousand population.

Decision Making

Decision making (Decision from Latin decidere "to decide, determine," literally "to cut off," from de- "off" and caedere "to cut") can be regarded as the mental processes (cognitive process) resulting in the selection of a course of action among several alternative scenarios. Every decision making process produces a final choice.

Decrease In Aggregate Demand

If there is a decrease in aggregate demand then the equilibrium level of output will tend to fall. Here it falls from Q1 to Q2.

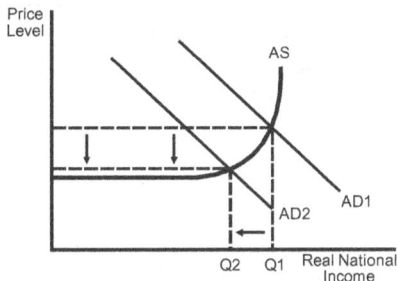

Aggregate demand is made up of consumption, investment, government expenditure and net exports. A decrease in any one of these components will shift the aggregate demand curve to the left and have the effect shown on the diagram.

Decrease In Marginal Cost

If a monopolist experiences significant economies of scale, then they may be able to sell the product cheaper than the equivalent industry in perfect competition. In the absence of economies of scale a monopolist would produce a quantity of Qm1 and at a price of Pm1. An industry in perfect competition would produce a quantity of Qpc at a price of Ppc. However, if the monopolist was able to gain significant economies of scale, that would shift the marginal cost curve to MC2. The monopolist would then produce a quantity of Qm2 at a price of Pm2 which is less than the equivalent industry in perfect competition.

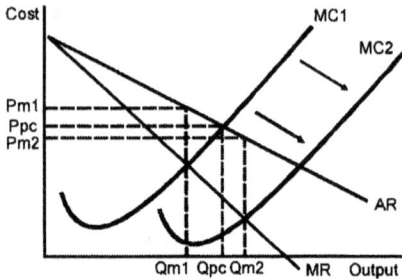

Decrease In Marginal Revenue Product

A decrease in the marginal revenue product of a factor will shift the MRP curve down.

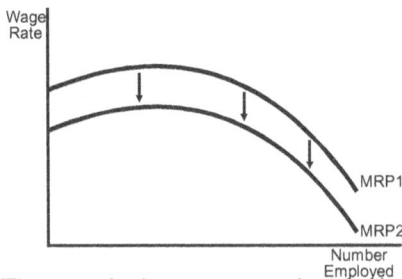

The marginal revenue product is the extra revenue earned by an additional factor, and is therefore the value of that factor to the firm. It is calculated by multiplying the marginal physical product (the extra output produced by one more factor) by the marginal

revenue (the additional revenue earned from selling the output). Any decrease in the MRP will shift the MRP curve downwards and may be caused by a reduction in the price of the good, a decrease in productivity of the factor or anything else that changes either the MPP or the MR.

Decrease In Supply And Demand

A decrease in supply shifts the supply curve to the left and a decrease in demand shifts the demand curve to the left. As a result of these changes there will definitely be a decrease in the equilibrium quantity in the market, but whether price is higher or lower will depend on whether the shift in supply or demand is greater and the elasticities of supply and demand.

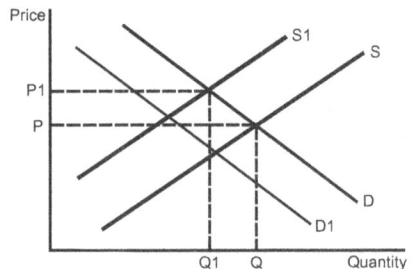

The supply and demand curves have shifted because there has been a change in the determinants of supply and demand. For example, there may have simultaneously been a decrease in the level of income and also an increase in the firm's costs.

Decreasing Returns To Scale

A situation in which output increases at a lower rate than inputs if the quantities of all inputs are increased at the same rate.

Decreasing-Cost Industry

An industry with a negatively sloped long-run supply curve; its expansion results in a decrease in average cost.

Deficit Spending

Deficit spending is the amount by which spending exceeds revenue over a particular period of time, also called simply deficit, or budget deficit; the opposite of budget surplus. The term may be applied to the budget of a government, private company, or individual.

Deflation

Deflation is a reduction in the level of national income and output, usually accompanied by a fall in the general price level.

Degrees Of Freedom (DF)

In multiple regression analysis, the number of observations minus the number of estimated parameters.

Demand

The maximum quantities of some good that people will choose (or buy) at different prices. An identical definition is the relative value of the marginal unit of some good when different quantities of that good are available.

Demand Curve

A graphic representation of the relationship between prices and the corresponding quantities demanded per time period. The relationship between quantity demanded of a good and the price, whether for an individual or for the market (all individuals) as a whole.

Demand Curve For Loanable Funds

Relationship between the quantity of loanable funds demanded and the interest rate.

Demand Decrease

A decrease in the quantity demanded at every price; a shift to the left of the demand curve.

Demand Deposits

Checking accounts in commercial banks. These banks are obliged to pay out funds when depositors write checks on those numbers. Checking accounts are not cash - they are numbers recorded in banks.

Demand Increase

An increase in the quantity demanded at every price; a shift to the right of the demand curve.

Demand Site Management

An attempt by utilities to reduce customers' demand for electricity or energy by encouraging efficiency.

Demand-Pull Inflation

Demand pull inflation is inflation caused by excess aggregate demand in the economy.

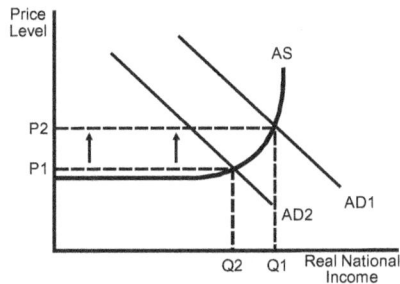

On the diagram the increase in demand from AD1 to AD2 has caused the price level to rise. If this continues then demand-pull inflation is the result. The rise in demand may have come from a variety of different sources; a decrease in the tax level, an increase in government expenditure or perhaps an increase in consumer expenditure.

Demographic Effects

Effects that arise from changes in characteristics of the population such as age, birthrates, and location.

Denominator Degrees Of Freedom

In an F test, the degrees of freedom in the unrestricted model.

Dependent Variable

The variable to be explained in a multiple regression model (and a variety of other models).

Deposit/Refund Systems

A surcharge paid when buying potentially polluting products is refunded when the product or container is returned for recycling or proper disposal. Examples include "Bottle bills" deposits on beverage bottles and cans, containerized hazardous or solid waste, such as motor vehicle batteries, oil, and tyres, and deposit-refund systems for car batteries. Recycling and environmentally safe disposal increase because the user is "paid" for doing it right.

Depository Institutions

Commercial banks, credit unions, savings and loan associations, mutual savings banks, and federal savings banks.

Depreciation

Reduction in the value of fixed assets due to wear and tear.

Depression

A phase of the business cycle in which economic activity is at low ebb and there is mass scale unemployment and under-employment of sources. Prices, profits, consumption, etc are also at a low level.

Deregulation

Reducing or eliminating government intervention to control particular market activities, especially of private firms. For example, removing price controls or monopoly privileges.

Descriptive Statistic

A statistic used to summarise a set of numbers; the sample average, sample median, and sample standard deviation are the most common.

Deseasonalizing

The removing of the seasonal components from a monthly or quarterly time series.

Determinants Of Demand

Factors that influence consumer purchases of goods, services, or resources.

Determinants Of Supply

Factors that influence producer decisions about goods, services, or resources.

Detrending

The practice of removing the trend from a time series.

Devaluation

Official reduction in the foreign value of domestic currency. It is done to encourage the country's exports and discourage imports.

Developed Countries

the wealthiest nations in the world, including Western Europe, the United States, Canada, Japan, Australia and New Zealand.

Developing Country

Less developed country, under-developed country or third world country: a country characterized by low levels of GDP and per capita income; typically dominated by agriculture and mineral products and majority of the population lives near subsistence levels.

Development Economics

A sub-discipline within economics specializing in the processes of long term growth and change, especially in the case of the less developed economies.

Difference In Slopes

A description of a model where some slope parameters may differ by group or time period.

Diminishing Marginal Utility

The principle that says that as an individual consumes more and more of a good, each successive unit increases her utility, or enjoyment, less and less.

Diminishing Relative Value

The principle that if all other factors remain constant, and individuals relative value of a good will decline as more of that good is obtained. Accordingly, the relative value of a good will increase, other factors remaining constant, as an individual gives up more of that good.

Diminishing Returns

The principle that says as one input increases, with other inputs fixed, the resulting increase in output tends to be smaller and smaller. As more and more of a productive resource is added to a given amount to other productive resources, additions to output will eventually diminish other factors, such as technology and the degree of specialization remaining constant.

Diminishing Returns To Scale

when all inputs are increased by a certain proportion, output increases by a similar proportion.

Dioxin

A man-made chemical by-product formed during the manufacturing of other chemicals and during incineration. Studies show that dioxin is the most potent animal carcinogen ever tested, as well as the cause of severe weight loss, liver problems, kidney problems, birth defects, and death.

Direct Investment

Foreign capital inflow in the form of investment by foreign-based companies into domestic based companies. Portfolio investment is foreign capital inflow by foreign investors into shares and financial securities. It is the ownership and management of production and/or marketing facilities in a foreign country.

Direct Tax

A direct tax is one imposed upon an individual person (juristic or natural) or on property, as distinct from a tax imposed upon a transaction. Indirect taxes such as a sales tax or a value added tax (VAT) are imposed only if and when a taxable transaction occurs; people have the freedom to engage in or refrain from such transactions; whereas a direct tax is imposed upon a person, typically in an unconditional manner, such as a poll-tax or head-tax, which is imposed on the basis of the person's very life or existence, or a property tax which is imposed upon the owner by virtue of ownership, rather than commercial use. Some commentators have argued that "a direct tax is one that cannot be shifted by the taxpayer to someone else, whereas an indirect tax can be."

Discount Rate

Degree to which future dollars are discounted relative to current dollars. Economic analysis generally assumes that a given unit of benefit or cost matters more if it is experienced now that if it occurs in the future. The degree to which the importance that is attached to gains and losses in the future is known as discounted. The present is more important due to impatience, uncertainty, and the productivity of capital. The interest a private bank pays for a loan from the U.S. Federal Reserve System.

Discrete Random Variable

A random variable that takes on at most a finite or countably infinite number of values.

Disequilibrium

The quantity demanded does not equal the quantity supplied at the going price.

Disequilibrium Unemployment

Disequilibrium unemployment occurs where imperfections in the labour market prevent it from reaching the full employment level of output.

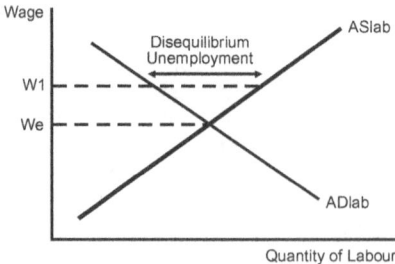

Quantity of Labour

At a wage level of W1 the supply of labour exceeds the demand and so there is unemployment. To get rid of this unemployment, classical economists argue that wages should fall until supply equals demand again. However, if imperfections in the market prevent wages falling then there will be disequilibrium unemployment.

Disinflation

Disinflation is a decrease in the rate of inflation – a slowdown in the rate of increase of the general price level of goods and services in a nation's gross domestic product over time. It is the opposite of reflation. Disinflation occurs when the increase in the "consumer price level" slows down from the previous period when the prices were rising. Disinflation is the reduction in the general price level in the economy but for a very short period of time. Disinflation takes place only when an economy is suffering from recession.

Disinvestment

Government makes a number of investment in public sector undertakings. But when it dilutes its stake in these undertakings, it is defined as disinvestment.

Disposable Income

Disposable income is total personal income minus personal current taxes. In national accounts definitions, personal income, minus personal current taxes equals disposable personal income. Subtracting personal outlays (which includes the major category of personal (or, private) consumption expenditure) yields personal (or, private) savings. Discretionary income is disposable income (after-tax income), minus all payments that are necessary to meet current bills. It is total personal income after subtracting taxes and typical expenses (such as rent or mortgage, utilities, insurance, medical, transportation, property maintenance, child support, food and sundries, etc.) to maintain a certain standard of living.

Dissaving

If individuals or households spend more than their current income they are said to be dissaving.

Distributed Lag Model

A time series model that relates the dependent variable to current and past values of an explanatory variable.

Distribution

The manner in which total output and income is distributed among individuals or factors (e.g., the distribution of income between labour and capital).

Diversifiable Risk

Risk that can be avoided by diversification.

Dividend

Dividends are payments made by a corporation to its shareholder members. It is the portion of corporate profits paid out to stockholders. When a corporation earns a profit or surplus, that money can be put to two uses: it can either be re-invested in the business (called retained earnings), or it can be distributed to shareholders. There are two ways to distribute cash to shareholders: share repurchases or dividends. Many corporations retain a portion of their earnings and pay the remainder as a dividend.

Division of Labour

Division of Labour is the specialization of cooperative labour in specific, circumscribed tasks and like roles. Historically an increasingly complex division of labour is closely associated with the growth of total output and trade, the rise of capitalism, and of the complexity of industrialization

processes. Division of labour was also a method used by the Sumerians to categorize different jobs, trade, and economic interdependence. In addition to this the division of labour helps to specialise and increase producer productivity. The division of labour makes trade necessary and is the source of economic interdependence. Division of labour is a process whereby the production process is broken down into a sequence of stages and workers are assigned to particular stages.

Domar, Evsey David (1914-1997)

Born in Lodz (Poland, then Russia) in 1914, Domar graduated with a Ph.D. from Harvard in 1947. His initial work was in the field of taxation, but he went on to study the theory of growth and the construction of Keynesian growth models. The basic Keynesian analysis of saving and investing was static in that equilibrium was achieved apparently at given levels of income when intended savings and intended investing were equal. But investing, Domar pointed out, like Roy Harrod some years earlier, must increase the capacity to produce and the question is, will that increased productivity capacity be used or wasted? Domar developed an analysis which showed that full employment could be maintained through time only if investment exceeded saving and income always grew sufficiently to produce the necessary level of saving. The policy implication of this, in Domar's view, was that modern capitalist economies, probably because of their monopolistic elements, tend to allow increased capacity arising from new investment to be less than fully utilized, a deflationary tendency not necessarily offset by technological advance. His major publication is *"Essays in the Theory of Economic Growth,"* 1957. His subsequent work has been on comparative economic systems, especially the economics of socialism.

Dominant Firm

In an oligopolistic industry, a single large firm that sets the price but lets the small firms in the industry sell all they want at that price.

Dominant Strategy

A strategy that is best for a player regardless of the other players' strategy.

Double Taxation

Double taxation is the levying of tax by two or more jurisdictions on the same declared income (in the case of income taxes), asset (in the case of capital taxes), or financial transaction (in the case of sales taxes). This double liability is often mitigated by tax treaties between countries. The term 'double taxation' is additionally used, particularly in the USA, to refer to the fact that corporate profits are taxed and the shareholders of the corporation are (usually) subject to personal taxation when they receive dividends or distributions of those profits. This use of the term 'double taxation' is politically freighted since it selectively concatenates, out of all describable sequences of taxation, two particular taxes on two particular transactions.

Downs, Anthony (1930-)

Born in Evanston, USA in 1930. He did Ph.D. from Stanford University: 1956. Downs is best known for his application of economic analysis to political theory, especially with respect to democratic political parties and bureaucratic organizations. His two major books are *An Economic Theory of Democracy,* 1957, and *Inside Bureaucracy,* 1967. He has subsequently published work on American urban issues, including the causes and effects of racial segregation in US cities.

Downward Bias

The expected value of an estimator is below the population value of the parameter.

Dummy Variable

A dummy variable (also known as an indicator variable) is one that takes the values 0 or 1 to indicate the absence or presence of some categorical effect that may be expected to shift the outcome. For example, in econometric time series analysis, dummy variables may be used to indicate the occurrence of wars, or major strikes. It could thus be thought of as a truth value represented as a numerical value 0 or 1 (as is sometimes done in computer programming).

Dummy Variable Regression

In a panel data setting, the regression that includes a dummy variable for each cross-sectional unit, along with the remaining explanatory variables. It produces the fixed effects estimator.

Dummy Variable Trap

The mistake of including too many dummy variables among the independent variables; it occurs when an overall intercept is in the model and a dummy variable is included for each group.

Dumping

Sale of a commodity at different prices in different markets, lower price being charged in a market where demand is relatively elastic.

Duopoly

A true duopoly is a specific type of oligopoly where only two producers exist in one market. In reality, this definition is generally used where only two firms have dominant control over a market. In the field of industrial organization, it is the most commonly studied form of oligopoly due to its simplicity.

Durable Goods

A durable good or a hard good is a good that does not quickly wear out, or more specifically, one that yields utility over time rather than being completely consumed in one use. Items like bricks could be considered perfectly durable goods, because they should theoretically never wear out. Highly durable goods such as refrigerators, cars, or mobile phones usually continue to be useful for three or more years of use, so durable goods are typically characterized by long periods between successive purchases.

Durables

Consumer goods expected to last longer than three years.

Durbin-Watson (Dw) Statistic

A statistic used to test for first order serial correlation in the errors of a time series regression model under the classical linear model assumptions.

E

Earn

Receive payment (income) for productive efforts.

Econometric Model

An equation relating the dependent variable to a set of explanatory variables and unobserved disturbances, where unknown population parameters determine the *ceteris paribus* effect of each explanatory variable.

Econometrics

The application of statistical and mathematical methods in the field of economics to test and quantify economic theories and the solutions to economic problems.

Economic Development

The process of improving the quality of human life through increasing per capita income, reducing poverty, and enhancing individual economic opportunities. It is also sometimes defined to include better education, improved health and nutrition, conservation of natural resources, a cleaner environment, and a richer cultural life.

Economic Efficiency

A situation in which all changes that harm no one and improve the well-being of some people have been accomplished.Such a situation is economically efficient (or Pareto efficient or Pareto optimal); no one can be made better off without hurting someone else.

Economic Growth

Economic growth is the increase in the amount of the goods and services produced by an economy over time. It is conventionally measured as the percent rate of increase in real gross domestic product, or real GDP. Growth is usually calculated in real terms, i.e. inflation-adjusted terms, in order to obviate the distorting effect of inflation on the price of the goods produced. In economics, "economic growth" or "economic growth theory" typically refers to growth of potential output, i.e., production at "full employment". As an area of study, economic growth is generally distinguished from development economics. The former is primarily the study of how countries can advance their economies. The latter is the study of the economic aspects of the development process in low-income countries.

Economic Inequality

Economic inequality (also known as the gap between rich and poor, income inequality, wealth disparity, or wealth and income differences) comprises disparities in the distribution of economic assets (wealth) and income within or between populations or individuals. The term typically refers to inequality among individuals and groups within a society, but can also refer to inequality among countries. The issue of economic inequality is related to the ideas of equity, equality of outcome, and equality of opportunity.

Economic Infrastructure

The underlying amount of physical and financial capital embodied in roads, railways, waterways, airways, and other forms of transportation and communication plus water supplies, financial institutions, electricity, and public services such as health and education. The level of infrastructural development in a country is a crucial factor determining the pace and diversity of economic development.

Economic Integration

The merging to various degrees of the economies and economic policies of two or more countries in a given region.

Economic Model

A relationship derived from economic theory or less formal economic reasoning.

Economic Policy

A statement of objectives and the methods of achieving these objectives (policy instruments) by government, political party, business concern, etc. Some examples of government economic objectives are maintaining full employment, achieving a high rate of economic growth, reducing income inequalities and regional development inequalities, and maintaining price stability. Policy instruments include fiscal policy, monetary and financial policy, and legislative controls (e.g., price and wage control, rent control).

Economic Profit

The difference between a firm's revenues and its costs, where the latter include the returns that could be gotten from the most lucrative alternative use of all of the firm's resources.

Economic Regulations

The control of entry into the market, pricing, the extension of service by established firms and issues of quality control.

Economic Rent

Any return a factor of production receives in excess of its opportunity cost (what it would have received in its next best use).

Economic Resource

A scarce resource that commands a nonzero price.

Economic Specialization

Concentration of activity in a few particular tasks or in producing only a few items.

Economic System

The collection of institutions, laws, activities, controlling values, and human motivations that collectively provide a framework for economic decision making.

Economic Wants

Desires that can be satisfied by consuming a good or a service. Some economic wants range from things needed for survival to things that are nice to have.

Economics

Economics is the social science that analyzes the production, distribution, and consumption of goods and services. A focus of the subject is how economic agents behave or interact and how economies work. Consistent with this, a primary textbook distinction is between microeconomics and macroeconomics. Microeconomics examines the behaviour of basic elements in the economy, including individual agents (such as households and firms or as buyers and sellers) and markets, and their interactions. Macroeconomics analyzes the entire economy and issues affecting it, including unemployment, inflation, economic growth, and monetary and fiscal policy. Economic analysis may be applied throughout society, as in business, finance, health care, and government, but also to such diverse subjects as crime, education,the family, law, politics, religion, social institutions, war, and science. At the turn of the 21st century, the expanding domain of economics in the social sciences has been described as economic imperialism. An increasing number of economists have called for increased emphasis on environmental sustainability; this area of research is known as Ecological economics.

Economies Of Scale

Economies of scale occur where the cost per unit of output decreases as production increases.

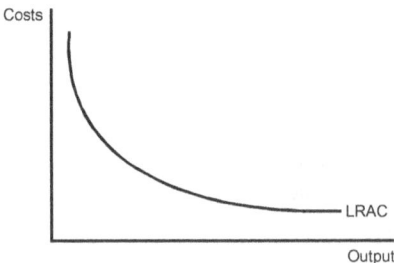

Economies of scale mean that as the firm grows in size, the cost per unit decreases. There may be external or internal economies of scale. There are various different types including marketing economies, technical economies, risk-bearing economies and financial economies.

Economies Of Scope

Economies resulting from the scope rather than the scale of the enterprise. They exist where it is less costly to combine two or more product lines in one firm than to produce them separately.

Efficiency

Efficiency in general describes the extent to which time, effort or cost is well used for the intended task or purpose. It is often used with the specific purpose of relaying the capability of a specific application of effort to produce a specific outcome effectively with a minimum amount or quantity of waste, expense, or unnecessary effort. "Efficiency" has widely varying meanings in different disciplines. The term "efficient" is very much confused and misused with the term "effective". In general, efficiency is a measurable concept, quantitatively determined by the ratio of output to input. "Effectiveness", is a relatively vague, non-quantitative concept, mainly concerned with achieving objectives. In several of these cases, efficiency can be expressed as a result as percentage of what ideally could be expected, hence with 100% as ideal case. This does not always apply, not even in all cases where efficiency can be assigned a numerical value, e.g. not for specific impulse.

Efficiency Wage

The wage at which total labour costs are minimized.

Efficiency Wage Theory

The theory that paying higher wages (up to a point) lowers total production costs, for instance by leading to a more productive labour force.

Efficient Markets Hypothesis

According to this hypothesis, investors quickly make effective use of available information in buying and selling stock. All that is known about the factors influencing a stock's price is already reflected in its price; thus technical analysis of stocks is useless, according to this theory.

Efficient Markets Theory

The theory that all available information is reflected in the current price of an asset.

Effluent Fee

A fixed tax rate per unit (litre or kilogram) of emissions. They are also referred to as emission charges or emission taxes.

Elastic Demand Curve

If the value of the price elasticity of demand for a product is between one and infinity, it is described as elastic in demand and the demand curve will tend to be relatively shallow.

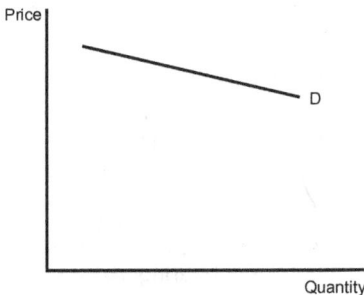

The price elasticity of demand is calculated by dividing the percentage change in demand by the percentage change in price. If the increase in demand is higher than the increase in price then the price elasticity is described as elastic. This is shown by a shallow demand curve as for a given change in price there is a larger change in demand.

Elastic Supply Curve

If the value of the price elasticity of supply for a product is between one and infinity, it is described as elastic in supply and the supply curve will tend to be relatively shallow.

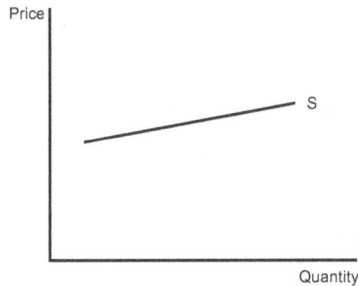

The price elasticity of supply is calculated by dividing the percentage change in supply by the percentage change in price. If the increase in supply is higher than the increase in price then the price elasticity is described as elastic. This is shown by a shallow supply curve as for a given change in price there is a larger change in supply.

Elasticity

When used without a modifier (such as "cross", or "income"), elasticity usually refers to price elasticity which is the percentage change in quantity demanded of a good or service divided by the percentage change in its (own) price.

Elasticity Of Demand

The degree to which consumer demand for a product or service responds to a change in price, wage or other independent variable. When there is no perceptible response, demand is said to be inelastic.

Elasticity Of Supply

The (price) elasticity of supply is the percentage change in the quantity supplied of a good or service divided by the percentage change in its (own) price.

Emission Charges

A fixed tax rate per unit (litre or kilogram) of emissions.

Emission Taxes

A fixed tax rate per unit (litre or kilogram) of emissions.

Empirical Analysis

A study that uses data in a formal econometric analysis to test a theory, estimate a relationship, or determine the effectiveness of a policy.

Endogeneity

A term used to describe the presence of an endogenous explanatory variable.

Endogenous Explanatory Variable

An explanatory variable in a multiple regression model that is correlated with the error term, either because of an omitted variable, measurement error, or simultaneity.

Endogenous Variables

In simultaneous equations models, variables that are determined by the equations in the system.

Endowment Position

A consumer's initial allocation of income or bundles of goods.

Engel Curve

An Engel curve describes how household expenditure on a particular good or service varies with household income. There are two varieties of Engel Curves. Budget share Engel Curves describe how the proportion of household income spent on a good varies with income. Alternatively,

Engel curves can also describe how real expenditure varies with household income. They are named after the German statistician Ernst Engel (1821–1896) who was the first to investigate this relationship between goods expenditure and income systematically in 1857. The best-known single result from the article is Engel's law which states that the poorer a family is, the larger the budget share it spends on nourishment.

Entitlements

Government transfer payments made to individuals having certain designated characteristics and circumstances, such as age or need.

Entrepreneur

The term entrepreneur is a loanword from French and was first defined by the Irish-French economist Richard Cantillon as the person who pays a certain price for a product to resell it at an uncertain price, thereby making decisions about obtaining and using the resources while consequently admitting the risk of enterprise.

Entrepreneurship

The ability and willingness to undertake the organization and management of production. As well as making the usual business decisions, entrepreneurship is often associated with the functions of innovating and bearing risks.

Envelope Curve

A curve enclosing, by just touching, a number of other curves

Equilibrium

The amount of output supplied equals the amount demanded. At equilibrium, the market has neither a tendency to rise nor fall but clears at the existing price.

Equilibrium Condition

A condition which must be satisfied for equilibrium to exist, equilibrium being defined as a situation in which there is no tendency for change. For example, in the Keynesian expenditure model, the equilibrium condition is that planned spending just equal the current level of national income. Once that condition is satisfied, there is no tendency for the level of national income to change.

Equilibrium Price

Economic equilibrium is a state of the world where economic forces are balanced and in the absence of external influences the (equilibrium) values of economic variables will not change. For example, in the standard text-book model of perfect competition, equilibrium occurs at the point at which quantity demanded and quantity supplied are equal.[1] Market equilibrium in this case refers to a condition where a market price is established through competition such that the amount of goods or services sought by buyers is equal to the amount of goods or services produced by sellers. This price is often called the competitive price or market clearing price and will tend not to change unless demand or supply changes.

Equilibrium Quantity

The quantity of a good demanded and supplied at the equilibrium price.

Equilibrium Unemployment

If the labour market is in equilibrium and there is still unemployment, then there must be a gap between the actual supply of labour and the potential supply of labour as this diagram shows. The labour supply curve shows the number of people who are willing and able to supply their labour at each given wage rate. If there is equilibrium in the labour market then that implies that everybody who is willing to work at the equilibrium wage rate is working, so any remaining unemployment must be people who could work but are not willing to work at the equilibrium wage. This is called equilibrium unemployment.

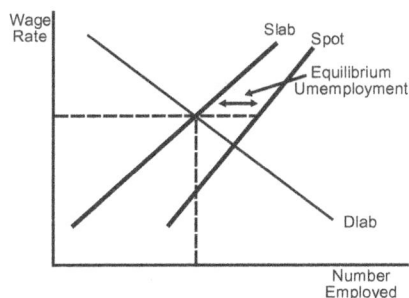

Equity

May be used in either of two unrelated senses. In the context of income distribution theory, refers to an objective, goal or principle implying "fairness". In a financial context may refer to a share or portion of ownership.

Equivalent Variation

The amount of money one would accept to forgo a benefit such as a price decrease or the amount of income one would pay to avoid a harm such as a price increase. Money required to leave an individual as well off as after the economic change. Amount an individual would be willing to accept to forgo the change, or willing to pay to avert the change.

Error Term

The variable in a simple or multiple regression equation that contains unobserved factors that affect the dependent variable. The error term may also include measurement errors in the observed dependent or independent variables.

Error Variance
The variance of the error term in a multiple regression model.

Errors-In-Variables
A situation where either the dependent variable or some independent variables arc measured with error.

Estimate
The numerical value taken on by an estimator for a particular sample of data.

Estimator
A rule for combining data to produce a numerical value for a population parameter; the form of the rule does not depend on the particular sample obtained.

Event Study
An econometric analysis of the effects of an event, such as a change in government regulation or economic policy, on an outcome variable.

Excess Capacity
The difference between the minimum-cost output and the actual output in a long-run equilibrium. A famous and controversial conclusion of the theory of monopolistic competition is that firms under this form of market structure will tend to operate with excess capacity.

Excess Demand
the situation in which the quantity demanded at a given price exceeds the quantity supplied. Opposite: excess supply

Excess Reserves
The difference between the amount of cash a bank wishes or is required to hold in relation to its deposit

liabilities and the amount it actually holds.

Excess Supply
If the price is above the equilibrium market price then supply will be greater than demand resulting in an excess supply.

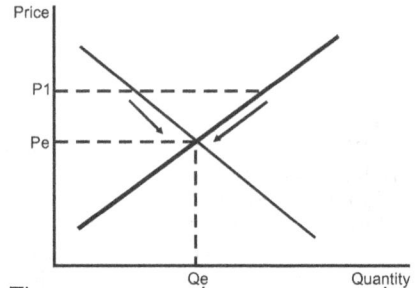

The excess supply means a surplus of the good. This will force the price down and as the price falls there will be an increase in the quantity demanded and a fall in the quantity supplied. This process will continue until the quantity demanded is equal to the quantity supplied. This will then be an equilibrium.

Excess Supply And Demand
If the price is above the equilibrium then there is an excess supply of the product and if the price is below the equilibrium, then there is an excess demand.

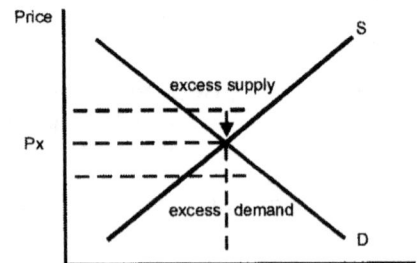

Any excess supply of a product will

tend to force the price down towards the equilibrium, while any excess demand will tend to force the price up as shortages of the product emerge.

Exchange

Trading goods and services with others for other goods and services or for money (also called trade). When people exchange voluntarily, they expect to be better off as a result.

Exchange Control

A governmental policy designed to restrict the outflow of domestic currency and prevent a worsened balance of payments position by controlling the amount of foreign exchange that can be obtained or held by domestic citizens. Often results from overvalued exchange rates

Exchange Rate

The price at which one currency converts to another. For example, on April 16, 2002, 3.8 Malaysian ringgits were equal to one U.S. dollar. In the Agricultural Exchange Rate Data Set, all exchange rates are given as foreign currency to the U.S. dollar. Nominal exchange rates are the current value of the foreign currency in terms of U.S. dollars. Real exchange rates are the nominal exchange rates adjusted for relative rates of inflation fixed to a given base year. The U.S. trade-weighted exchange rate is an index of exchange rates across countries where relative exports determine the weight of the country's exchange rate in the overall index. The sum of the weights equals one.

Exchange Value

The purchasing power of a unit of currency for goods and services in the marketplace.

Excise Duties

The foods manufactured within the country are imposed with some duties. Those duties are known as Excise duties.

Excise Duty

Tax imposed on the manufacture, sale and consumption of various commodities, such as taxes on textiles, cloth, liquor, etc.

Excise Tax

An excise or excise tax (sometimes called a duty of excise special tax) is an inland tax on the sale, or production for sale, of specific goods or a tax on a good produced for sale, or sold, within a country or licenses for specific activities. Excises are distinguished from customs duties, which are taxes on importation. Excises are inland taxes, whereas customs duties are border taxes.

Excluding A Relevant Variable

In multiple regression analysis, leaving out a variable that has a nonzero partial effect on the dependent variable.

Exclusion Principle

The owner of a private good may exclude others from use unless they pay.

Exclusion Restrictions

Restrictions which state that certain variables are excluded from the model (or have zero population coefficients).

Existence Value

Value from knowing environmental goods exist independent of use or option value. If we lose a species in the wild, such as the Bengal tiger, very few of us will have our welfare directly affected by not being able to see it, photograph it or hear it. That "use value" is very small. But many people will lose the option to do that in the future, should they care to. Economists call that "option value." Further, many people around the world derive some benefit just from knowing that Bengal tigers exist in the wild. That is "existence value.".

Exogenous Explanatory Variable

An explanatory variable that is uncorrelated with the error term.

Exogenous Variable

Any variable that is unconnected with the error term in the model of interest.

Expansion Path

(a) The locus of points where the isoquants corresponding to various outputs are tangent to the isocost curves (no inputs are fixed). (MY)

(b) assuming technology, P_K & P_L remain fixed, for each level of production (isoquant) there will be a corresponding tangency with an isocost curve. The set of these tangency will trace out the expansion path for the firm.

Expectations-Augmented Phillip's Curve

The expectations-augmented Phillips Curve was developed by Milton Friedman to explain the breakdown of the Phillips Curve in the 1970's. He argued that in the long run there would be no trade-off between inflation and unemployment. Friedman incorporated people's price expectations, and said that there would be a number of short run Phillips Curves (PC1, PC2 and so on) - one for each level of price expectations. However, in the long run there would be no trade-off between unemployment and inflation

and any attempt to reduce unemployment to below its natural rate would simply be inflationary.

Expected Monetary Value

To determine the expected monetary value of an uncertain situation, multiply the amount of money gained (or lost) with each outcome by the probability of its occurrence and add the resulting expected outcomes.

Expected Profit

The long-term average value of profit-that is, the (weighted) sum of the various possible levels of profit. The probabilities of occurrence are used as the weights.

Expected Utility

To determine the expected utility of an uncertain situation, multiply the utility associated with each possible outcome by the probability of its occurrence and add the resulting value.

Expected Value

A measure of central tendency in the distribution of a random variable, including an estimator.

Experiment

In probability, a general term used to denote an event whose outcome is uncertain. In econometric analysis, it denotes a situation where data are collected by randomly assigning individuals to control and treatment groups.

Experimental Data

Data that have been obtained by running a controlled experiment.

Explained Sum Of Squares (ESS)

The total sample variation of the fitted values in a multiple regression model.

Explanatory Variable

In regression analysis, a variable that is used to explain variation in the dependent variable.

Explicit Costs

The ordinary expenses of the firm that accountants include, such as payroll costs and payments for raw materials.

Exponential Function

A mathematical function defined for all values that has an increasing slope but a constant proportionate change.

Export Incentives

Public subsidies, tax rebates, and other kinds of financial and nonfinancial measures designed to promote a greater level of economic activity in export industries.

Exports

The value of all goods and nonfactor services sold to the rest of the world; they include merchandise, freight, insurance, travel, and other nonfactor services. The value of factor services (such as investment receipts and workers' remittances from abroad) is excluded from this measure.

External Diseconomy

An uncompensated cost to one person or firm resulting from the consumption or output of another person or firm.

External Economy

An uncompensated benefit to one person or firm resulting from the consumption or output of another person or firm.

Externalities

A benefit or cost associated with an economic transaction which is not taken into account by those directly involved in making it. A beneficial or adverse side effect of production or consumption.

F

F Distribution

The probability distribution obtained by forming the ratio of two independent chi-square random variables, where each has been divided by its degrees of freedom.

F Statistic

A statistic used to test multiple hypotheses about the parameters in a multiple regression model.

Factor Demand

The amount of an input demanded by a firm, given the price of the input and the quantity of output being produced; an input will be demanded up to the point where the value of the input's marginal product equals the price of the input.

Factors Of Production

Factors of production may also refer specifically to the 'primary factors', which are stocks including land, labour (the ability to work), and capital goods applied to production. Materials and energy are considered secondary factors in classical economics because they are obtained from land, labour and capital. The primary factors facilitate production but neither become part of the product (as with raw materials) nor become significantly transformed by the production process (as with fuel used to power machinery). 'Land' includes not only the site of production but natural resources above or below the soil. The factor land may, however, for simplification purposes be merged with capital in some cases (due to land being of little importance in the service sector and manufacturing). Recent usage has distinguished human capital (the stock of knowledge in the labour force) from labour. Entrepreneurship is also sometimes considered a factor of production. Sometimes the overall state of technology is described as a factor of production. The number and definition of factors varies, depending on theoretical purpose, empirical emphasis, or school of economics.

Fall In Marginal Cost

If marginal cost falls, the curve will shift to the right. This should lead to an increased level of output and a reduced price for the good or service.

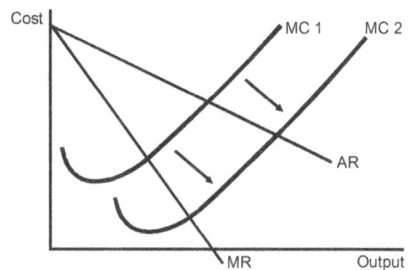

A decrease in marginal cost means that the firms variable costs have fallen. A change in fixed costs will not affect the marginal cost curve. Since profit-maximising firms produce where MC=MR a reduction in MC should lead to an increased level of profit-maximising output.

Federal Reserve System

Federal Reserve System (also known as the Federal Reserve, and informally as the Fed) is the central banking system of the United States. It was created on December 23, 1913, with the enactment of the Federal Reserve Act, largely in response to a series of financial panics, particularly a severe panic in 1907. Over time, the roles and responsibilities of the Federal Reserve System have expanded and its structure has evolved. Events such as the Great Depression were major factors leading to changes in the system.

Federation Of Indian Chambers Of Commerce And Industry

Set up in 1927, it is a business association with over 1,500 corporate members–www.ficci.com

Fiat Money

A type of money which has little or no intrinsic value in itself, but which is decreed to be money by the government and is generally accepted in exchange. Modern paper currencies are all fiat money, as are most coins in active circulation.

Final Goods

Any tangible commodity which is produced and subsequently consumed by the consumer, to satisfy its current want or need, is a consumer good or final good. Consumer goods are goods that are ultimately consumed rather than used in the production of another good. For example, a microwave oven or a mixer grinder which is sold to a consumer is a final good or consumer good, where as the components which are sold to be used in to final good those goods are called intermediate goods.

Finance Bill

It is a bill that is passed in the Parliament by the government. This bill is government's plan for imposing new taxes beyond the period. The plans may include continuation of present tax structure or modifications in the it. The finance bill seeks approval from by the Parliament.

Financial Year

Usually April 1 to March 31; e.g. FY 04 would refer to the period, April 1, 2003 to March 31, 2004. Also referred to as 2003-04.

Firms

Economic entities which buy or employ factors of production and organize them to create goods and services for sale.

First Difference

A transformation on a time series constructed by taking the difference of adjacent time periods, where the earlier time period is subtracted from the later time period.

First Order Autocorrelation

For a time series process ordered chronologically, the correlation coefficient between pairs of adjacent observations.

First Order Conditions

The set of linear equations used to solve for the OLS estimates.

First-Mover Advantages

The advantages that accrue to the player who makes the first move in a game.

Fiscal Deficit

The gap between the government's total spending and the sum of its revenue receipts and non-debt capital receipts. The fiscal deficit represents the total amount of borrowed funds required by the government to completely meet its expenditure

Fiscal Policy

The use of government expenditure and taxation to try to influence the level of economic activity. An expansionary (or reflationary) fiscal policy could mean: cutting levels of direct or indirect tax increasing government expenditure The effect of these policies would be to encourage more spending and boost the economy. A contractionary (or deflationary) fiscal policy could be: increasing taxation - either direct or indirect cutting government expenditure These policies would reduce the level of demand in the economy and help to reduce inflation

Fitted Input

A resource used in the production process (such as plant or equipment) whose quantity cannot be changed during the period under consideration.

Fitted Values

The estimated values of the dependent variable when the values of the independent variables for each observation are plugged into the OLS regression line.

Fixed Capital

Fixed capital is a concept in economics and accounting, first theoretically analysed in some depth by the economist David Ricardo. It refers to any kind of real or physical capital (fixed asset) that is not used up in the production of a product and is contrasted with circulating capital

such as raw materials, operating expenses and the like. Fixed capital is that portion of the total capital that is invested in fixed assets (such as land, buildings, vehicles, plant and equipment) that stay in the business almost permanently, or at the very least, for more than one accounting period. Fixed assets can be purchased by a business, in which case the business owns them, but also leased, hired or rented, if that is cheaper or more convenient, or if owning the fixed assets is practically impossible.

Fixed Capital Formation

Investment, the creation of capital goods such as structures, machinery and equipment.

Fixed Cost

Fixed costs are costs that do not vary with the level of output. They are therefore constant.

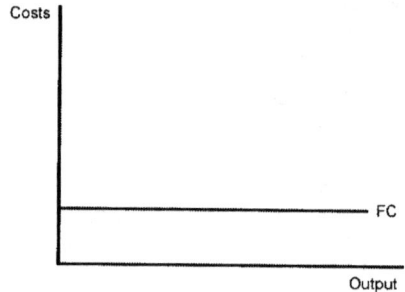

Fixed costs may include costs like loan repayments, marketing and administration costs, security and other costs that are independent of the level of output. A cost incurred in the general operations of the business that is not directly attributable to the costs of producing goods and services. These "Fixed" or "Indirect" costs of doing business will be incurred whether or not any sales are made during the period, thus the designation "Fixed", as opposed to "Variable".

Fixed Exchange Rate

The exchange value of a national currency fixed in relation to another (usually the U.S. dollar), not free to fluctuate on the international money market.

Fixed Inputs

Inputs that do not change depending on the quantity of output, at least over the short term. Inputs that cannot be changed over a given time interval.

Flat Organisational Structure

In a fairly flat organisational structure there will be few layers of managers. Each manager will have larger groups of people reporting to them.

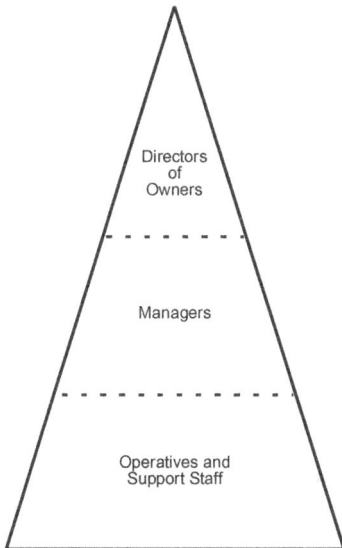

Directors
of
Owners

Managers

Operatives and
Support Staff

In a flat organisational structure there will be a large span of control. In other words each person will be responsible for far more people than in a more hierarchical structure. The advantage of this sort of structure is improved communication and giving people more responsibility for their own work.

Forecast Error

The difference between the actual outcome and the forecast of the outcome.

Forecast Interval

In forecasting, a confidence interval for a yet unrealised future value of a time series variable.

Foreign Aid

The international transfer of public funds in the form of loans or grants either directly from one government to another (bilateral assistance) or indirectly through the vehicle of a multilateral assistance agency like the World Bank.

Foreign Direct Investment (FDI)

Foreign direct investment (FDI) is direct investment into production or business in a country by a company in another country, either by buying a company in the target country or by expanding operations of an existing business in that country. Foreign direct investment is in contrast to portfolio investment which is a passive investment in the securities of another country such as stocks and bonds.

Foreign Exchange

Claims on a country by another, held in the form of currency of that country. Foreign exchange system enables one currency to be exchanged for another, thus facilitating trade between countries.

Foreign Exchange Reserves

The stock of liquid assets denominated in foreign currencies held by a government's monetary authorities (typically, the finance ministry or central bank). Reserves enable the monetary authorities to intervene in foreign exchange markets to affect the exchange value of their domestic currency in the market. Reserves are invested in low-risk and liquid assets, often in foreign government securities.

Foreign Institutional Investments

Portfolio Investments by Foreign Asset Management Companies, Pension Funds, Mutual Funds etc., which are registered with the SEBI. FIIs can buy and sell listed as well as unlisted securities.

Foreign Investment Promotion Board

FIPB is a specially empowered board, chaired by Secretary, Department of Economic Affairs, which acts as the approving authority for foreign investment not falling under the automatic approval route and as a facilitator/single-window clearance agency for large foreign investment proposals.

Free Good

Free goods are needed by the society and are available without limits. The free good is a term used in economics to describe a good that is not scarce. A free good is available in as great a quantity as desired with zero opportunity cost to society. A good that is made available at zero price is not necessarily a free good. For example, a shop might give away its stock in its promotion, but producing these goods would still have required the use of scarce resources. Examples include ideas and works that are reproducible at zero cost, or almost zero cost. For example, if someone invents a new device, many people could copy this invention, with no danger of this

"resource" running out. Other examples include computer programmes and web pages.

Free Resource

A resource that is so abundant it can be had for a zero price.

Free Rider

One who receives something without paying.

Free Rider Problem

The undersupplying of a public good caused by the fact that individuals can consume or benefit from the good without paying for it.

Free Trade

Free trade in which goods can be imported and exported without any barriers in the forms of tariffs, quotas, or other restrictions. Free trade has often been described as an engine of growth because it encourages countries to specialize in activities in which they have comparative advantages, thereby increasing their respective production efficiencies and hence their total output of goods and services.

Free-Market Exchange Rate Rate

It is a rate of exchange determined solely by international supply and demand for domestic currency expressed in terms of, say, U.S. dollars.

Free-Rider Problem

Problem that occurs when someone thinks he may be able to enjoy something without paying for it, and fails to contribute ever a portion of the cost.

Free-Trade Area

A form of economic integration in which there exists free internal trade among member countries but each member is free to levy different external tariffs against non-member nations.

Frictional Unemployment

Unemployment caused by the loss of jobs due to technological change, the entry of new participants into a labour market, or other normal labour market adjustments.

Friedman, Milton (1912-2006)

Born New York City in 1912. Degrees from Rutgers, Chicago, and Columbia. Associated with the University of Chicago since 1946. Best known for his advocacy of monetary explanations of the course of economic events and fierce opposition to Keynesian economics, Friedman is usually credited with (or blamed for) establishing the "monetarist school" of economics which gained great influence on government policy in both the US and the UK in the 1970s.

Fringe Benefit

A benefit in addition to salary offered to employees such as use of company's car, house, lunch coupons, health care subscriptions etc.

Full Employment

A term that is used in many senses. Historically, it was taken to be that level of employment at which no (or minimal) involuntary unemployment exists. Today economists rely upon the concept of the natural rate of unemployment to indicate the highest sustainable level of employment over the long run.

Functional Distribution Of Income

The division of total income in an economy into shares according to the kind of service provided-usually labour or property (land and capital).

Functional Form Misspecification

A problem that occurs when a model has omitted functions of the explanatory variables (such as quadratics) or uses the wrong functions of either the dependent variable or some explanatory variables.

Functions Of Money

The roles played by money in an economy. These roles include medium of exchange, standard of value, and store of value.

G

Gains From Trade

The addition to output and consumption resulting from specialization in production and free trade with other economic units including persons, regions, or countries.

Gains of Exchange

The difference between the relative values of a good to the buyer and the seller. How this difference is divided between buyer and seller will depend upon the price of the good. Exchange will not occur unless both the buyer and the seller expect to receive some of this gain.

Gauss-Markov Assumptions

The Gauss–Markov, named after Carl Friedrich Gauss and Andrey Markov, states that in a linear regression model in which the errors have expectation zero and are uncorrelated and have equal variances, the best linear unbiased estimator (BLUE) of the coefficients is given by the ordinary least squares estimator. Here "best" means giving the lowest possible mean squared error of the estimate. The errors need not be normal, nor independent and identically distributed (only uncorrelated and homoscedastic).

Gauss-Markov Theorem

The theorem which states that, under the five Gauss-Markov assumptions (for cross-sectional or time series models), the OLS estimator is BLUE (conditional on the sample values of the explanatory variables).

GDP

Gross domestic product (GDP) is the market value of all officially recognized final goods and services produced within a country in a given period of time. GDP per capita is often considered an indicator of a country's standard of living; GDP per capita is not a measure of personal income (See Standard of living and GDP). Under economic theory, GDP per capita exactly equals the gross domestic income (GDI) per capita. GDP is related to national accounts, a subject in macroeconomics. GDP is not to be confused with gross national product (GNP) which allocates production based on ownership.

GDI

The Gross Domestic Income (GDI) is the total income received by all sectors of an economy within a nation. It includes the sum of all wages, profits, and taxes, minus subsidies. Since all income is derived from production (including the production of services), the gross domestic income of a country should exactly equal its gross domestic product (GDP). The GDP is a very commonly cited statistics measuring the economic activity of countries, and the GDI is quite uncommon.

General Agreement On Tariffs And Trade (GATT)

An international body set up in 1947 to probe into the ways and means of reducing tariffs on internationally traded goods and services. Between 1947 and 1962, GATT held seven conferences but met with only moderate success. Its major success was achieved in 1967 during the so-called Kennedy Round of talks when tariffs on primary commodities were drastically slashed and then in 1994 with the signing of the Uruguay Round agreement. Replaced in 1995 by World Trade Organization (WTO).

General Equilibrium

The condition reached when all markets (for products and productive factors) have cleared, that is, established equilibrium prices and quantities.

General Equilibrium Analysis

An analysis that (in contrast to a partial equilibrium analysis) takes account of the interrelationships among various markets and prices.

General Equilibrium Theory

General equilibrium theory is a branch of theoretical economics. It seeks to explain the behaviour of supply, demand, and prices in a whole economy with several or many interacting markets, by seeking to prove that a set of prices exists that will result in an overall equilibrium, hence general equilibrium, in contrast to partial equilibrium, which only analyzes single markets. As with all models, this is an abstraction from a real economy; it is proposed as being a useful model, both by considering

equilibrium prices as long-term prices and by considering actual prices as deviations from equilibrium. General equilibrium theory both studies economies using the model of equilibrium pricing and seeks to determine in which circumstances the assumptions of general equilibrium will hold. The theory dates to the 1870s, particularly the work of French economist Léon Walras in his pioneering 1874 work Elements of Pure Economics.

General Linear Regression (GLR) Model

A model linear in its parameters, where the dependent variable is a function of independent variables plus an error term.

Giffen's Paradox

A situation in which the quantity demanded of a good is directly related to its price. This occurs when the substitution effect of a price change is not strong enough to offset an inferior good's income effect.

Gini Coefficient

The ratio of the area between the 45 degree line depicting complete equality and a Lorenz curve to the entire area of the triangle below the 45 degree line.

Global Warming Theory

A theory that world climate is slowly warming as a result of both MDC and LDC industrial and agricultural activities.

GNP

Gross national product (GNP) is the market value of all products and services produced in one year by labour and property supplied by the residents of a country. Unlike Gross Domestic Product (GDP), which defines production based on the geographical location of production, GNP allocates production based on ownership. GNP does not distinguish between qualitative improvements in the state of the technical arts (e.g., increasing computer processing speeds), and quantitative increases in goods (e.g., number of computers produced), and considers both to be forms of "economic growth". Basically, GNP is the total value of all final goods and services produced within a nation in a particular year, plus income earned by its citizens (including income of those located abroad), minus income of non-residents located in that country. GNP measures the value of goods and services that the country's citizens produced regardless of their location. GNP is one measure of the economic condition of a country, under the assumption that a higher GNP leads to a higher quality of living, all other things being equal.

GNP Deflator

Measure of the percentage increase in the average price of products in GNP over a certain base year (now 1972) published by the Commerce Department.

Good

A good is something that is intended to satisfy some wants or needs of a consumer and thus has economic utility. It is normally used in the plural form—goods—to denote tangible commodities such as products and materials. Although in economic theory, all goods are considered tangible, in reality certain classes of goods, such as information, only are in intangible forms. For example, among other goods an apple is a tangible object, while news belongs to an intangible class of goods and can be perceived only by means of an instrument such as print, broadcast or computer. Goods are contrasted with services, which are intangible commodities.

Good With Negative Externalities

If there are negative externalities then the marginal social cost will be less than the marginal private benefit. To correct this market failure the government may consider taxing the good.

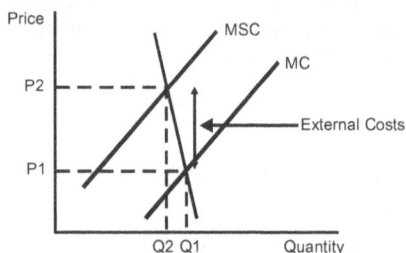

If the government want to fully correct the market failure then the amount of the tax needs to be equivalent to the external costs. This would then shift the supply curve to be identical to the marginal social cost curve and correct the market failure. In practice this is very difficult as it can be a problem quantifying the value of the external costs.

Goodness-of-Fit Measure

A statistic that summarises how well a set of explanatory variables explains a dependent or response variable.

Government

A government is the group of people with the authority to govern a country or a political state. In British English (and that of the Commonwealth of Nations), a government more narrowly refers to the particular administrative set-up in control of a state at a given time—known in American English as an administration. In American English, government refers to the larger system by which any state is organized.Furthermore, government is occasionally used in English as a synonym for governance.

Government Bond

A government bond is a bond issued by a national government, generally promising to pay a certain amount (the face value) on a certain date, as well as periodic interest payments. Bonds are debt investments whereby an investor loans a certain amount of money, for a certain amount of time, with a certain interest rate, to a company or country. Government bonds are usually denominated in the country's own currency. Bonds issued by national governments in foreign currencies are normally referred to as sovereign bonds, although the term "sovereign bond" may also refer to bonds issued in a country's own currency.

Government Budget Balance

The government budget balance, also commonly referred to as general government balance, public budget balance, or public fiscal balance, is the overall result of a country's general government budget over the course of an accounting period, usually one year. It includes all government levels (from national to local) and public social security funds. The budget balance is the difference between government revenues (e.g., tax) and spending. A positive balance is called a government budget surplus, and a negative balance is called a government budget deficit.

Government Budget Constraint

Total government outlays (the sum of expenditures on goods and services, transfer payments and interest on debt)

must equal total revenue (the sum of taxes and U.S. government loans).

Government Security

A contract of the government promising to pay a lender a fixed rate of interest per year and repay the original loan at a fixed future date.

Government Spending

The total outlays by government on goods and services during some accounting period, usually a year. Government outlays such as welfare benefits to households, for example, are normally excluded from this amount on the grounds that they are merely transfers of income from taxpayers to the beneficiaries of such programmes.

Government Transfer Payment

A transfer payment (or government transfer or simply transfer) is a redistribution of income in the market system. These payments are considered to be exhaustive because they do not directly absorb resources or create output. In other words, the transfer is made without any exchange of goods or services. Examples of certain transfer payments include welfare (financial aid), social security, and government making subsidies for certain businesses (firms).

Graph

A visual representation of a relationship between two variables, usually drawn to some specified scale.

Gross Domestic Product

The domestic goods & services produced in a financial year have a total market value.

Gross Domestic Product (GDP) Deflator

Nominal GDP divided by real (constant dollar GDP) multiplied by 100. Nominal GDP is the value of output measured in terms of the prices prevailing in the accounting period in question. Real GDP is that output measured in terms of the prices prevailing in some base period. The value of the deflator in the base period is always 100.

Gross Domestic Product (GDP), Real

Real Gross Domestic Product (real GDP) is a macroeconomic measure of the value of economic output adjusted for price changes (i.e., inflation or deflation). This adjustment transforms the money-value measure, nominal GDP, into an index for quantity of total output.

Gross Investment

Total investment during the accounting period. It includes both additions to the capital stock (net investment) and investment to replace worn out capital (to make up for depreciation).

Gross National Expenditure (GNE)

The sum of all spending on consumption and investment plus government spending on goods and services and net exports (total exports minus imports). It is equivalent in value to GDP.

Gross National Product

The gross value determined of the finished goods & services that are produced in the country in a financial year and the total income of the citizens from investments that are made abroad. This value does not include the foreigners' income in the domestic market.

Growth Rate

The proportionate change in a time series from the previous period. It may be approximated as the difference in logs or reported in percentage form.

H

Harrod, Sir Roy F. (1900-78)

Born in Norfolk, England. Harrod was an influential British economist. He was educated at Oxford, who was an early proponent of Keynesian economics, a prominent adviser to the British government during the years of World War II, and subsequently Keyne's official biographer. Harrod wrote extensively on a number of topics such as business cycles, monetary problems, international trade, and the theory of economic growth. In the latter field, he pointed out as early as 1939 that in the Keynesian model investment played the role of an offset to saving- a way of getting spending withdrawn from the income stream by savers back into it. But investment also increases the productive capacity of the economy.

Hedonic Pricing Approach

Derives values by decomposing market prices into components encompassing environmental and other characteristics through studying property values, wages and other phenomena. The premise of the approach is that the value of an asset depend on the stream of benefits derived, including environmental amenities.

Heteroskedasticity

A collection of random variables is heteroscedastic (often spelled heteroskedastic, and commonly pronounced with a hard k sound regardless of spelling) if there are sub-populations that have different variabilities from others. Here "variability" could be quantified by the variance or any other measure of statistical dispersion. Thus heteroscedasticity is the absence of homoscedasticity. The possible existence of heteroscedasticity is a major concern in the application of regression analysis, including the analysis of variance, because the presence of heteroscedasticity can invalidate statistical tests of significance that assume that the modelling errors are uncorrelated and normally distributed and that their variances do not vary with the effects being modelled. Similarly, in testing for differences between sub-populations using a location test, some standard tests assume that variances within groups are equal.

Hicks, John R. (1904-1989)

One of the leading British economic theorists of the 20th century, Hicks was educated at Oxford to which he returned to teach after holding positions at the London School of Economics, Cambridge, and Manchester. Hicks made important contributions on a variety of topics, but is best known for his work on consumer behaviour as published in his major work, *Value and Capital*. In it Hicks utilized the indifference curve concept first developed by Vilfredo Pareto to construct a theory of demand which was independent of any cardinal measure of utility such as was implicit in the traditional approach perpetuated by Alfred Marshall in his famous *Principles*. Hicks also provided a way of incorporating the interest rate in the Keynesian model which has become a standard feature of intermediate level text-book treatments of the Keynesian model. He was joint winner (with the American economist Kenneth Arrow) of the Nobel prize in economics in 1972.

High MPC

When the consumption line is steep, this indicates a high value of the marginal propensity to consume.

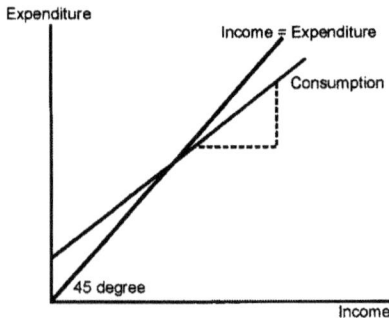

A steep consumption line shows that the level of consumption rises quickly as the level of income increases. This means a high value for the marginal propensity to consume. This will cause the AD line to be similarly steep.

High-Powered Money

The monetary base, or the total of currency in circulation and commercial bank deposits with the central bank.

Hirsch, Fred (1931-1978)

Born in Vienna, Fred Hirsch graduated from the London School of Economics in 1952. After working as an economic journalist and with the International Monetary Fund he became a professor of economics at the University of Warwick in 1975. He published a large amount of work on international monetary issues and the subject of inflation, but he became more widely known only at the end of his tragically short life when he published his book, *The Social Limits to Growth*. Its broad theme, as he put it in an interview reported in the *New York Times*, was that material growth can "no longer deliver what has long been promised for it-to make everyone middle-class."

Homoskedasticity

It is a sequence or a vector of random variables is homoscedastic if all random variables in the sequence or vector have the same finite variance. This is also known as homogeneity of variance. The complementary notion is called heteroscedasticity. The spellings homoskedasticity and heteroskedasticity are also frequently used. The assumption of homoscedasticity simplifies mathematical and computational treatment. Serious violations in homoscedasticity (assuming a distribution of data is homoscedastic when in actuality it is heteroscedastic) may result in overestimating the goodness of fit as measured by the Pearson coefficient.

Households

Individuals and family units which, as consumers, buy goods and services from firms and, as resource owners, sell or rent productive resources to business firms.

Human Capital

Human capital is the stock of competencies, knowledge, social and personality attributes, including creativity, embodied in the ability to perform labour so as to produce economic value. It is an aggregate economic view of the human being acting within economies, which is an attempt to capture the social, biological, cultural and psychological complexity as they interact in explicit and/or economic transactions. Many theories explicitly connect investment in human capital development to education, and the role of human capital in economic development, productivity growth, and innovation has frequently been cited as a justification for government subsidies for education and job skills training.

Human Capital Productive Investments

Embodied in human persons. These include skills, abilities, ideals, and health resulting from expenditures on education, on-the-job training programmes, and medical care.

Human Resources

Human resources is the set of individuals who make up the workforce of an organization, business sector or an economy. "Human capital" is sometimes used synonymously with human resources, although human capital typically refers to a more narrow view; i.e., the knowledge the individuals embody and can contribute to an organization. Likewise, other terms sometimes used include "manpower", "talent", "labour" or simply "people". The professional discipline and business function that oversees an organization's human resources is called human resource management (HRM, or simply HR).

Hypothesis Test

A statistical test of the null, or maintained, hypothesis against an alternative hypothesis.

Hypothetical Bias

Difference in actual willingness to pay and willingness to pay revealed in a survey arising from the fact that in actual markets purchasers suffer real costs, while in surveys they do not.

Hypothetical Budget Line

It is a budget curve derived from a fixed level of I and P_y but changed P_x that is tangent to the original indifference curve - assuming the consumer was somehow allowed to maintain the same level of staisfaction but at the new price ratio.

I

Impact Elasticity
In a distributed lag model, the immediate percentage change in the dependent variable given a 1% increase in the independent variable.

Impact Propensity
In a distributed lag model, the immediate change in the dependent variable given a one-unit increase in the independent variable.

Imperfect Competition
In economic theory, imperfect competition is the competitive situation in any market where the sellers in the market sell different/ dissimilar of goods, (heterogenous) that does not meet the conditions of perfect competition. Forms of imperfect competition include:
1. **Monopoly**, in which there is only one seller of a good.
2. **Oligopoly**, in which there are few sellers of a good.
3. **Monopolistic competition**, in which there are many sellers producing highly differentiated goods.
4. **Information asymmetry** when one competitor has the advantage of more or better information.

There may also be imperfect competition due to a time lag in a market. An example is the "jobless recovery". There are many growth opportunities available after a recession, but it takes time for employers to react, leading to high unemployment. High unemployment decreases wages, which makes hiring more attractive, but it takes time for new jobs to be created.

Imperfect Market
A market where the theoretical assumptions of perfect competition are violated by the existence of, for example, a small number of buyers and sellers, barriers to entry, nonhomogeneity of products, and incomplete information. The three imperfect markets commonly analyzed in economic theory are monopoly, oligopoly, and monopolistic competition.

Implicit Costs
The alternative costs of using the resources owned by the firm's owner, such as his or her time and capital.

Import Duty
A tariff on imports.

Import Elasticity
Usually means the import demand elasticity.

Import Liberalization
Trade liberalization

Import Licence
The licence to import under an import quota or under exchange controls.

Import Monitoring

A practice introduced by the US, first for steel and later for textiles and apparel, whereby the Department of Commerce records the volume of imports of specified products in order to make these data publicly available earlier than would otherwise be possible. Implicitly, these procedures are intended to facilitate faster administered protection.

Import Parity Price

The price that a purchaser pays or can expect to pay for an imported good, thus the c.i.f. import price plus tariff plus transport cost to the purchaser's location. This and the export parity pricetogether define a range of the possible equilibrium prices for an equivalent domestically produced good.

Import Penetration

A measure of the importance of imports in the domestic economy, either by sector or overall, usually defined as the value of imports divided by the value of apparent consumption.

Import Price Index

Price index of the goods that a country imports.

Import Promotion

Any policy that encourages imports. A policy of export promotion generally has the side effect of stimulating imports as well. Today the term is more commonly used for policies used by developed countries intended to assist developing countries in exporting to them.

Import Propensity

The marginal propensity to import (or sometimes the average propensity, if they are different).

Import Quantity Index

Quantity index of the goods that a country imports.

Import Relief

Usually refers to some form of restraint of imports in a particular sector in order to assist domestic producers, and with the connotation that these producers have been suffering from competition with imports. If done formally under existing statutes, it is administered protection, but it may also be done informally using a VER.

Import Substitute

A good produced on the domestic market that competes with imports, either as a perfect substitute or as a differentiated product.

Import Substituting Industrialization

A strategy for economic development based on replacing imports with domestic production.

Import Substitution

A deliberate effort to replace major consumer imports by promoting the emergence and expansion of domestic industries such as textiles, shoes, and household appliances. Import substitution requires the imposition of protective tariffs and quotas to get the new industry started.

Import Surcharge

A tax levied uniformly on most or all imports, in addition to already-existing tariffs.

Import Surveillance

The monitoring of imports, usually by means of automatic licensing.

Import-Export Company

A firm whose business consists mainly of international trade: buying goods in one country and selling them in another, thus both exporting and importing. Same as export-import company.

Imports
The quantity or value of all that is imported into a country.

Impossible Trinity
The impossibility of combining all three of the following: monetary independence, exchange rate stability, and full financial market integration.

Impost
A tax or tariff. (This is not a commonly used word.)

Improve The Terms Of Trade
To increase the terms of trade; that is, to increase the relative price of exports compared to imports. Because it represents an increase in what the country gets in return for what it gives up, this is associated with an improvement in the country's welfare, although whether that actually occurs depends on the reason prices change.

Improve The Trade Balance
This conventionally refers to an increase in exports relative to imports, which thus causes the balance of trade to become larger if positive or smaller if negative. The terminology ignores that exports drain resources while imports satisfy domestic needs, and reflects instead the association of exports with either accumulation of wealth or jobs.

In Kind
Referring to a payment made with goods instead of money.

Incentives
An incentive is something that motivates an individual to perform an action. The study of incentive structures is central to the study of all economic activity (both in terms of individual decision-making and in terms of co-operation and competition within a larger institutional structure). Economic analysis, then, of the differences between societies (and between different organizations within a society) largely amounts to characterizing the differences in incentive structures faced by individuals involved in these collective efforts. Ultimately, incentives aim to provide value for money and contribute to organizational success.

Inclusion Of An Irrelevant Variable
The including of an explanatory variable in a regression model that has a zero population parameter in estimating an equation by OLS.

Income
1. The amount of money (nominal or real) received by a person, household, or other economic unit per unit time in return for services provided or goods sold.
2. National income.
3. The return earned on an asset per unit time.

Income Disparity
Inequality of income, usually referring to differences in average per capita incomes across countries.

Income Distribution
A description of the fractions of a population that are at various levels of income. The larger are the differences in income, the "worse" the income distribution is usually said to be, the smaller the "better." International trade and factor movements can alter countries' income distributions by changing prices of low- and high-paid factors.

Income Effect

The consumer's preferences, money income and prices play an important role in solving the consumer's optimization problem (maximization of their utility subject to a budget constraint). The income effect in economics can be defined as the change in consumption resulting from a change in real income. The comparative statics of consumer behaviour investigates the effects of changes in the exogenous or independent variables i.e. prices and money incomes of the consumers on the equilibrium values of the endogenous or dependent variables i.e. the consumer's demand for goods. When the income of the consumer rises with the prices held constant, the optimal bundle chosen by the consumer changes as the feasible set available to him changes. The income–consumption curve is the set of optimal points of intersection of the points of tangency of the sets of budget constraint lines and indifference curves as income varies, with prices held constant.

Income Elastic

Having an income elasticity greater than one.

Income Elasticity

The percent change in quantity demanded induced by a percent change in income. If a 1-percent change in income induces a change in quantity demanded by more than 1 percent, then the demand is said to be elastic. If the response is less than 1 percent, the demand is said to be inelastic. Since elasticity is a relative measure, it is independent of scale and thus provides a useful measure of comparison across all ranges and scales of quantities.

Income Elasticity Of Demand

In economics, income elasticity of demand measures the responsiveness of the demand for a good to a change in the income of the people demanding the good, ceteris paribus. It is calculated as the ratio of the percentage change in demand to the percentage change in income. For example, if, in response to a 10% increase in income, the demand for a good increased by 20%, the income elasticity of demand would be 20%/ 10% = 2.

Income elasticity of demand can be used as an indicator of industry health, future consumption patterns and as a guide to firms investment decisions. For example, the "selected income elasticities" below suggest that an increasing portion of consumer's budgets will be devoted to purchasing automobiles and restaurant meals and a smaller share to tobacco and margarine.

Income Inelastic

Having an income elasticity less than one.

Income Inequality

The existence of disproportionate distribution of total national income among households whereby the share going to rich persons in a country is far greater than that going to poorer persons (a situation common to most LDCs). This is largely due to differences in the amount of income derived from ownership of property and to a lesser extent the result of differences in earned income. Inequality of personal incomes can be reduced by progressive income taxes and wealth taxes. This is measured by the Gini coefficient.

Income Redistribution Argument For A Tariff

The argument that tariffs should be used in order to redistribute income towards the poor. In a rich country, where unskilled labour is the scarce factor, this can make sense as explained in the Stolper-Samuelson Theorem, but it is a second-best argument.

Income Tax

An income tax is a tax levied on the income of individuals or businesses (corporations or other legal entities). Various income tax systems exist, with varying degrees of tax incidence. Income taxation can be progressive, proportional, or regressive. When the tax is levied on the income of companies, it is often called a corporate tax, corporate income tax, or profit tax. Various systems define income differently and often allow notional reductions of income (such as a reduction based on number of children supported)

Income Terms Of Trade

The purchasing power, in terms of the price of imports, P_m, of the value (price times quantity) of a country's exports: $ITT = P_x Q_x / P_m$.

Income-Compensated Demand Curve

A curve showing how much of a good the consumer demands at each price, when the consumer's income is adjusted so that, regardless of the price, the original market basket can be purchased.

Income-Consumption Curve

(a) A curve connecting points representing equilibrium market baskets corresponding to all possible levels of the consumer's money income. Curves of this sort can be used to derive Engel curves.

(b) the locus of tangents of budget lines with indifference curves forms the income-consumption curve or the set of commodity combinations (x, y) purchased as income increases assuming constant prices and taste.

Income-Expenditure Analysis

The simplest Keynesian model for determining national income, in which desired expenditure (consumption plus investment plus government purchases) depends on income, which is in turn determined so that desired expenditure equals income.

Incomplete Specialization

Production of goods that compete with imports.

Inconsistency

The difference between the probability limit of an estimator and the parameter value.

Incoterms

International commercial terms; that is, the language of international commerce. Examples include CIF, ex works, and FOB. The name was coined by the International Chamber of Commerce, which maintains and updates their definitions.

Increase In Aggregate Demand

If there is an increase in the level of aggregate demand then the curve will shift to the right. Aggregate demand is made up of consumption, investment, government expenditure and net exports. The curve will shift to the right if there is an increase in any of these components. The increase will usually lead to an increase in output in the economy, but may also lead to an increase in the price level.

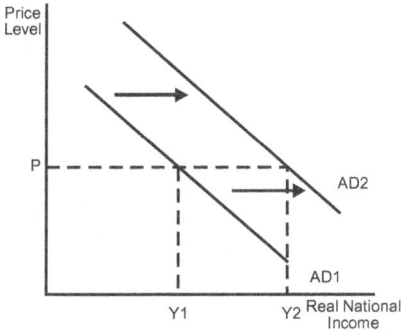

Increase In Aggregate Supply - Keynesian

When aggregate supply increases the supply curve shifts to the right. Here a Keynesian aggregate supply curve is shown.

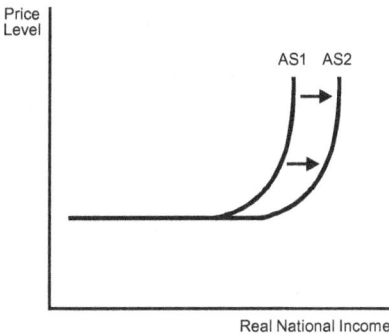

Keynesians believe that the aggregate supply curve will be the same in the short and long run, and so an increase in aggregate supply will shift the edge of the curve to the right. This may be caused by a change in productivity, changes in the tax and benefit system or some other factor affecting the amount of output that can be produced in the economy.

Increase In Long Run Aggregate Supply

An increase in aggregate supply will shift the long run aggregate supply curve right. According to Classical economists the LRAS curve will be vertical.

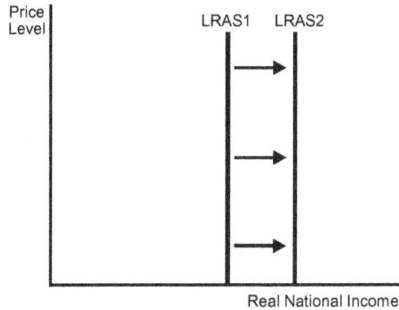

Classical economists believe that in the long run the economy will settle automatically at the full employment level of income. If something happens to increase the full employment potential of the economy, this will shift the LRAS curve to the right. Possible causes could be an increase in productivity, an improvement in skill levels or a change in the tax and benefits system.

Increase In Marginal Revenue Product

An increase in the marginal revenue product of a factor will shift the MRP curve upwards.

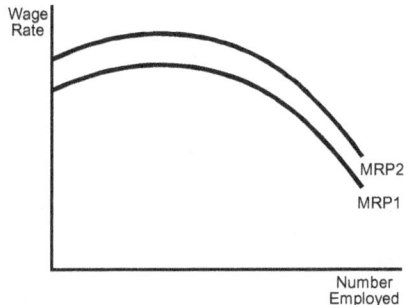

The marginal revenue product is the extra revenue earned by an additional factor, and is therefore the value of that factor to the firm. It is calculated

117

by multiplying the marginal physical product (the extra output produced by one more factor) by the marginal revenue (the additional revenue earned from selling the output). Any increase in the MRP will shift the MRP curve upwards and may be caused by an increase in the price of the good, an increase in productivity of the factor or anything else that changes either the MPP or the MR.

Increase In Productivity

When the same amount of an output can be produced with fewer inputs; more output can be produced with the same amount of inputs; or a combination of the two.

Increased Aggregate Supply

Classical economists would argue that governments should use supply-side policy to increase the potential level of output in the economy. The effect of this is to shift the aggregate supply curve to the right.

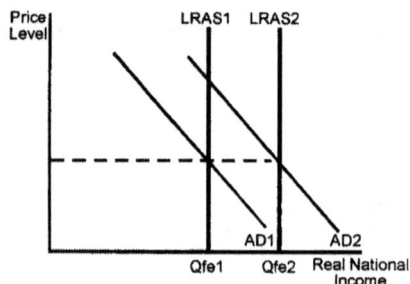

If the LRAS curve shifts to the right then the level of aggregate demand can be correspondingly higher before there is any effect on inflation. In this diagram full employment output (and equilibrium) grows from Qfe1 to Qfe2 without any impact on the price level.

Increasing Cost

1. Referring to a single firm or industry, the rise in cost of production that occurs when output

is increased by expanding variable inputs while holding some fixed input constant. A corollary of the Law of Diminishing Returns.

2. In general equilibrium, increasing opportunity cost.

Increasing Opportunity Cost

The characteristic of an economy that the opportunity cost of a good rises as it produces more of it, resulting in a transformation curve that is concave to the origin. In the HO Model, this happens in spite of CRTS if sectors have different factor intensities.

Increasing Returns To Scale

A property of a production function such that changing all inputs by the same proportion changes output more than in proportion. Common forms include homogeneous of degree greater than one and production with constant marginal cost but positive fixed cost. Also called economies of scale, scale economies, and simply increasing returns.

Increasing-Cost Industry

An industry with a positively sloped long-run supply curve; its expansion results in an increase in input prices.

Incremental Capital Output Ratio

The amount of additional capital that a developing country requires to increase its output by one unit; thus the reciprocal of the marginal product of capital. Used as an (inverse) indicator of how efficiently a country is using the scarce capital it acquires.

Indebtedness

The amount that is owed; thus amount of an entity's (individual, firm, or government's) financial obligations to creditors.

Independent Random Variables

Random variables whose joint distribution is the product of the marginal distributions.

Index

A quantitative measure, usually of something the measurement of which is not straightforward, such as an average of many diverse prices, or a concept such as economic development or human rights.

Index Number

A numerical index, usually indicating, by comparison with a base value of 100, the size of the index relative to a base year or other benchmark for comparison. Thus, for example, a CPI of 115 in 2004 with a base year of 1999 means that prices have risen 15% from 1999 to 2004.

Index Number Problem

A question the answer to which depends on a choice of weights. e.g., the effect of trade on thereal wage of labour in the specific factors model is an index number problem, depending on how much workers consume of (lower-priced) imported and (higher-priced) exported goods.

Index Of Industrial Production

A quantity index that is designed to measure changes in the physical volume or production levels of industrial goods over time.

Index Of Sustainable Economic Welfare

An alternative to GDP intended as a measure of welfare rather than simply production. As such it would take account of such things as income distribution, environmental impact, and leisure. No single measure of ISEW seems to have been agreed upon.

Indexation

Modifying contracts so that their dollar terms adjust to the inflation rate as measured in an index, such as the consumer price index.

India Brand Equity Foundation

IBFF is a public-private partnership between the Ministry of Commerce and Industry, Government of India and the Confederation of Indian Industry. It collects, collates and disseminates comprehensive and current information on the Indian economy and business -www.ibef.org

Indifference Curve

A means of representing the preferences and well being of consumers. Formally, it is a curve representing the combinations of arguments in a utility function that yield a given level of utility.

1. The locus of points representing market baskets among which the consumer is indifferent.

2. for any level of utility, say U1, there is a set of commodity combinations which graphically form an indifference curve representing all combinations yielding the same level of utility - U1. Indifference curves are sometimes called preference curves, i.e. a curve reflecting a constant level of preference, or isoquants, i.e. a curve reflecting a constant quantity of satisfaction or utility.

Indifference Theory

The analysis of consumer demand using indifference curves and an income constraint to demonstrate the reason for the inverse relationship between price and quantity demand. An alternative to the older marginal utility explanation of this phenomenon.

Indigenous Innovation Policy

A policy introduced by China in 2009 requiring that purchases by government agencies favour products whose intellectual property has been developed, owned, and registered in China.

Indirect Exchange Rate

The foreign-currency price of a unit of domestic currency.

Indirect Export

Export of a good by someone other than the firm that produced it, such as by a trading company or by a foreign purchaser.

Indirect Tax

The term indirect tax has more than one meaning. In the colloquial sense, an indirect tax (such as sales tax, a specific tax, value added tax (VAT), or goods and services tax (GST)) is a tax collected by an intermediary (such as a retail store) from the person who bears the ultimate economic burden of the tax (such as the consumer). The intermediary later files a tax return and forwards the tax proceeds to government with the return. In this sense, the term indirect tax is contrasted with a direct tax which is collected directly by government from the persons (legal or natural) on which it is imposed. Some commentators have argued that "a direct tax is one that cannot be shifted by the taxpayer to someone else, whereas an indirect tax can be." An indirect tax may increase the price of a good so that consumers are actually paying the tax by paying more for the products. Examples would be fuel, liquor, and cigarette taxes. An excise duty on motor cars is paid in the first instance by the manufacturer of the cars; ultimately the manufacturer transfers the burden of this duty to the buyer of the car in form of a higher price. Thus, an indirect tax is such which can be shifted or passed on. The degree to which the burden of a tax is shifted determines whether a tax is primarily direct or primarily indirect. This is a function of the relative elasticity of the supply and demand of the goods or services being taxed. Under this definition, even income taxes may be indirect.

Indirect Trade Deflection

Same as internal trade deflection. This term seems to be more commonly used than internal trade deflection.

Industrial Concentration

The extent to which a small number of firms dominates an industry, often measured by aconcentration ratio or by a Herfindahl index. Concentration is, in effect, the opposite of competition, although in an open economy imports complicate the relationship.

Industrial Policy

Government policy to influence which industries expand and, perhaps implicitly, which contract, via subsidies, tax breaks, and other aids for favoured industries. The purpose, aside from political favour, may be to foster competitive advantage where there are beneficial externalities and/or scale economies.

Industrialization

Industrialisation (or industrialization) is the period of social and economic change that transforms a human group from an agrarian society into an industrial one. It is a part of a wider modernisation process, where social change and economic development are closely related with technological innovation, particularly with the development of large-scale energy and metallurgy production. It is the extensive organisation of an economy for the purpose of manufacturing. Industrialisation also introduces a form of philosophical change where people obtain a different attitude towards their perception of nature, and a sociological process of ubiquitous rationalisation.

Industrialized

Having experienced substantial industrialization. Industrialized countries are usually the same as developed countries.

Industry

1. The portion of an economy that produces a particular related group of products; e.g., the motor vehicle industry, the tourism industry, the mining industry. A list of industries might well include agriculture.
2. One of three main sectors of an economy, the other two being the agriculture and service sectors. Industry in turn includes mining and manufacturing.

Inelastic

Having an elasticity less than one. For a price elasticity of demand, this means that expenditure falls as price falls. For an income elasticity it means that expenditure share falls with rising income.

Inelastic Demand

A term used when the percentage change in quantity demanded is smaller than the percentage change in price.

Inelastic Offer Curve

An offer curve with inelastic demand for imports. That inelasticity implies that exports decline as imports increase, and it therefore means that the offer curve is backward bending. Strictly speaking, the natural definition

of an offer curve's elasticity would be negative in this case, not just less than one, but that definition is seldom used.

Inequality

Differences in per capita income or household income across populations within a country or across countries.

Infant Industry Argument

The theoretical rationale for infant industry protection.

Infant Industry Protection

Protection of a newly established domestic industry that is less productive than foreign producers. If productivity will rise with experience enough to pass Mill's and Bastable's tests, there is a second-best argument for protection. The term is very old, but a classic treatment may be found in Baldwin (1969).

Inferior Good

An inferior good is a good that decreases in demand when consumer income rises, unlike normal goods, for which the opposite is observed. Normal goods are those for which consumers' demand increases when their income increases. This would be the opposite of a superior good, one that is often associated with wealth and the wealthy, whereas an inferior good is often associated with lower socio-economic groups. Inferiority, in this sense, is an observable fact relating to affordability rather than a statement about the quality of the good. As a rule, these goods are affordable and adequately fulfill their purpose, but as more costly substitutes that offer more pleasure (or at least variety) become available, the use of the inferior goods diminishes. Depending on consumer or market indifference curves, the amount of a good bought can either increase, decrease, or stay the same when income increases.

Infinite Distributed Lag (IdL) Model

A distributed lag model where a change in the explanatory variable can have an impact on the dependent variable into the indefinite future.

Infinitely Elastic

Having an elasticity that is infinitely large, usually with respect to price, in which case what it means in effect is that the price is constant, given, or fixed. A small open economy, usually by definition, faces world supply and demand that are infinitely elastic at a given world price.

Inflation

In economics, inflation is a rise in the general level of prices of goods and services in an economy over a period of time. When the general price level rises, each unit of currency buys fewer goods and services. Consequently, inflation also reflects an erosion in the purchasing power of money – a loss of real value in the internal medium of exchange and unit of account within the economy. A chief measure of price inflation is the inflation rate, the annualized percentage change in a general price index (normally the Consumer Price Index) over time. Inflation's effects on an economy are various and can be simultaneously positive and negative. Negative effects of inflation include an increase in the opportunity cost of holding money, uncertainty over future inflation which may discourage investment and savings, and if inflation is rapid enough, shortages of goods as consumers begin hoarding out of concern that prices will increase in the future. Positive effects include ensuring that central banks can adjust real interest rates (intended to mitigate recessions), and encouraging investment in non-monetary capital projects.

Inflation Adjusted

Adjusted for inflation.

Inflation Rate

In economics, the inflation rate is a measure of inflation, or the rate of increase of a price index such as the consumer price index. It is the percentage rate of change in price level over time, usually one year. The rate of decrease in the purchasing power of money is approximately equal. The inflation rate is used to calculate the real interest rate, as well as real increases in wages. Official measurements of this rate are input variables to COLA adjustments and inflation derivatives prices.

Inflation Targeting

A principle of monetary policy that the rate of inflation should be kept within a pre-specified range, using expansionary policy when the rate is below that range and contractionary policy above it.

Information Set

In forecasting, the set of variables that we can observe prior to forming our forecast.

Inframarginal

Inside of, as opposed to at, the margin. Example: for a firm that is producing 100 units, marginal cost is the cost of the 101st unit, while inframarginal cost refers, usually only qualitatively and without a precise definition, to the cost of units 1,...,100.

Inframarginal Rent

The quasi rent earned by a perfectly competitive firm in the short run. If price equals marginal cost, then it earns nothing on the marginal unit, but if marginal cost increases with output due to a fixed factor, then price exceeds marginal cost for inframarginal units.

Infrastructure

The facilities that must be in place in order for a country or area to function as an economy and as a state, including the capital needed for transportation, communication, and provision of water and power, and the institutions needed for security, health and education.

Injury

Harm to an industry's owners and/or workers. Import protection under the safeguards, AD, and CVD provisions of the GATT require a finding of serious (for safeguards) or material (for AD/CVD) injury (as determined by, in the U.S., the ITC). Known as the injury test.

Injury Margin

In cases of anti-dumping and counterailing duties, the difference between the import price and the price that would be needed to prevent injury.

Innovation

Innovation is the development of new customers value through solutions that meet new needs, inarticulate needs, or old customer and market needs in value adding new ways. This is accomplished through more effective products, processes, services, technologies, or ideas that are readily available to markets, governments, and society. Innovation differs from invention in that innovation refers to the use of a better and, as a result, novel idea or method, whereas invention refers more directly to the creation of the idea or method itself. Innovation differs from improvement in that innovation refers to the notion of doing something different (Lat. innovare: "to change") rather than doing the same thing better.

Input

1. Anything that is used in a production process, including both the services of primary factors and intermediate inputs.
2. Sometimes input refers only to intermediate inputs, as distinct from primary factors.

Input-Output

Refers to the structure of intermediate transactions among industries, in which one industry's output is an input to another, or even to itself.

Input-Output Table

A table of all inputs and outputs of an economy's industries, including intermediate transactions, primary inputs, and sales to final users. As developed by Wassily Leontief, the table can be used to calculate gross outputs and primary factor inputs needed to produce specified net outputs. Leontief (1954) used this to find the factor content of U.S. trade, generating the Leontief Paradox.

In-Sample Criteria

Criteria for choosing forecasting models that are based on goodness-of-fit within the sample used to obtain the parameter estimates.

Inshoring

Term used occasionally as an opposite to offshoring, when a foreign firm relocates a part of its productive activity into the domestic economy.

Insignificant

1. Too small to matter, usually meaning that the size of a variable or effect is small enough that it will not be noticed in comparison to whatever else is going on.
2. Not statistically significant.

Insourcing

Insourcing is the cessation by a company of contracting a business function and the commencement of performing it internally. Insourcing is the opposite of outsourcing. Insourcing is a business decision that is often made to maintain control of critical production or competencies. Insourcing is widely used in production to reduce costs of taxes, labour and transportation. Insourcing is also defined as bringing a third party outsourcer to work inside a company's facility. An IT outsourcing provider, for example, will be hired to service a company's IT department while working inside the company's facilities. In addition to contracting an entire team of workers from an outsourcing provider, outside experts are sometimes hired as consultants (to improve certain processes etc.) and the internal staff thereafter implements their recommendations. It may also refer to bringing in foreign nationals to do jobs at lower wages. An example would be a coal mine which lists a foreign language(ie Mandarin Chinese) as a job prerequisite that citizens tend not to study. Since the labour pool does not have the listed skill a foreign worker permit can be obtained allowing the importation of Chinese workers.

Instability

The property of not being stable; thus, moving around over time, and/or uncertain in its movement over time.

Institute For International And Development Economics

A web-based network of research economists in Europe and North America focusing on the global economy, trade and financial integration, and international development.

Institutional Investor

An owner of financial assets other than a person, and for whom such ownership is a main part of its business. Main examples are banks, hedge funds, insurance companies, mutual funds, and pension funds.

Instrument

An economic variable that is controlled by policy makers and can be used to influence other variables, called targets. Examples are monetary and fiscal policies used to achieve external and internal balance.

Insurance

Insurance is the equitable transfer of the risk of a loss, from one entity to another in exchange for payment. It is a form of risk management primarily used to hedge against the risk of a contingent, uncertain loss. An insurer, or insurance carrier, is a company selling the insurance; the insured, or policyholder, is the person or entity buying the insurance policy. The amount to be charged for a certain amount of insurance coverage is called the premium. Risk management, the practice of appraising and controlling risk, has evolved as a discrete field of study and practice. The transaction involves the insured assuming a guaranteed and known relatively small loss in the form of payment to the insurer in exchange for the insurer's promise to compensate (indemnify) the insured in the case of a financial (personal) loss. The insured receives a contract, called the insurance policy, which details the conditions and circumstances under which the insured will be financially compensated.

Intangible Service

Same as service, since all services are intangible.

Integrated World Economy

A hypothetical, theoretical benchmark in which both goods and factors move costlessly between countries. The IWE is associated with a rectangular diagram depicting allocation of factors to countries, showing conditions for FPE. The name was coined by Dixit and Norman (1980), but the concept and technique was introduced by Travis (1964).

Integrated World Economy Diagram

A box diagram, somewhat analogous to an Edgeworth box, depicting alternative allocations of world endowments of two factors between two countries. It is used to illustrate the conditions for factor price equalization.

Integration

Economic integration refers to reducing barriers among countries to transactions and to movements of goods, capital, and labour, including harmonization of laws, regulations, and standards. Common forms include FTAs, customs unions, and common markets.

Intellectual Property

Intellectual property (IP) is a juridical concept which refers to creations of the mind for which exclusive rights are recognized. Under intellectual property law, owners are granted certain exclusive rights to a variety of intangible assets, such as musical, literary, and artistic works; discoveries and inventions; and words, phrases, symbols, and designs. Common types of intellectual property rights include copyright, trademarks, patents, industrial design rights and in some jurisdictions trade secrets.

Intellectual Property Protection

Laws that establish and maintain ownership rights to intellectual property. The principal forms of IP protection are patents, trademarks, and copyrights.

Intellectual Property Right

The right to control and derive the benefits from something one has invented, discovered, or created.

Intensity

The amount that something is used, as compared to something else.

Intensive

Of production, using a relatively large amount of an input.

Intensive Margin

Refers to varying the amount of trade (or other activity) of a firm, industry, or country by varying the quantity that it trades of a given number of products, as opposed to the extensive margin at which it would vary the number of products.

Interaction Effect

In multiple regression, the partial effect of one explanatory variable depends on the value of a different explanatory variable.

Interaction Term

An independent variable in a regression model that is the product of two explanatory variables.

Inter-American Development Bank

A development bank for the countries of Latin America and the Caribbean.

Interbank Rate

The rate of interest charged by a bank on a loan to another bank.

Intercept Parameter

The parameter in a multiple linear regression model that gives the expected value of the dependent variable when all the independent variables equal zero.

Intercept Shift

The intercept in a regression model differs by group or time period.

Interdependence

Dependence on others for goods and services; occurs as a result of specialization.

Interdependence Inter-relationship

Interdependence inter-relationship between economic and noneconomic variables. Also, in international affairs, the situation in which one nation's welfare depends to varying degrees on the decisions and policies of another nation, and vice versa.

Interest

Interest is a fee paid by a borrower of assets to the owner as a form of compensation for the use of the assets. It is most commonly the price paid for the use of borrowed money, or money earned by deposited funds. When money is borrowed, interest is typically paid to the lender as a percentage of the principal, the amount owed to the lender. The percentage of the principal that is paid as a fee over a certain period of time (typically one month or year) is called the interest rate. A bank deposit will earn interest because the bank is paying for the use of the deposited funds. Assets that are sometimes lent with interest include money, shares, consumer goods through hire purchase, major assets such as aircraft, and even entire factories in finance lease arrangements. The interest is calculated upon the value of the assets in the same manner as upon money.

Interest Arbitrage

A form of arbitrage intended to profit from a difference in interest rates in different markets. It consists of simultaneously borrowing at the low interest rate and lending at the higher interest rate in order to profit from the difference. If done in two different currencies, it may be coveredor uncovered.

Interest Bearing Account

An account in a bank or other financial institution that pays interest to the depositor.

Interest Equalization Tax

A tax levied between 1963 and 1974 by the United States of 15% on interest received from foreign borrowers, intended to discourage capital outflows.

Interest Parity

Equality of returns on otherwise identical financial assets denominated in different currencies. May be uncovered, with returns including expected changes in exchange rates, or covered, with returns including the forward premium or discount. Also called interest rate parity and interest parity condition.

Interest Rate

The rate of return on bonds, loans, or deposits. When one speaks of "the" interest rate, it is usually in a model where there is only one.

Intergenerational Equity

Intergenerational equity in economic, psychological, and sociological contexts, is the concept or idea of fairness or justice in relationships between children, youth, adults and seniors, particularly in terms of treatment and interactions. It has been studied in environmental and sociological settings.

Intergovernmental Organization

An organization the members of which are national governments, including the United Nations, its subsidiary organizations such as UNCTAD, and a great many others.

Interindustry Trade

Trade in which a country's exports and imports are in different industries. Typical of models of comparative advantage, such as the Ricardian Model and Heckscher-Ohlin Model.

Intermediate Good

A good that is used to produce other goods and ser- vices.

Intermediate Input

An input to production that has itself been produced and that, unlike capital, is used up in production. As an input it is in contrast to a primary input and as an output it is in contrast to a final good. A very large portion of international trade is in intermediate inputs.

Intermediate Transaction

The sale of a product by one firm to another, presumably to be used as an intermediate input.

Intermittent Dumping

Dumping that occurs for short periods of time, presumably to dispose of temporary surpluses of goods and not intended to eliminate competition.

Intermodalism

The use of more than one form (mode) of transportation, as when a shipment travels by both sea and rail.

Internal Balance

A target level for domestic aggregate economic activity, such as a level of GDP that minimizes unemployment without being inflationary.

Internal Debt

The amount owed by a country to, in effect, itself. It includes, for example, the portion of the government debt that is denominated in the country's own currency and held by domestic residents.

Internal Economies Of Scale

Economies of scale that are internal to a firm; that is, the firm's average costs fall as its own output rises. Likely to be inconsistent with perfect competition.

Internal Equilibrium

Internal balance.

Internal Market

Term used for a target of European integration, which would remove all barriers between national markets so that they would become, in effect, a single European market.

Internal Rate Of Return

The internal rate of return (IRR) or economic rate of return (ERR) is a rate of return used in capital budgeting to measure and compare the profitability of investments. It is also called the discounted cash flow rate of return (DCFROR) or the rate of return (ROR). In the context of savings and loans the IRR is also called the effective interest rate. The term internal refers to the fact that its calculation does not incorporate environmental factors (e.g., the interest rate or inflation).

Internal Trade Deflection

The shift of domestic sales from a low-tariff member of an FTA to a high-tariff member, displacing imports there and inducing additional imports at home, thus having the same effects as trade deflection without potential for interruption by rules of origin. Identified and named by Richardson (1995), though others have used the equivalent indirect trade deflection.

Internalization

One of the three pillars of the OLI paradigm for understanding FDI and the formation of multinational enterprises, this refers to the advantage that a firm derives from keeping multiple activities within the same organization.

Internalize

To cause, usually by a tax or subsidy, an external cost or benefit of someone's actions to be experienced by them directly, so that they will take it into account in their decisions.

International

Involving transactions or relations between nations. The term, according to Suganami (1978), was coined by Bentham (1789).

International Accounting Standards Board

An independent body, based in London, that sets accounting standards in the form of the International Financial Reporting Standards.

International Adjustment Process

1. Any mechanism for change in international markets.

2. The mechanism by which payments imbalances diminish under pegged exchange rates and nonsterilization. Similar to the specie flow mechanism, exchange-market intervention causesmoney supplies of surplus countries to expand and vice versa, leading to price and interest rate changes that correct the current and capital account imbalances.

International Bank For Reconstruction & Development

The largest of the five institutions that comprise the World Bank Group, IBRD provides loans and development assistance to middle-income countries and creditworthy poorer countries.

International Capital Movement

The acquisition or sale of assets, financial or real, across international borders. Measured in thefinancial account of the balance of payments.

International Centre For Settlement Of Investment Disputes

One of the five institutions that comprise the World Bank Group, ICSID provides facilities for the settlement - by conciliation or arbitration - of investment disputes between foreign investors and their host countries.

International Chamber Of Commerce

Calling itself the "voice of world business," the ICC promotes the cause of international business and open markets.

International Cocoa Organization

An intergovernmental organization set up in 1973 to administer the International Cocoa Agreement, the most recent version of which was negotiated in 2001.

International Coffee Organization

An intergovernmental organization set up in 1963 that administers the International Coffee Agreement.

International Commodity

Agreement Formal agreement by sellers of a common internationally traded commodity (coffee, sugar) to coordinate supply to maintain price stability.

International Commodity Agreement

An international commodity agreement is an undertaking by a group of countries to stabilize trade, supplies, and prices of a commodity for the benefit of participating countries. An agreement usually involves a consensus on quantities traded, prices, and stock management. A number of international commodity agreements serve solely as forums for information exchange, analysis, and policy discussion. USTR leads United States participation in two commodity trade agreements: the International Tropical Timber Agreement and the International Coffee Agreement (ICA). Both agreements establish inter-governmental organizations with governing councils .

International Comparison Programme

A programme currently coordinated by the World Bank to gather extensive information about prices in many countries so as to ascertain the purchasing power of their currencies and thus permit international comparisons of real incomes.

International Competition Network

The International Competition Network is an informal, virtual network that seeks to facilitate cooperation between competition law authorities globally. It was established in 2001 after the publication of a Final Report of the International Competition Policy Advisory Committee to the US Attorney General and Assistant Attorney General for Antitrust (or the ICPAC report, for short). Competition law experts in the US recommended that increased collabouration with overseas authorities could contribute to the coordination of enforcement and sharing of information on competition policy globally.

International Cotton Advisory Committee

The International Cotton Advisory Committee (ICAC) is an association of governments of cotton producing, consuming and trading countries which acts as the international commodity body for cotton and cotton textiles.

International Development Association (IDA)

The International Development Association (IDA) is an international financial institution which offers concessional loans and grants to the world's poorest developing countries. The IDA is a member of the World Bank Group and is headquartered in Washington, D.C., United States. It was established in 1960 to complement the existing International Bank for Reconstruction and

Development by lending to developing countries which suffer from the lowest gross national income, from troubled creditworthiness, or from the lowest per capita income. Together, the International Development Association and International Bank for Reconstruction and Development are collectively known as the World Bank, as they follow the same executive leadership and operate with the same staff.

International Economics

The study of economic interactions among countries — including trade, investment, financial transactions, and movement of people — and the policies and institutions that influence them.

International Externality

An externality that extends across national borders. A negative example is emission of greenhouse gases that contribute to global warming. A positive example is technological innovation that diffuses to other countries.

International Factor Movement

The international movement of any factor of production, including primarily labour and capital. Thus includes migration and foreign direct investment. Also may include the movement offinancial capital in the form of international borrowing and lending.

International Finance

The monetary side of international economics, in contrast to the real side, or real trade. Often called also international monetary economics or international macroeconomics, each term has a slightly different meaning, and none seems entirely right for the entire field. "International finance" is best for the study of international financial markets including exchange rates.

International Finance Corporation

One of the five institutions that comprise the World Bank Group, IFC promotes growth in the developing world by financing private sector investments and providing technical assistance and advice to governments and businesses.

International Financial Institution

Usually refers to intergovernmental organizations dealing with financial issues, most often the IMF and/or the World Bank.

International Financial Reporting Standards

A set of accounting standards set by the International Accounting Standards Board and required for use throughout Europe and parts of Asia, Africa and Latin America. Other countries have committed to adopt or converge toward these standards, and the United States permits non-US companies to report under them, although US companies use the Generally Accepted Accounting Priciples.

International Fisher Effect

The theory that exchange-rate changes will match, or be expected to match, international differences in nominal interest rates. It follows from the (domestic) Fisher Effect together withpurchasing power parity.

International Forum Of Sovereign Wealth Funds

A voluntary group of sovereign wealth funds that meets to exchange views and propagate the Santiago Principles. As of July 2011, it had 23 member countries.

International Fund For Agricultural Development

A United Nations specialized agency that finances projects primarily for food production in developing countries.

International Grains Council

An intergovernmental organization, concerned with grains trade, that administers the Grains Trade Convention of 1995.

International Indebtedness

The amount that a country's government and/or its private sector has borrowed from other countries and/or international financial institutions.

International Institution

An organization established by multiple national governments, usually to administer a programme or pursue a purpose that the governments have agreed upon.

International Investment

1. International capital movement
2. Foreign direct investment.

International Investment Position

The total value of assets, real and financial, owned abroad by a country's people, firms, and government, minus the total value of foreign-owned assets in the country.

International Jute Organization

The organization set up in 1984 to implement the International Agreement on Jute and Jute Products,

1982, now called the International Jute Study Group.

International Labour Organization (ILO)

One of the functional organizations of the United Nations, based in Geneva, Switzerland, whose central task is to look into problems of world labour supply, its training, utilization, domestic and international distribution, etc. Its aim in this endeavour is to increase world output through maximum utilization of available human resources and thus improve levels of living.

International Lead And Zinc Study Group

The international organization formed in 1959 to share information about lead and zinc.

International Liquidity

Refers to the adequacy of a country's, or the world's, international reserves. Under the Bretton Woods System, liquidity was a problem, since it depended on US dollars and thus a US deficit. The SDR was an attempt to fix this.

International Macro-economics

Same as international finance, but with more emphasis on the international determination of macroeconomic variables such as national income and the price level.

International Monetary Economics

Same as international finance, but with more emphasis on the role of money and less on other financial assets.

International Monetary Fund

An autonomous international financial institution that originated in the Bretton

Woods Conference of 1944. Its main purpose is to regulate the international monetary exchange system, which also stems from that conference but has since been modified. In particular, one of the central tasks of the IMF is to control fluctuations in exchange rates of world currencies in a bid to alleviate severe balance of payments problems.

International Olive Oil Council

The intergovernmental organization in charge of administering the International Olive Oil Agreement, which originated in 1956.

International Organization For Migration

International organization assisting migrants and the management of migration.

International Organization For Standardization

An NGO that develops and publishes international standards. It is a network of national standards institutes from 161 countries. Some of these institutes are parts of governments, while others are private-sector partnerships of industry associations.

International Parity Conditions

Refers collectively to purchasing power parity and interest parity.

International Political Economy

A field of study within social science, especially political science, that addresses the interrelationships between international economics and political forces and institutions.

International Poverty Line

An arbitrary international real income measure, usually expressed in constant dollars (e.g., $270), used as a basis for estimating the proportion of the world's population that exists at bare levels of subsistence.

International Price

World price.

International Price Programme

The origins of the International Price Programme (IPP) can be traced to a 1961 report on Federal Price Statistics prepared by the National Bureau of Economic Research. The report for Congress' Joint Economic Committee suggested that indexes be assigned to a federal statistical agency "to obtain the attention and resources for these indexes that we believe are essential." A further study undertaken for NBER by Professors Irving Kravis and Robert Lipsey gave more impetus to the project. In their study, "Price Competitiveness in World Trade," Kravis and Lipsey outlined the need for such measures and the feasibility of producing them. During this time, the Bureau's Division of Price and Index Number Research, largely because of its expertise in the development of other price measures, had also begun research on the feasibility of producing import and export price indexes. The IPP was a natural result of this research and was established in 1971.

International Relations

1. All aspects of interactions among nations.
2. The field within the discipline of political science that studies the mechanisms and institutions through which countries interact.

International Reserves

The assets denominated in foreign currency, plus gold, held by a central bank, sometimes for the purpose of intervening in the exchange market to influence or peg the exchange rate. Usually includes foreign currencies themselves (especially US dollars), other assets denominated in foreign currencies, gold, and a small amount of SDRs.

International Rubber Study Group

An intergovernmental organization, founded in 1944, that provides a forum for the discussion of matters affecting the supply and demand for both synthetic and natural rubber.

International Standard Industrial Classification

A classification system for industries, organized by the activity performed by the industry, and used for recording and reporting data on industrial activities, including output and employment.

International Sugar Organization

An intergovernmental body that administers the International Sugar Agreement of 1992.

International Tax

1. This could mean, if it existed, a tax levied by an international body on the governments or private sector actors throughout the world. This does not exist, however, except among small groups of countries that have agreed to share resources, such as the European Union.
2. The field of study that deals with how separate national taxing authorities interact and how private sector actors respond to international differences in taxing regimes.

International Trade

International trade is the exchange of capital, goods, and services across international borders or territories. In most countries, such trade represents a significant share of gross domestic product (GDP). While international trade has been present throughout much of history (see Silk Road, Amber Road), its economic, social, and political importance has been on the rise in recent centuries. Industrialization, advanced transportation, globalization, multinational corporations, and outsourcing are all having a major impact on the international trade system. Increasing international trade is crucial to the continuance of globalization. Without international trade, nations would be limited to the goods and services produced within their own borders. International trade is, in principle, not different from domestic trade as the motivation and the behaviour of parties involved in a trade do not change fundamentally regardless of whether trade is across a border or not. The main difference is that international trade is typically more costly than domestic trade. The reason is that a border typically imposes additional costs such as tariffs, time costs due to border delays and costs associated with country differences such as language, the legal system or culture.

International Trade Administration

A part of the United States Department of Commerce, the ITA acts on behalf of U.S. businesses in global competition. In trade policy, its Import Administration has the duty of determining whether imports are dumped or subsidized.

International Trade Centre

An international agency whose purpose is to help developing countries increase export. It is a "joint technical cooperation agency" of UNCTAD and the WTO.

International Trade Organization

Conceived as a complement to the Bretton Woods institutions — the IMF and World Bank -- the ITO was to provide international discipline in the uses of trade policies. The Havana Charterfor the ITO was not approved by the United States Congress, however, and the initiative died, replaced by the continuing and growing importance of the GATT.

International Tropical Timber Organization

An organization created in 1983 for consultation among producers and consumers of tropical timber. An objective was that all timber traded by members should originate from sustainably managed forests.

International Working Group of Sovereign Wealth Funds

A group of countries that maintain sovereign wealth funds and that formulated the Santiago Principles. In 2009 the group established the International Forum of Sovereign Wealth Funds.

Intertemporal

Occurring across time, or across different periods of time.

Intertemporal Trade

Trade across time, as when a country imports in one time period paying for the imports with exports in a different time period, earlier or later. An imbalance in the balance of trade is presumed to reflect intertemporal trade.

Interval Estimator

A rule that uses data to obtain lower and upper bounds for a population parameter.

Intervention Currency

A currency that is commonly used by central banks for exchange market intervention.

Intrafirm Trade

International trade conducted within a firm, as when a subsidiary of a company exports to or imports from another subsidiary or the parent company in a different country.

Intraindustry Trade

Trade in which a country exports and imports in the same industry, in contrast to interindustry trade. Ubiquitous in the data, much IIT is due to aggregation. Can be horizontal or vertical.Grubel and Lloyd (1975) wrote the book on IIT and introduced the Grubel-Lloyd index to measure it.

Intra-Mediate Trade

Another term for fragmentation. Used by Antweiler and Trefler (2002).

Intra-Product Specialization

Another term for fragmentation. Used by Arndt (1997).

Intrinsic Values

Intrinsic value refers to the value of a security which is intrinsic to or contained in the security itself. It is also frequently called fundamental value. It is ordinarily calculated by summing the future income generated by the asset, and discounting it to the present value. Simply put, it is the actual value of a security as opposed to the market or book value.

Inventories

The word inventory is commonly used in American English to describe the goods and materials that a business holds for the ultimate purpose of resale. In the rest of the English speaking world stock is more commonly used, although the word inventory is recognised as a synonym. In British English, the word inventory is more commonly thought of as a list compiled for some formal purpose, such as the details of an estate going to probate, or the contents of a house let furnished. In American English, the word stock is commonly used to describe the capital invested in a business, while in British English, the word share is more widely used in the same context. In both British and American English, stock is the collective noun for one hundred shares as shares were usually traded in stocks on Stock Exchanges. For this reason that the word stock is used by both American and British English forms in the context of the term Stock Exchange.

Inventory

A stock of goods or resources held by a buyer or seller in order to reduce the cost of exchange or production.

Inverse Demand Function

A function representing the relationship between quantity demanded and price, specified for convenience with price as a function of quantity instead of the more usual quantity as a function of price.

Inverse Supply Function

A function representing the relationship between quantity supplied and price, specified for convenience with price as a function of quantity instead of the more usual quantity as a function of price.

Invertible

Said of a matrix if its inverse exists. That is, a matrix A is invertible if there exists another matrix B such that $BA=I$, where I is the identity matrix.

Investing

Creating capital goods. Acquiring or producing structures, machinery and equipment or inventories.

Investment

1. Addition to the stock of capital of a firm or country.
2. Purchase of an asset, real or financial.
3. The use of resources today for the purpose of increasing productivity or income in the future.

Investment Bank

A commercial institution that provides a variety of services to firms and other entities that seek to raise funds and/or invest their own funds. These services include underwriting, advising, managing assets, and providing their own or borrowed funds. The largest investment banks today operate in many countries.

Investment Demand Curve

The relationship between the total amount of investment and the rate of return from an extra dollar of investment.

Investment Expenditures

Dollar expenditures by firms on capital goods (factories, office buildings and others structures, machinery and equipment, inventories and residential housing) used to produce other new goods and services.

Investment In Capital Goods

Occurs when savings are used to increase the economy's productive capacity by financing the construction of new factories, machines, means of communication, and the like.

Investment In Capital Resources

Business purchases of new plant and equipment.

Investment In Human Capital

An action taken to increase the productivity of workers. These actions can include improving skills and abilities, education, health, or mobility of workers.

Investment Spending

The total amount of spending during some period of time on capital goods.

Invisible

In referring to international trade, used as a synonym for "service." "Invisibles trade" is trade in services.

Invoice

An invoice or bill is a commercial document issued by a seller to the buyer, indicating the products, quantities, and agreed prices for products or services the seller has provided the buyer. An invoice indicates the sale transaction only. Payment terms are independent of the invoice and are negotiated by the buyer and the seller. Payment terms are usually included on the invoice. The buyer could have already paid for the products or services listed on the invoice. Buyer can also have a maximum number of days in which to pay for these goods and is sometimes offered a discount if paid before the due date. In the rental industry, an invoice must include a specific reference to the duration of the time being billed, so in addition to quantity, price and discount the invoicing amount is also based on duration. Generally each line of a rental invoice will refer to the actual hours, days, weeks, months, etc., being billed.

Involuntary Unemployment

Potential workers able and willing to work at the existing market wage rate, are unable to find jobs.

Inward FDI

Foreign direct investment by a foreign firm establishing a facility within the domestic country.

Inward-Oriented Development

A strategy of promoting development by encouraging production, as well as research and development, for domestic markets. Seems to be the same as import substitution, although proponents make a distinction between them.

Irreversibility

If an asset is not preserved it is likely to be eliminated with little or no chance of regeneration.

Isocost Curve

1. A curve showing the combinations of inputs that can be obtained for a fixed total outlay.
2. Plotted assuming Cost, P_K and P_L are fixed showing all combinations of K & L that a firm can afford.

Isoprofit Curve

A curve showing all input combinations that can produce a given level of profit.

Isoquant

An isoquant (derived from quantity and the Greek word iso, meaning equal) is a contour line drawn through the set of points at which the same quantity of output is produced while changing the quantities of two or more inputs. While an indifference curve mapping helps to solve the utility-maximizing problem of consumers, the isoquant mapping deals with the cost-minimization problem of producers. Isoquants are typically drawn on capital-labour graphs, showing the technological tradeoff between capital and labour in the production function, and the decreasing marginal returns of both inputs. Adding one input while holding the other constant eventually leads to decreasing marginal output, and this is reflected in the shape of the isoquant. A family of isoquants can be represented by an isoquant map, a graph combining a number of isoquants, each representing a different quantity of output. Isoquants are also called equal product curves.

Isorevenue Line

A line showing all combinations of outputs of two commodities that result in the same total revenue.

J

J-Curve

The J-Curve shows the possible effects of a devaluation on the balance of payments. If the Marshall-Lerner condition is true then the balance of payments may intially deteriorate and then improve later.

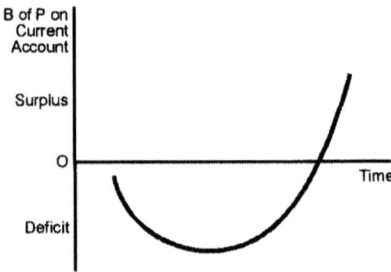

B of P on Current Account

Surplus

O

Time

Deficit

The Marshall-Lerner condition says that if the sum of the price elasticities of demand for imports and exports is greater than 1 then the balance of payments will improve following a devaluation. It is thought that the Marshall-Lerner condition will not be true in the short runbut may be true in the long run. It is this that gives rise to the J curve.

Jevons, William Stanley (1835-1882)

An English philosopher and scientist instrumental in developing the marginal utility theory of consumer choice. He demonstrated that consumers will purchase increasing quantities of goods until the marginal utility derived from the last penny's worth of one good is equal to the marginal worth of every other good. His major work was *The Theory of Political Economy* published in 1871.

Joint Distribution

The probability distribution determining the probabilities of outcomes involving two or more random variables.

Joint Hypothesis Test

A test involving more than one restriction on the parameters in a model.

Joint Implementation

The method of achieving reductions in CO_2 emissions whereby rich countries (which will probably have made binding commitments to cut emissions) can get partial credit for emission reductions projects which are funded by them, but which are undertaken in poor countries. This is now referred to as the Clean Development Mechanism (CDM) to denote respect for developing countries' right to develop. This mechanism is an attempt to make a system of marketable permits more equitable.

Joint Supply

Where goods are in joint supply, it means they are supplied together. This means that changes in the market for one good will have knock-on effects on the other market. In the diagram an increase in the demand for Good

A has led to a higher price and more of the good being supplied. Since the goods are in joint supply, this means that there will be increased supply for Good B, lowering its price.

Jointly Statistically Significant

The null hypothesis that two or more explanatory variables have zero population coefficients is rejected at the chosen significance level.

K

Keynes, John Maynard (1883-1946)

The most important economist of the 20th century. Keynes first came to prominence with his attack on the 1919 treaty with Germany (*The Economic Consequences of the Peace*, 1919). During the 1920s he became dissatisfied with the mainstream economics based on the tradition established by Alfred Marshall. The conventional analysis of individual markets appeared inadequate to explain the economic problems then being experienced in England. Keynes became convinced that deflationary policies were the cause of the difficulties and published several works on money, notably a two volume work, *The Treatise on Money*. From this he went on to develop the analysis subsequently elaborated in *The General Theory of Employment, Interest and Money*, 1936. Within ten years of its publication, Keynes had, as he expected to do, brought about a revolution in the discipline of economics. Keynes' lifetime achievements went beyond his theoretical work. He played a prominent role in the intellectual and cultural life of his time and was a very influential adviser to the British government up to the time of his death.

Keynesian

A branch of economics, based, often loosely, on the ideas of Keynes, characterised by a belief in active government and suspicion of market outcomes. It was dominant in the 30 years following the second world war, and especially during the 1960s, when fiscal policy became bigger-spending and looser in most developed countries as policymakers tried to kill off the business cycle. During the 1970s, widely blamed for the rise in inflation, Keynesian policies gradually gave way to monetarism and microeconomic policies that owed much to the neo-classical economics that Keynes had at times opposed. Even so, the idea that public spending and taxation have a crucial role to play in managing demand, in order to move towards full employment, remained at the heart of macroeconomic policy in most countries, even after the monetarist and supply-side revolution of the 1980s and 1990s. Recently, a school of new, more pro-market Keynesian economists has emerged, believing that most markets work, but sometimes only slowly.

Keynesian Aggregate Supply

Keynes argued that in the long run, the economy can settle at an equilibrium below the full employment level of output. As a result, the AS curve looks like this.

Price Level

AS

Real National Income

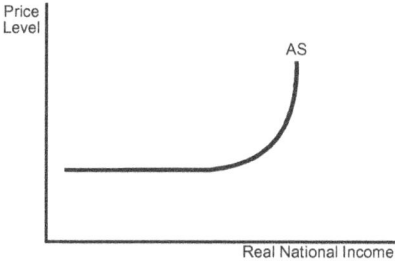

As the economy approaches full employment shortages will gradually emerge in the system and this will cause the price level to rise. This upward-sloping section of the aggregate supply curve can cause what is sometimes termed "bottleneck inflation".

Keynesian Growth Models

Models in which a long run growth path for an economy is traced out by the relations between saving, investing and the level of output.

Keynesian Macroeconomics

The theory that shows how a market-based capitalist economy may reach equilibrium with large scale unemployment and how government spending may be used to raise it out of this to a new equilibrium at the full-employment level of output.

Kleptocracy

Corrupt, thieving government, in which the politicians and bureaucrats in charge use the powers of the state to feather their own nests. Russia in the years immediately after the fall of communism was a clear-cut example, with Mafia-friendly government members allocating themselves valuable shares during the privatisation of state-owned companies, accepting bribes from foreign businesses, not collecting taxes from "helpful" companies and siphoning off international aid into their personal offshore bank accounts.

Kondratieff wave

It is a 50 year-long business cycle, named after Nikolai Kondratieff, a Russian economist. He claimed to have identified cycles of economic activity lasting half a century or more in his 1925 book, *The Long Waves in Economic Life*. Because this implied that capitalism was, ultimately, a stable system, in contrast to the Marxist view that it was self-destructively unstable, he ended up in one of Stalin's prisons, where he died. Alas, there is little hard evidence to support Kondratieff's conclusion.

141

L

Labelling

A requirement to label imported goods with information about how they were produced. This is often suggested as an alternative to trade restrictions as a means to pursue particular trade-related objectives involving, for example, environment or labour standards.

Labour

Human effort, physical or mental, used to produce goods and services.

Labour Abundant

A country is labour abundant if its endowment of labour is large compared to other countries. Relative labour abundance can be defined by either the quantity definition or the price definition.

Labour Augmenting

Said of a technological change or technological difference if one production function produces the same as if it were the other, but with a larger quantity of labour. Same as factor augmentingwith labour the augmented factor.

Labour Economics

Labour economics seeks to understand the functioning and dynamics of the markets for labour. Labour markets function through the interaction of workers and employers. Labour economics looks at the suppliers of labour services (workers), the demands of labour services (employers), and attempts to understand the resulting pattern of wages, employment, and income. In economics, labour is a measure of the work done by human beings. It is conventionally contrasted with such other factors of production as land and capital. There are theories which have developed a concept called human capital (referring to the skills that workers possess, not necessarily their actual work), although there are also counter posing macro-economic system theories that think human capital is a contradiction in terms.

Labour Force

The labour force of a country (or other geographic entity) consists of everyone of working age, typically above a certain age (around 14 to 16) and below retirement (around 65) who are participating workers, that is people actively employed or seeking employment. People not counted include students, retired people, stay-at-home parents, people in prisons or similar institutions, people employed in jobs or professions with unreported income, as well as discouraged workers who cannot find work.

Labour Intensive

Describing an industry or sector of the economy that relies relatively heavily on inputs of labour, usually relative to capital but sometimes to human capital or skilled labour, compared to other industries or sectors.

Labour Intensive Methods

Use of low quantity of capital per worker.

Labour Law

Labour law (also called labour law or employment law) is the body of laws, administrative rulings, and precedents which address the legal rights of, and restrictions on, working people and their organizations. As such, it mediates many aspects of the relationship between trade unions, employers and employees. In Canada, employment laws related to unionized workplaces are differentiated from those relating to particular individuals. In most countries however, no such distinction is made. However, there are two broad categories of labour law. First, collective labour law relates to the tripartite relationship between employee, employer and union. Second, individual labour law concerns employees' rights at work and through the contract for work. The labour movement has been instrumental in the enacting of laws protecting labour rights in the 19th and 20th centuries. Labour rights have been integral to the social and economic development since the Industrial Revolution. Employment standards are social norms (in some cases also technical standards) for the minimum socially acceptable conditions under which employees or contractors will work. Government agencies (such as the former U.S. Employment Standards Administration) enforce employment standards codified by labour law (legislative, regulatory, or judicial).

Labour Market

A market for labour. Can refer to anything from local interactions between workers and employers to country-wide (not usually world-wide) markets dominated by broadly based labour unions, industry associations, and sometimes governments.

Labour Market Restriction

A market restriction in the labour market, most often limits on wages and on the ability of firms to terminate workers.

Labour Mobility

The ability of workers to move between industries and locations to obtain higher wages or more favourable working conditions. Most models of international trade assume that labour is perfectly mobile within a country between industries and locations but not mobile at all between countries.

Labour Productivity

The ratio of real output per unit of labour input; growth is measured by a higher ratio of outputs to inputs.

Labour Scarce

A country is labour scarce if its endowment of labour is small compared to other countries. Relative labour scarcity can be defined by either the quantity definition or the price definition.

Labour Standard

Any of many conditions of workers in the workplace that are viewed as important for their well being, and minimum levels of which are advocated by labour rights activists and have been agreed to by many of the countries that are members of the ILO.

Labour Standards Argument For Protection

The view that trade restrictions (trade sanctions) should be used as a tool to improve labour standards, limiting imports, for example, from countries that do not enforce such labour rights as freedom of association and collective bargaining.

Labour Theory Of Value

The theory that the value of any produced good or service is equal to the amount of labour used, directly and indirectly, to produce it. Sometimes said to underlie the Ricardian Model of international trade.

Labour Union

A trade union (British English), labour union (Canadian English) or labour union (American English) is an organization of workers who have banded together to achieve common goals such as protecting the integrity of its trade, achieving higher pay, increasing the number of employees an employer hires, and better working conditions. The trade union, through its leadership, bargains with the employer on behalf of union members (rank and file members) and negotiates labour contracts (collective bargaining) with employers. The most common purpose of these associations or unions is "maintaining or improving the conditions of their employment".

Labour-Saving

A technological change or technological difference that is biased in favour of using less labour, compared to some definition of neutrality.

Labour-Using

A technological change or technological difference that is biased in favour of

using more labour, compared to some definition of neutrality.

Lafay Index

An index of specialization or revealed comparative advantage that takes account of both exports and imports and is therefore more suitable for a country with intraindustry trade. Due to Lafay (1992).

Laffer Curve

An inverse-U-shaped curve representing tax revenue as a function of the tax rate, attributed to Arthur Laffer. Although the idea that a rise in tax rate can reduce tax revenue is mostly based on induced reduction of work effort, for some types of taxes — especially corporate — movement of activity to another tax jurisdiction or country can have the same effect.

Lag Distribution

In a finite or infinite distributed lag model, the lag coefficients graphed as a function of the lag length.

Lagged Dependent Variable

An explanatory variable that is equal to the dependent variable from an earlier time period.

Lagged Endogenous Variable

In a simultaneous equations model, a lagged value of one of the endogenous variables.

Lagging Indicator

A measurable economic variable that varies over the business cycle, reaching peaks and troughs somewhat later than other macroeconomic variables such as GDP and unemployment.

Lagrangian

A function constructed in solving economic models that include maximization of a function (the "objective function") subject to constraints. It equals the objective function minus, for each constraint, a variable "Lagrange multiplier" times the amount by which the constraint is violated.

Laissez – Faire

A doctrine advocating a minimum role for government in the economy, such as providing for defence against external enemies, a system of law to protect individuals and their property, and production of such goods and services which for some reason are needed, but would not be produced by private firms.

Land

Natural resources or gifts of nature that are used to produce goods and services.

Land Reform

A deliberate attempt to reorganize and transform existing agrarian systems with the intention of improving the distribution of agricultural incomes and thus fostering rural development. Among its many forms, land reform may entail provision of secured tenure rights to the individual farmer, transfer of land ownership away from small classes of powerful landowners to tenants who actually till the land, appropriation of land estates for establishing small new settlement farms, or instituting land improvements and irrigation schemes.

Landed Duty Paid

The landed value of a good plus any import duties.

Large Country

A country that is large enough for its international transactions to affect economic variables abroad, usually

for its trade to matter for world prices. Contrasts with a small open economy.

Latin American Debt Crisis

The default on government debt, and subsequent rescheduling, by more than two dozen less developed countries including many in Latin America, in the early 1980s starting with Mexico on August 12, 1982.

Latin American Free Trade Association

A group of Latin American countries formed in 1960 with the aim of establishing a free trade area. This aim was never achieved, and LAFTA was replaced in 1980 with the Latin American Integration Association.

Latin American Integration Association

An organization of Latin American countries that replaced the failed LAFTA. LAIA has the more limited goal of encouraging free trade but with no timetable for achieving it.

Laurel-Langley Agreement

The Laurel-Langley Agreement was a trade agreement between the Philippines and the United States which was signed in 1955 and expired in 1974. Although it proved deficient, the final agreement satisfied nearly all of the diverse Filipino economic interests. While some have seen the Laurel-Langley agreement as a continuation of the 1946 trade act, Jose P. Laurel and other Philippine leaders recognized that the agreement substantially gave the country greater freedom to industrialize while continuing to receive privileged access to US markets. The agreement replaced the unpopular Bell Trade Act, which tied the economy of the Philippines to that of the United States.

Law Of Comparative Advantage

The principle that, given the freedom to respond to market forces, countries will tend to export goods for which they have comparative advantage and import goods for which they have comparative disadvantage, and that they will experience gains from trade by doing so.

Law Of Demand

The law of demand is an economic law, which states that consumers buy more of a good when its price is lower and less when its price is higher (ceteris paribus). When the price of a product is increased then less will be demanded. Also is the same for the opposite, when the price of a product is decreased then more will be demanded. The Law of demand states that the quantity demanded and the price of a commodity are inversely related, other things remaining constant. That is, if the income of the consumer, prices of the related goods, and preferences of the consumer remain unchanged, then the change in quantity of good demanded by the consumer will be negatively correlated to the change in the price of the good. There are some exceptions to this rule, however. see Giffen's Paradox.

Law Of Diminishing Marginal Returns

Diminishing returns (also called diminishing marginal returns) is the decrease in the marginal (per-unit) output of a production process as the amount of a single factor of production is increased, while the amounts of all other factors of production stay constant. The law of diminishing returns (also law of diminishing marginal returns or law of increasing relative cost) states

that in all productive processes, adding more of one factor of production, while holding all others constant ("ceteris paribus"), will at some point yield lower per-unit returns.[1] The law of diminishing returns does not imply that adding more of a factor will decrease the total production, a condition known as negative returns, though in fact this is common.

Law Of Diminishing Marginal Utility

According to this law, as a person consumes more and more of a given commodity (the consumption of other commodities being held constant), the marginal utility of the commodity eventually will tend to decline.

Law Of Diminishing Returns

The principle that, in any production function, as the input of one factor rises holding other factors fixed, the marginal product of that factor must eventually decline.

Law Of One Price

The principle that identical goods should sell for the same price throughout the world if trade were free and frictionless.

Law Of Similars

Regulations that limit imports of a good, or alter its tariff if a "similar" good is produced in the country. Also called a market reserve policy.

Law Of Supply

The "law of supply" is a fundamental principal of economic theory which is that quantities respond in the same direction as price changes. In other words, the law of supply states that (all other things unchanged) an increase in price results in an increase in quantity supplied. This means that producers are willing to offer more products for sale on the market at higher prices by increasing production as a way of increasing profits.

Law Of Supply And Demand

Law of supply and demand is an economic model of price determination in a market. It concludes that in a competitive market, the unit price for a particular good will vary until it settles at a point where the quantity demanded by consumers (at current price) will equal the quantity supplied by producers (at current price), resulting in an economic equilibrium for price and quantity.

The four basic laws of supply and demand are:

1. If demand increases and supply remains unchanged, a shortage occurs, leading to a higher equilibrium price.
2. If demand decreases and supply remains unchanged, a surplus occurs, leading to a lower equilibrium price.
3. If demand remains unchanged and supply increases, a surplus occurs, leading to a lower equilibrium price.
4. If demand remains unchanged and supply decreases, a shortage occurs, leading to a higher equilibrium price.

Lawson Doctrine

The view, attributed to Nigel Lawson, U.K. Chancellor of the Exchequer in the 1980s, that a current account deficit that results from a shift in private-sector savings or investment, is not a cause for concern.

LDC

A developing country, also known as a less-developed country (LDC), is a nation with a low living standard, undeveloped industrial base, and low Human Development Index (HDI) relative to other countries. Countries with more advanced economies than other developing nations, but which have not yet fully demonstrated the signs of a developed country, are categorized under the term newly industrialized countries.

Lead Time

The amount of time between when an action is initiated and when it is completed, and thus the amount of time before you want it to be done that you must initiate the action. In commerce, this often refers to how long before you want something to be delivered that you must order it, a time that is likely to be longer if it involves transport from abroad.

Leading Indicator

A measurable economic variable that varies over the business cycle, reaching peaks and troughs somewhat earlier than other macroeconomic variables such as GDP and unemployment, and therefore useful for forecasting them. Contrasts with lagging indicator.

League Of Arab States

An association of mainly Arabic-speaking countries founded in Cairo in 1945 to strengthen ties amoung the members, coordinate policies among them, and promote their common interests. As of August 2012, it had 22 members.

League Of Nations

An intergovernmental organization founded at the end of World War I to prevent wars. Its main tool was economic sanctions to curb aggressive behaviour. The US did not join, however, and although the League had some successes, it failed to prevent World War II and was replaced after that by the United Nations.

Leamer Triangle

A diagram introduced by Leamer (1987) depicting both relative factor endowments and relative factor intensities with three factors and any number of goods.

Leaning Against The Wind

Use of exchange market intervention to try to slow the movement of the exchange rate under a managed float, and/or to reduce the amplitude of its fluctuations.

Learning By Doing

Refers to the improvement in technology that takes place in some industries, early in their history, as they learn by experience, so that average cost falls as accumulated output rises.

Learning Curve

A relationship representing either average cost or average product as a function of the accumulated output produced. Usually reflecting learning by doing, the learning curve shows cost falling, or average product rising.

Least Absolute Deviations

A method for estimating the parameters of a multiple regression model based on minimising the sum of the absolute values of the residuals.

Least Developed Country

A country designated by the UN as least developed based on criteria of low per capita GDP, weak human resources (life expectancy, calorie intake, etc.), and a low level of economic diversification (share of manufacturing and other measures). As of August 2012, 49 countries were designated as LDCs.

Leibenstein, Harvey (1922-1994)

An American economist, born in 1922. Leibenstein taught at the University of California Berkeley in the 1950s and 60s, and subsequently at Harvard. He has published widely in area of economic growth and development, but remains best known for his theory of X-efficiency, which postulates that individuals are non-maximizers when there is little pressure on them and that convention plays a large part in determining the amount of effort they put into their work.

Leisure

Leisure, or free time, is time spent away from business, work, and domestic chores. It also excludes time spent on necessary activities such as eating, sleeping and, where it is compulsory, education. The distinction between leisure and unavoidable activities is not a rigidly defined one, e.g. people sometimes do work-oriented tasks for pleasure as well as for long-term utility. A distinction may also be drawn between free time and leisure. For example, Situationist International maintains that free time is illusory and rarely free; economic and social forces appropriate free time from the individual and sell it back to them[clarification needed] as the commodity known as "leisure". Certainly most people's leisure activities are not a completely free choice, and may be constrained by social pressures, e.g. people may be coerced into spending time gardening by the need to keep up with the standard of neighbouring gardens.

Lender Of Last Resort

An institution that has the capacity and willingness to make loans when no one else can. Within a country, the central bank may play that role, since it can create money. Some have argued that the IMF or other institution should play that role internationally, to avert financial crises.

Lenin (Vladimir Ilyich Ulyanov) (1870-1924)

A Russian-born intellectual who masterminded the formation of the Russian Communist Party and successfully seized power with the revolutionary uprising of November 7, 1917. Although he produced a considerable volume of writing, ranging from polemical tracts to serious scholarly works (notably a history of capitalism in Russia), Lenin (the name he began using while living in exile in Germany) was above all else a master politician who succeeded in welding the disputatious radical factions in Russia together to create a well-disciplined political machine. His adaptation of the principles of Karl Marx to the situation in Russia was built on the idea of using the Party as the instrument for forging a revolutionary working class.

Leontief Composite

A composite of two or more goods or factors that includes them in fixed proportions, analogous to the Leontief technology.

Leontief Paradox

The finding of Leontief (1954) that U.S. imports embodied a higher ratio of capital to labour than U.S. exports. This was surprising because it was thought that the U.S. was capital abundant, and the Heckscher-Ohlin Theorem would then predict that U.S. exports would be relatively capital intensive.

Leontief Technology

A production function in which no substitution between inputs is possible: $F(V) = \min_i(V_i/a_i)$, where V is a vector of inputs V_i, and a_i are the constant per unit input requirements. Isoquants are L-shaped.

Lerner Index

A measure of the amount of monopoly power possessed by a firm. Specifically, it equals $(P - MC)/P$, where P is the firm's price and MC is its marginal cost.

Lerner Paradox

The possibility, identified by Lerner (1936), that a tariff might worsen a country's terms of trade. This can happen only if the country spends a disproportionately large fraction of the tariff revenue on the imported good, and it will not happen (from a stable equilibrium) if the tariff revenue is redistributed.

Lerner Symmetry Theorem

The proposition that a tax on all imports has the same effect as an equal tax on all exports, if the revenue is spent in the same way. The result depends critically on balanced trade, as in a real model, so that a change in imports leads to an equal change in the value of exports.

Lerner, Abba P (1903-1982)

An American academic economist, born in Russia, and educated largely in England, Lerner was one of the first and most enthusiastic converts to Keynesian economics. He subsequently taught at a number of different universities in the US including Michigan State and UCLA Berkeley. His major publication was *The Economics of Control* (1944) which combined Keynesian principles with welfare economics to produce a complete system of economic management equally applicable to capitalist or socialist economies.

Lerner-Pearce Diagram

This name is sometimes given (for years, by me at least) to the Lerner Diagram. In fact, Pearce's (1952) diagram uses unit isoquants rather than unit value isoquants and is much more cumbersome.

Less Developed Country

Refers to any country whose per capita income is low by world standards. Same as developing country.

Lesser Duty Rule

Setting an anti-dumping duty equal to the injury margin when that is smaller than the dumping margin. This is the practice in the European Union, but not in the United States.

Less-Than-Fair-Value

Less than fair value in a case of dumping.

Letter Of Credit

A common means of payment in international trade, this is a written commitment by a bank to make payment to an exporter on behalf of an importer, under specified conditions.

Level Playing Field

The goal of those who advocate protection on the grounds that foreign firms have an unfair advantage. A level playing field would remove such advantages, although it is unclear what sorts of advantage (including comparative advantage) could remain.

Level-Level Model

A regression model where the dependent variable and the independent variables are in level (or original) form.

Level-Log Model

A regression model where the dependent variable is in level form and (at least some of) the independent variables are in logarithmic form.

Levy

1. To impose and collect a tax or tariff.
2. A tax or tariff.

LHS

Left-hand side, usually referring to what appears to the left of the equal sign in an equation, and therefore usually the dependent variable that is explained by the right-hand side.

Liabilities

In general, debts owed by individuals or firms. In the case of commercial banks, their liabilities are largely in the form of what they owe their customers, that is, the total amount of deposits held.

Liability

A liability is defined as an obligation of an entity arising from past transactions or events, the settlement of which may result in the transfer or use of assets, provision of services or other yielding of economic benefits in the future. A liability is defined by the following characteristics:

1. Any type of borrowing from persons or banks for improving a business or personal income that is payable during short or long time;
2. A duty or responsibility to others that entails settlement by future transfer or use of assets, provision of services, or other transaction yielding an economic benefit, at a specified or determinable date, on occurrence

of a specified event, or on demand;

3. A duty or responsibility that obligates the entity to another, leaving it little or no discretion to avoid settlement; and,

4. A transaction or event obligating the entity that has already occurred.

Liabilities in financial accounting need not be legally enforceable; but can be based on equitable obligations or constructive obligations. An equitable obligation is a duty based on ethical or moral considerations. A constructive obligation is an obligation that is implied by a set of circumstances in a particular situation, as opposed to a contractually based obligation.

Liberal

Associated with freedom and/or generosity. Thus in England to be liberal (or to be a liberal) is to favour free markets, including free trade. But in the U.S. it tends to mean favouring a generous, active government pursuing social and redistributive policies, with no implication for views on free trade.

Liberal Trade

Free trade, or something approximating that. Thus a trade regime in which tariffs are low or zero and in which nontariff barriers are largely absent.

Liberalism

The set of views associated with being liberal, in the sense of freedom.

Liberalization

1. The process of making policies less constraining of economic activity.
2. Reduction of tariffs and/or removal of nontariff barriers.

Licensing

1. The requirement that importers and/or exporters get government approval prior to importing or exporting. Licensing may be automatic, or it may be discretionary, based on a quota, aperformance requirement, or some other criterion.

2. Granting of permission, in return for a licensing fee, to use a technology. When done by firms in one country to firms in another, it is a form of technology transfer.

Life Expectancy

The expected value of the number of years a person has yet to live at a given age or, if age is unspecified, at birth, based on the distribution of actual deaths in the population to which the person belongs. Life expectancy in a country is an important indicator of its level of development and well-being.

Lifetime Employment

The practice, common in Japan since the early 20th century and covering about 20% of the labour force, of (male) workers remaining employed by the same large firm from graduation to retirement. This results from a non-contractual understanding that firms would not lay off workers and workers would not resign.

Light Manufacturing

Sectors of the economy that produce manufactured goods without large amounts of physical capital, thus likely to be labour intensive.

Limit Price

A limit price is the price set by a monopolist to discourage entry into a market, and is illegal in many countries. The limit price is the price that a potential entrant would face upon entering as long as the incumbent firm did not decrease output. The limit price is often lower than the average cost of production or just low enough to make entering not profitable. Such a pricing strategy is called limit pricing. The quantity produced by the incumbent firm to act as a deterrent to entry is usually larger than would be optimal for a monopolist, but might still produce higher economic profits than would be earned under perfect competition. The problem with limit pricing as strategic behaviour is that once the entrant has entered the market, the quantity used as a threat to deter entry is no longer the incumbent firm's best response. This means that for limit pricing to be an effective deterrent to entry, the threat must in some way be made credible. A way to achieve this is for the incumbent firm to constrain itself to produce a certain quantity whether entry occurs or not. An example of this would be if the firm signed a union contract to employ a certain (high) level of labour for a long period of time. Another example is to build excess production capacity as a commitment device.

Limited Liability

The maximum that an owner (or partial owner, such as a stockholder or partner) of a business can be required to lose in the event that the business fails or acquires financial obligations greater than its value. Some forms of business organization, such as a corporation or a limited partnership, set that maximum at the amount that the owner has contributed to the business.

Linder Hypothesis

The theory that a country's ability to export depends on domestic demand, so that countries that demand similar goods will trade more with each other than will countries with dissimilar demands.

Linear Function

A function where the change in the dependent variable, given it one-unit change in an independent variable, is constant.

Linear Regression Model

A linear relationship between a dependent variable Y and one or more independent variables X plus a stochastic disturbance u:

$$Y_i = b_0 + b_1 X_{1i} + ... + b_n X_{ni} + u_i.$$

Linear Unbiased Estimator

In multiple regression analysis, an unbiased estimator that is a linear function of the outcomes on the dependent variable.

Linearly Homogeneous

Homogeneous of degree 1. Sometimes called linear homogeneous.

Liner Code

The United Nations Convention on a Code of Conduct for Liner Conferences.

Liner Conference

An agreement between two or more shipping companies to coordinate schedules and prices. Likely to be anti-competitive.

Linking Scheme

A requirement that, in order to get an import license, the importer must buy a certain amount of the same product from local producers.

Liquid

Possessing liquidity.

Liquid Assets

In business, economics or investment, market liquidity is an asset's ability to be sold without causing a significant movement in the price and with minimum loss of value. Money, or cash, is the most liquid asset, and can be used immediately to perform economic actions like buying, selling, or paying debt, meeting immediate wants and needs. However, currencies, even major currencies, can suffer loss of market liquidity in large liquidation events. For instance, scenarios considering a major dump of US dollar bonds by China or Saudi Arabia or Japan, each of which holds trillions in such bonds, would certainly affect the market liquidity of the US dollar and US dollar denominated assets. There is no asset whatsoever that can be sold with no effect on the market. An act of exchange of a less liquid asset with a more liquid asset is called liquidation. Liquidity also refers both to a business's ability to meet its payment obligations, in terms of possessing sufficient liquid assets, and to such assets themselves.

A liquid asset has some or all of the following features. It can be sold rapidly, with minimal loss of value, any time within market hours. The essential characteristic of a liquid market is that there are always ready and willing buyers and sellers. Another elegant definition of liquidity is the probability that the next trade is executed at a price equal to the last one. A market may be considered deeply liquid if there are ready and willing buyers and sellers in large quantities. This is related to market depth that can be measured as the units that can be sold or bought for a given price impact. The opposite is that of market breadth measured as the price impact per unit of liquidity.

Liquidity

The capacity to turn assets into cash, or the amount of assets in a portfolio that have that capacity. Cash itself (i.e., money) is the most liquid asset.

Liquidity Crisis

A financial crisis that occurs due to lack of liquidity. In international finance, it usually means that a government or central bank runs short of international reserves needed to peg its exchange rate and/or to service its foreign loans.

Liquidity Trap

A situation in which expansionary monetary policy fails to stimulate the economy. As used by Keynes (1936), this meant interest rates so low that expectations of their increase made people unwilling to hold bonds. Today it usually means a nominal interest rate so near zero that lowering it further is impossible or ineffective.

Lisbon Treaty

The treaty that went into force on December 1, 2009, revising the institutions of the European Union. It is intended to make the EU more democratic and more efficient.

Living Wage

A real wage that is high enough for the worker and family to survive and remain healthy and comfortable, sometimes called meeting basic needs. Term is used in calling for higher wages in both developed and developing countries, where concepts of basic needs may be very different.

LM-Curve

In the IS-LM model, the curve representing combinations of income and interest rate at which demand for money equals the money supply in the domestic money market. It is normally upward sloping because an increase in income increases demand for money while an increase in the interest rate reduces demand for money.

Loan

An amount, usually of money, given by one to another in the expectation that it will be returned, perhaps with specified interest, at a later date. When the lender and borrower are in different countries with separate monetary and legal systems, loans bear extra risk.

Lobby

To attempt to influence government policy by talking to lawmakers and bureaucrats, and perhaps by using other means such as monetary contributions or assistance. Lobbyists often play a role in influencing trade policies, including tariffs and administered protection.

Local Content Requirement

Same as domestic content requirement.

Local Optimum

An allocation that by some criterion is better than all those in its neighbourhood.

Locational Advantage

Any reason for a firm to locate production, or a stage of production, in a particular place, such as availability of a natural resource, transport cost, or barriers to trade. May explain why a country's firms succeed in trade, or why a multinational firm locates there.

Locomotive Effect

The effect that economic expansion in one large country can have on other parts of the world economy, causing them to expand as well, as the large country demands more of their exports.

Logarithm

A particular mathematical transformation often used to express economic variables. Advantages:

1. If a variable grows at a constant percentage rate over time, the graph of its logarithm is a straight line.
2. A small change in the logarithm of a variable is approximately its percentage change.

Logarithmic Function

A mathematical function defined for positive arguments that has a positive, but diminishing, slope.

Log-Level Model

A regression model where the dependent variable is in logarithmic form and the independent variables are in level (or original) form.

Logrolling

The exchange of political favours, especially among legislators who agree to support each others' initiatives. Logrolling contributed importantly to the Smoot-Hawley Tariff.

London Interbank Offered Rate

The interest rate that the largest international banks charge each other for loans, usually of Eurodollars. In fact, LIBOR includes rates quoted each day for many currencies, excluding the euro, but it is the rate for dollar loans that is used as a benchmark for other transactions.

London International Financial Futures And Options Exchange

An organized market for a variety of financial instruments, including short term interest ratefutures, bonds, swaps, equities, and commodities.

Long Position

A long position in a security, such as a stock or a bond, or equivalently to be long in a security, means the holder of the position owns the security and will profit if the price of the security goes up. Going long is the more conventional practice of investing and is contrasted with going short. An investor goes long on the underlying instrument by buying call options or writing put options on it.

Long Run

Referring to a long time horizon. This is not always well defined, but in trade models it usually means long enough for industries to vary the amounts of all factors they employ, and therefore for the factors to be mobile across industries.

Long Run Average Cost Curve

The long run average cost curve shows the least cost combination of producing each level of output.

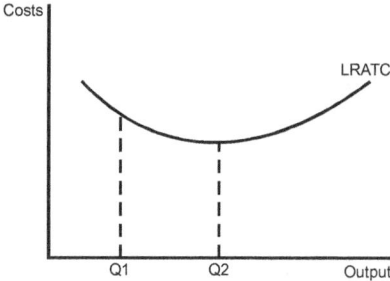

In this diagram the long run cost curve initially slopes downwards and this shows economies of scale. At Q1 cost per unit will be higher than at Q2 because the firm has not derived all the possible economies of scale. Beyond an output level of Q2 diseconomies of scale set in and cost per unit begins to rise.

Long Run Average Costs

Total costs divided by the number of units of output. The long run average cost curve plots the relationship

between output and the lowest possible average total cost when all inputs can be varied.

Long Run Costs

Production costs when the firm is using its economically most efficient size of plant.

Long-Run Elasticity

The long-run propensity in a distributed lag model with the dependent and independent variables in logarithmic form; thus, the long-run elasticity is the eventual percentage increase in the explained variable, given a permanent 1% increase in the explanatory variable.

Long-Run Propensity

In a distributed lag model, the eventual change in the dependent variable given a permanent, one-unit increase in the independent variable.

Long-Term Capital

In the capital account of the balance of payments, long-term capital movements include FDI and movements of financial capital with maturity of more than one year (including equities).

Lorenz Curve

The Lorenz curve is a graphical representation of the cumulative distribution function of the empirical probability distribution of wealth; it is a graph showing the proportion of the distribution assumed by the bottom y% of the values. It is often used to represent income distribution, where it shows for the bottom x% of households, what percentage y% of the total income they have. The percentage of households is plotted on the x-axis, the percentage of income on the y-axis. It can also be used to show distribution of assets. In such use, many economists consider it to be a measure of social inequality. It was developed by Max O. Lorenz in 1905 for representing inequality of the wealth distribution. The concept is useful in describing inequality among the size of individuals in ecology, and in studies of biodiversity, where cumulative proportion of species is plotted against cumulative proportion of individuals. It is also useful in business modeling: e.g., in consumer finance, to measure the actual delinquency Y% of the X% of people with worst predicted risk scores.

Loss

Business situation in which total cost of production exceeds total revenue; negative profit.

Lost Decade

There is, sadly, no single meaning for this term, as it has been applied to many episodes of economies that stagnated for most of a decade. Examples: Argentina and other Latin America in the 1980s; Japan in the 1990s; and the least developed countries in the 1990s.

Louvre Accord

Louvre Accord was signed by the then G6 (France, West Germany, Japan, Canada, the United States and the United Kingdom) on February 22, 1987 in Paris, France. Italy had been an invited member, but declined to finalize the agreement. The goal of the Louvre Accord was to stabilize the international currency markets and halt the continued decline of the US Dollar caused by the Plaza Accord (of which a primary aim was depreciation of the US dollar in relation to the Japanese yen and German Deutsche Mark by the mutual agreement of the G7 Minister of Finance meeting (i.e. a conference of ministers of the "group of seven") that had been held in Louvre

in Paris in 1987. Since the Plaza accord, the dollar rate had continued to slide, reaching an exchange rate of ¥150 per US$1 in 1987. The ministers of the G7 nations gathered at the Louvre in Paris to "put the brakes" on this decline.

Low Income Country

The bottom income group in the World Bank's classification of countries by GNI per capita, calculated by the Atlas Method. Based on July 2010 data, these were countries with incomes of $1,005 or less. Other groups are Middle Income Countries and High Income Countries.

Low Marginal Propensity To Consume

When the consumption line is shallow, this indicates a low value of the marginal propensity to consume.

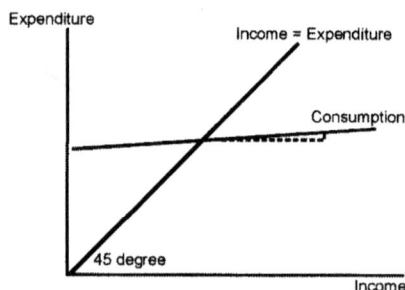

A shallow consumption line shows that the level of consumption rises slowly as the level of income increases. This means a low value for the marginal propensity to consume. This will cause the AD line to be similarly shallow.

LSE

1. London School of Economics and Political Science, an excellent university with a traditional strength in international economics.

2. London Stock Exchange, a company that handles the trading of the stocks of around 3000 companies from over 70 countries.

LTD

The abbreviation used in the United Kingdom to represent a limited liability company, thus analogous to "Inc", for incorporated, in the United States and AG in German speaking countries.

Lucas Critique

The observation that economic equations estimated under one policy regime are unlikely to be valid under another policy regime, since market participants will take the policy regime into account in forming their behaviour. What is needed is to model rational expectations, which internalize all information, including the policy regime.

Lump Sum

Describes a tax or subsidy that does not distort behaviour. By using a tax (or subsidy) in an amount (the lump sum) independent of any aspect of the payer's or recipient's behaviour, it does not alter behaviour. Nondistorting lump sum taxes and subsidies do not exist, but they are a convenient fiction for theoretical analysis, especially of gains from trade.

M

Macroeconomic Stabilization Policies

Macroeconomic Stabilization Policies designed to eliminate macroeconomic instability.

Macroeconomics

Macroeconomics (from Greek prefix "makros-" meaning "large" + "economics") is a branch of economics dealing with the performance, structure, behaviour, and decision-making of an economy as a whole, rather than individual markets. This includes national, regional, and global economies. With microeconomics, macroeconomics is one of the two most general fields in economics. Macroeconomists study aggregated indicators such as GDP, unemployment rates, and price indices to understand how the whole economy functions. Macroeconomists develop models that explain the relationship between such factors as national income, output, consumption, unemployment, inflation, savings, investment, international trade and international finance. In contrast, microeconomics is primarily focused on the actions of individual agents, such as firms and consumers, and how their behaviour determines prices and quantities in specific markets. While macroeconomics is a broad field of study, there are two areas of research that are emblematic of the discipline: the attempt to understand the causes and consequences of short-run fluctuations in national income (the business cycle), and the attempt to understand the determinants of long-run economic growth (increases in national income). Macroeconomic models and their forecasts are used by both governments and large corporations to assist in the development and evaluation of economic policy and business strategy.

Majority Goods

Goods which are generally available to consumers because they can be mass produced in whatever quantities there is a demand for. Fast food and consumer electronics are good examples.

Malthus, Thomas (1766-1834)

Son of an eccentric country gentleman-scholar, Malthus was educated at Cambridge, studying mainly social studies and mathematics in preparation for his intended career as a cleric. He wrote widely on economic issues of his day, maintaining a close correspondence with David Ricardo. His most famous work, however, was on the subject of population. His recognition of what subsequently came to be called the "principle of diminishing returns" underlay his famous proposition that production of the means of subsistence increases as an arithmetic progression (1,2,3,4, etc.)

whereas human population has a tendency to increase geometrically (2,4,16, etc.). Malthus argued that it was useless to try to solve this problem by producing more food. The only cure could be to prevent population from increasing at its biological potential. Unless people learned to control their rate of increase (by postponing marriage until children could be adequately supported), nature would control population through the instruments of what Malthus referred to as "misery" and "vice" (which as far as he was concerned included the use of contraceptive measures).The success of his writings enabled Malthus to escape the life of a country cleric and led him to an appointment in 1805 as professor of history and political economy at a small college operated by the East India Company, Haileybury College, in the south of England. Malthus is often called the first professional economist. He spent the rest of his life teaching and writing. He published a general treatise on economic principles, *Political Economy*, in 1820, although it attracted less attention than his first book, *An Essay on the Principle of Population as it Affects the Future Improvement of Society*.

Malthusian Trap
The Malthusian trap, named after political economist Thomas Robert Malthus, suggests that for most of human history, income was largely stagnant because technological advances and discoveries only resulted in more people, rather than improvements in the standard of living. It is only with the onset of the Industrial Revolution in about 1800 that the income per person dramatically increased in some countries, and they broke out of the Trap; it has been shown, however, that the escape from the Malthusian trap can also generate serious political upheavals.

Marginal
The additional or extra quantity of something. If one drinks six sodas in a day, the marginal soda would be the sixth soda.

Marginal Analysis
An analytical technique which focuses attention on incremental changes in total values, such as the last unit of a good consumed, or the increase in total cost.

Marginal Benefit
The increase in total benefit consequent upon a one unit increase in the production of a good.

Marginal Cost
Marginal cost is the change in total cost that arises when the quantity produced changes by one unit. That is, it is the cost of producing one more unit of a good. If the good being produced is infinitely divisible, so the size of a marginal cost will change with volume, as a non-linear and non-proportional cost function includes the following:
1. Variable terms dependent to volume,
2. Constant terms independent to volume and occurring with the respective lot size,
3. Jump fix cost increase or decrease dependent to steps of volume increase.

Marginal Cost And Average Cost Curves
The marginal cost and average cost curves are both normally drawn u-shaped due to increasing and then diminishing returns. Marginal cost will always intersect the average cost at the minimum point of the average cost curve.

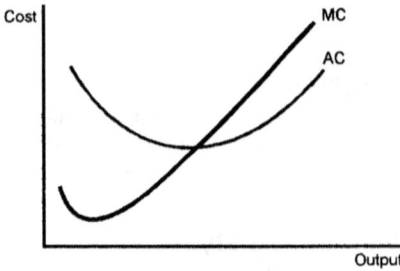

Both these curves are short run curves. The firm will be constrained in the short run by their fixed factors. As these cannot be changed, they can only alter their variable factors. As they do this, they will initially experience increasing returns and so MC and AC will both fall. However, eventually they will experience diminishing returns and MC and AC will start to rise again.

Marginal Cost Curve

The marginal cost is the increase in cost from producing one more unit. It tends to be drawn U-shaped.

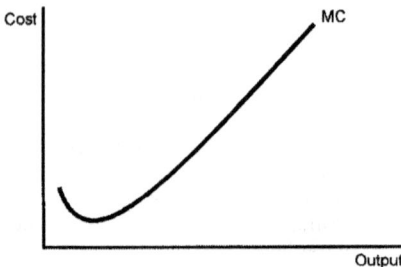

The marginal cost is calculated by taking the change in total cost. In the short run the marginal cost will eventually start to rise due to diminishing returns and that is why it is drawn u-shaped. Initially there may be increasing returns to the variable factor and marginal cost will fall, but eventually there will be diminishing returns and the marginal cost will start to rise.

Marginal Cost Pricing

A pricing rule whereby firms or government-owned enterprises set price equal to marginal cost.

Marginal Effect

The effect on the dependent variable that results from changing an independent variable by a small amount.

Marginal Efficiency Of Capital

The marginal efficiency of capital (MEC) is that rate of discount which would equate the price of a fixed capital asset with its present discounted value of expected income.

The term "marginal efficiency of capital" was introduced by John Maynard Keynes in his General Theory, and defined as "the rate of discount which would make the present value of the series of annuities given by the returns expected from the capital asset during its life just equal its supply price".

Marginal Expenditure Curve

A curve showing the additional cost to the firm of increasing its utilization of input X by 1 unit.

Marginal Physical Product

The change in total product measured in physical terms caused by a one unit increase in a variable input.

Marginal Product

The addition to total output due to the addition of the last unit of an input (when the quantity of other inputs is held constant).

Marginal Productivity

The marginal revenue productivity theory of wages, also referred to as the marginal revenue product of labour and the value of the marginal product or VMPL, is the change in total revenue earned by a firm that results from employing one more unit of labour. It is a neoclassical model that determines, under some conditions, the optimal number of workers to employ at an exogenously determined market wage rate. The idea that payments to factors of production equilibrate to their marginal productivity had been laid out early on by such as John Bates Clark and Knut Wicksell, who presented a far simpler and more robust demonstration of the principle. Much of the present conception of that theory stems from Wicksell's model. The marginal revenue product (MRP) of a worker is equal to the product of the marginal product of labour (MP) and the marginal revenue (MR), given by MRXMP = MRP. The theory states that workers will be hired up to the point where the Marginal Revenue Product is equal to the wage rate by a maximizing firm, because it is not efficient for a firm to pay its workers more than it will earn in revenues from their labour.

Marginal Propensity To Consume

The marginal propensity to consume (MPC) quantifies induced consumption, the concept that the increase in personal consumer spending (consumption) occurs with an increase in disposable income (income after taxes and transfers). The proportion of the disposable income which individuals desire to spend on consumption is known as propensity to consume. MPC is the proportion of additional income that an individual desires to consume. For example, if a household earns one extra dollar of disposable income, and the marginal propensity to consume is 0.65, then of that dollar, the household will spend 65 cents and save 35 cents.

Marginal Propensity To Save

The marginal propensity to save (MPS) refers to the increase in saving (non-purchase of current goods and services) that results from an increase in income i.e. The marginal propensity to save might be defined as the proportion of each additional dollar of household income that is used for saving. It is also used as an alternative term for the slope of the saving line. For example, if a household earns one extra dollar, and the marginal propensity to save is 0.35, then of that dollar, the household will spend 65 cents and save 35 cents. It can also go the other way, referring to the decrease in saving that results from a decrease in income. The MPS plays a central role in Keynesian economics as it quantifies the saving-income relation, which is the flip side of the consumption-income relation, and thus it reflects the fundamental psychological law. Marginal Propensity to Save is also a key variable in determining the value of the multiplier.

Marginal Rate Of Product Transformation

The negative of the slope of the production possibilities curve. It represents the amount of one good that must be sacrificed to allow resources to be devoted to the production of one more unit of some other good.

Marginal Rate Of Substitution

The number of units of good Y that must be given up if the consumer, after receiving an extra unit of good X, is to maintain a constant level of satisfaction.

Marginal Revenue

The addition to total revenue as one additional unit is produced and sold.

Marginal Revenue

Marginal revenue (R') is the additional revenue that will be generated by increasing product sales by 1 unit. It can also be described as the unit revenue the last item sold has generated for the firm. In a perfectly competitive market, the additional revenue generated by selling an additional unit of a good is equal to price the firm is able to charge the buyer of the good. This is because a firm in a competitive market will always get the same price for every unit it sells regardless of the number of units the firm sells since the firm's sales can never impact the industry's price. However, a monopoly determines the entire industry's sales. As a result, it will have to lower the price of all units sold to increase sales by 1 unit. Therefore the marginal revenue generated is always less (lower) than the price the firm is able to charge for the unit sold since each reduction in price causes unit revenue to decline on every good the firm sells. The marginal revenue (the increase in total revenue) is the price the firm gets on the additional unit sold, less the revenue lost by reducing the price on all other units that were sold prior to the decrease in price.

Marginal Revenue Curve

The marginal revenue curve is affected by the same factors as the demand curve - changes in income, change in the prices of complements and substitutes, change in populations. These factors can cause the R curve to shift and rotate

Marginal Revenue Product

The marginal revenue product is the extra revenue earned by the firm when one more unit of the variable factor is employed. The marginal revenue product is calculated by multiplying together the marginal physical product (the extra output produced) by the marginal revenue (the extra revenue earned). The result is the value of the output produced to the firm.

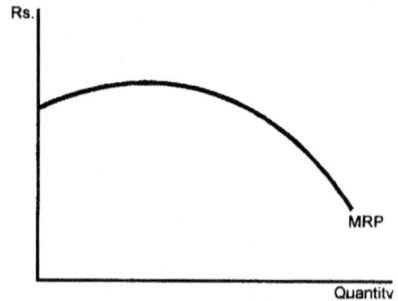

The increase in total revenue due to the use of an additional unit of input X. It equals the marginal product of input X times the firm's marginal revenue.

Marginal Tax Rate

The tax rate charged on the taxpayers last dollar earned; in a progressive tax system the marginal tax rate is always greater than the average tax rate.

Marginal Utility

The additional satisfaction (utility) derived from an additional unit of a commodity (when the levels of consumption of all other commodities are held constant).

Market

A market is one of many varieties of systems, institutions, procedures, social relations and infrastructures whereby parties engage in exchange. While parties may exchange goods and services by barter, most markets rely on sellers offering their goods or services (including labour) in exchange for money from buyers. It can be said that a market is the process by which the prices of goods and services are established.

For a market to be competitive, there

must be more than a single buyer or seller. It has been suggested that two people may trade, but it takes at least three persons to have a market, so that there is competition on at least one of its two sides. However, competitive markets, as understood in formal economic theory, rely on much larger numbers of both buyers and sellers. A market with single seller and multiple buyers is a monopoly. A market with a single buyer and multiple sellers is a monopsony. These are the extremes of imperfect competition.

Market Clearing Price

A market clearing price is the price of goods or a service at which quantity supplied is equal to quantity demanded, also called the equilibrium price. Another market clearing price may be a price below equilibrium price to stimulate demand. In simple terms, this means that markets tend to move towards prices which balance the quantity supplied and the quantity demanded, such that the market will eventually be cleared of all surpluses and shortages (excess supply and demand). The first version assumes that this process occurs instantaneously.

Market Demand

Supply and demand is an economic model of price determination in a market. It concludes that in a competitive market, the unit price for a particular good will vary until it settles at a point where the quantity demanded by consumers (at current price) will equal the quantity supplied by producers (at current price), resulting in an economic equilibrium for price and quantity. The four basic laws of supply and demand are:

1. If demand increases and supply remains unchanged, a shortage occurs, leading to a higher equilibrium price.
2. If demand decreases and supply remains unchanged, a surplus occurs, leading to a lower equilibrium price.
3. If demand remains unchanged and supply increases, a surplus occurs, leading to a lower equilibrium price.
4. If demand remains unchanged and supply decreases, a shortage occurs, leading to a higher equilibrium price.

Market Demand Curve

A curve that shows the relationship between a product's price and the quantity of it demanded in the entire market.

Market Demand Schedule

A table that shows the relationship between a product's price and the quantity of it demanded in the entire market.

Market Economy

A market economy is an economy in which decisions regarding investment, production and distribution are based on supply and demand, and prices of goods and services are determined in a free price system. The major defining characteristic of a market economy is that decisions regarding investments and the allocation of producer goods is accomplished primarily through markets. This is contrasted with a planned economy, where investment and production decisions are embodied in a plan of production. Market economies can range from hypothetical laissez-faire and free market variants to regulated markets and interventionist variants. In reality market economies do not exist in pure form, since societies and governments regulate them to varying degrees. Most existing market economies include a degree of economic planning or state-directed activity, and are thus classified as mixed economies. The term free-market economy is sometimes used synonymously with market economy but may also refer to laissez-faire or Free-market anarchism.

Market Failure

A phenomenon that results from the existence of market imperfections (e.g., monopoly power, lack of factor mobility, significant externalities, lack of knowledge) that weaken the functioning of a free-market economy it fails to realize its theoretical beneficial results. Market failure often provides the justification for government interference with the working of the free market.

Market Mechanism

The system whereby prices of stocks & shares, commodities or services freely rise or fall when the buyer's demand for them rises or falls or the seller's supply of them decreases or increases.

Market Period

A period of time during which the quantity that is supplied of a good is fixed.

Market Prices

Market price is the economic price for which a good or service is offered in the marketplace. It is of interest mainly in the study of microeconomics. Market value and market price are equal only under conditions of market efficiency, equilibrium, and rational expectations. Market pricing is primarily determined by the interaction of supply and demand. Price is interrelated with both of these measures of value. The relationship

between price and supply is generally negative, meaning that the higher the price climbs, the lower amount of the supply is demanded. Conversely, the lower the price, the greater the supply is demanded. Market price is just the price at which goods and services are sold.

Market Structure

Four general types of market structure are perfect competition, monopoly, monopolistic competition, and oligopoly. The structure of a market depends on the number of buyers and sellers, as well as the extent of product differentiation and other factors.

Market Supply Schedule

A table showing the quantity of a good that would be supplied at various prices. Supply curves do not exist for all forms of market structure (e.g., monopolists do not have supply curves).

Market-Friendly Approach

World Bank notion that successful development policy requires governments to create an environment in which markets can operate efficiently and to intervene selectively in the economy in areas where the market is inefficient (e.g., social and economic infrastructure, investment coordination, economic "safety net").

Markets

Any coming together of buyers and sellers of produced goods and services or the services of productive factors.

Markup

A percentage (or absolute) amount added to a product's estimated average (or marginal) cost to obtain its price; this amount is meant to include costs that cannot be allocated to any specific product and to provide a return on the firm's investment.

Marshall, Alfred (1842-1924)

One of the great synthesizers of economic theory who also developed and refined many of the most useful analytical tools of the discipline. His famous student at Cambridge, John Maynard Keynes, called him the greatest economist of the 19th century. His influential textbook, *Principles of Economics*, first published in 1890, served for more than a quarter of a century as the standard reference on the subject. In it he set out clearly such basic concepts as price elasticity of demand, competitive short-run and long-run equilibrium of the firm, consumer surplus, increasing and decreasing cost industries, and economies of scale. Trained in mathematics, Marshall relegated the mathematical expression of his principles to footnotes.

Marx, Karl (1818-83)

One of the most influential social philosophers in history, Marx lived a life of almost constant conflict and adversity. Despite a Ph.D. in philosophy from the University of Jena he was unable to secure a university teaching position and his involvement in revolutionary political activity led to his expulsion from Germany. He was also subsequently forced to leave Belgium and France before finally settling in London where he made a meagre living by journalism (serving as a correspondent for the *New York Herald-Tribune*). While continuing to involve himself in radical political affairs he devoted as much time as he could to an extraordinary scholarly undertaking, which was nothing less than an attempt to synthesize all human knowledge since the time of Aristotle. The fruits of this labour, much of it pursued in the Reading Room of the British Museum, was eventually published in his massive work, *Das Kapital* which established the intellectual foundation of the Marxist interpretation of history and which posited the coming of a new world order following the inevitable collapse of capitalism. Key elements of his analysis were embodied in an easily-understood pamphlet written with his benefactor Frederick Engels, *The Communist Manifesto,* published in London in 1848.

Mass Balance Condition

The mass of all the inputs used to produce goods and services (output) must equal the mass of the resulting output(s) plus the mass of the wastes.

Matrix

An array of numbers.

Matrix Notation

A convenient mathematical notation, grounded in matrix algebra, for expressing and manipulating the multiple regression model.

Mean Absolute Error (Mae)

A performance measure in forecasting, computed as the average of the absolute values of the forecast errors.

Mean Squared Error

The expected squared distance that an estimator is from the population value; it equals the variance plus the square of any bias.

Measurement Error

The difference between an observed variable and the variable that belongs in a multiple regression equation.

Median

In a probability distribution, it is the value where there is a 50% chance of being below the value and a 50% chance of being above it. In a sample of numbers, it is the middle value after the numbers have been ordered.

Median Voter Theorem

The proposition that political parties will tend to adopt moderate policies to appeal to voters near the middle of the political spectrum.

Medium of Exchange

A medium of exchange is an intermediary used in trade to avoid the inconveniences of a pure barter system. Money is the common Medium of Exchange and its most important and essential function is that it is 'measure of value'... Hifzur Rab has shown that market measures or sets value of various goods and services using the medium of exchange/money as 'unit' i.e., standard or the Yard Stick of Measurement of Wealth. There is no other alternative to the mechanism used by market to set or determine or measure value of various goods and services and therefore wealth. Just determination of prices is an essential condition for justice in exchange, efficient allocation of resources, economic growth welfare and justice.Money helps us in gaining power of buying.

Mercantilism

A body of policy recommendations designed to promote the development of the early nation states of western Europe in the 17th and 18th centuries. The emphasis was on utilizing trade to increase national wealth at the expense of the countries being traded with through fostering a "favourable balance of trade", by which was meant an excess of exports over imports.

Merchandise Exports And Imports

All international changes in ownership of merchandise passing across the customs borders of the trading countries. Exports are valued f.o.b. (free on board). Imports are valued c.i.f. (cost, insurance, and freight).

Merchandise Trade Balance

Balance on commodity exports and imports.

Method Of Moments Estimator

An estimator obtained by using the sample analog of population moments; ordinary least squares and two stage least squares are both method of moments estimators.

Microeconomics

Microeconomics is a branch of economics that studies the behaviour of individual households and firms in making decisions on the allocation of limited resources. Typically, it applies to markets where goods or services are bought and sold. Microeconomics examines how these decisions and behaviours affect the supply and demand for goods and services, which determines prices, and how prices, in turn, determine the quantity supplied and quantity demanded of goods and services. This is in contrast to macroeconomics, which involves the "sum total of economic activity, dealing with the issues of growth, inflation, and unemployment." Microeconomics also deals with the effects of national economic policies (such as changing taxation levels) on the aforementioned aspects of the economy. Particularly in the wake of the Lucas critique, much of modern macroeconomic theory has been built upon 'microfoundations'—i.e. based upon basic assumptions about micro-level behaviour. One of the goals of microeconomics is to analyze market mechanisms that establish relative prices amongst goods and services and allocation of limited resources amongst many alternative uses. Microeconomics analyzes market failure, where markets fail to produce efficient results, and describes the theoretical conditions needed for perfect competition. Significant fields of study in microeconomics include general equilibrium, markets under asymmetric information, choice under uncertainty and economic applications of game theory. Also considered is the elasticity of products within the market system.

Middle-Income Countries (MICS)

LDCs with per capita income above $1006 and below $12275 in 2011 according to World Bank measures.

Minimum Efficient Size Of Plant

The smallest size of plant where long-run average cost is at or close to its minimum value.

Minimum Variance Unbiased Estimator

An estimator with the smallest variance in the class of all unbiased estimators.

Minimum Wage

A minimum wage is the lowest hourly, daily or monthly remuneration that employers may legally pay to workers. Equivalently, it is the lowest wage at which workers may sell their labour. Although minimum wage laws are in effect in many jurisdictions, differences of opinion exist about the benefits and drawbacks of a minimum wage.

Minimum Wage Law

Minimum wage law is the body of law which prohibits employers from hiring employees or workers for less than a given hourly, daily or monthly minimum wage. More than 90% of all countries have some kind of minimum wage legislation. Until recently, minimum wage laws were usually very tightly focused. In the U.S. and Great Britain, for example, they applied only to women and children. Only after the Great Depression did many industrialized economies extend them to the general work force. Even then, the laws were often specific to certain industries. In France, for example, they were extensions of existing trade union legislation. In the U.S., industry specific wage restrictions were held to be unconstitutional. The country's Fair Labour Standards Act of 1938 established a uniform national minimum wage for nonfarm, nonsupervisory workers. Coverage was later extended to most of the labour force.

Minority Goods

Goods which have a very low elasticity of supply. That is, even large increases in their price can call forth little, if any, additional supply, which means that only the very wealthy can afford them. Large, secluded waterfront properties might be an example.

Mishan, Ezra Joshua (1917-)

Born in Manchester England, Mishan taught at the London School of Economics from 1956 to 1977. He published a large number of articles in professional journals and several books, the best known of which is *The Costs of Economic Growth*, 1967. In later years he has been a frequent contributor to more popular journals writing on variety of issues, including what he has refereed to as "the pretensions of economists."

Missing Data

A data problem that occurs when we do not observe values on some variables for certain observations (individuals, cities, time periods, and so on) in the sample.

Misspecification Analysis

The process of determining likely biases that can arise from omitted variables, measurement error, simultaneity, and other kinds of model misspecification.

Mixed Economic Systems

Economic systems that are a mixture of both capitalist and socialist economies. Most developing countries have mixed systems. Their essential feature is the coexistence of substantial private and public activity within a single economy.

Mixed Economy

Mixed economy is an economic system in which both the state and private sector direct the economy, reflecting characteristics of both market economies and planned economies. Most mixed economies can be described as market economies with strong regulatory oversight, and many mixed economies feature a variety of government-run enterprises and governmental provision of public goods. The basic idea of the mixed economy is that the means of production are mainly under private ownership; that markets remain the dominant form of economic coordination; and that profit-seeking enterprises and the accumulation of capital remain the fundamental driving force behind economic activity. However, unlike a free-market economy, the government would

wield considerable indirect influence over the economy through fiscal and monetary policies designed to counteract economic downturns and capitalism's tendency toward financial crises and unemployment, along with playing a role in interventions that promote social welfare. Subsequently, some mixed economies have expanded in scope to include a role for indicative economic planning and/or large public enterprise sectors.

Model

A theory based on assumptions that simplify and abstract from reality and from which predictions or conclusions about the real world are deduced.

Monetarism

A view that market economies are inherently self-stabilizing and that variations in the quantity of money are the main cause of fluctuations in the level of aggregate demand.

Monetary Base

The same as "high-powered money": cash in commercial banks, plus cash in circulation and deposits of the commercial bank at the central bank.

Monetary Policy

Monetary policy is the process by which the monetary authority of a country controls the supply of money, often targeting a rate of interest for the purpose of promoting economic growth and stability. The official goals usually include relatively stable prices and low unemployment. Monetary theory provides insight into how to craft optimal monetary policy. It is referred to as either being expansionary or contractionary, where an expansionary policy increases the total supply of money in the economy more rapidly than usual, and contractionary policy expands the money supply more slowly than usual or even shrinks it. Expansionary policy is traditionally used to try to combat unemployment in a recession by lowering interest rates in the hope that easy credit will entice businesses into expanding. Contractionary policy is intended to slow inflation in hopes of avoiding the resulting distortions and deterioration of asset values. Monetary policy rests on the relationship between the rates of interest in an economy, that is, the price at which money can be borrowed, and the total supply of money. Monetary policy uses a variety of tools to control one or both of these, to influence outcomes like economic growth, inflation, exchange rates with other currencies and unemployment. Where currency is under a monopoly of issuance, or where there is a regulated system of issuing currency through banks which are tied to a central bank, the monetary authority has the ability to alter the money supply and thus influence the interest rate (to achieve policy goals). The beginning of monetary policy as such comes from the late 19th century, where it was used to maintain the gold standard.

Monetised Deficit

This deficit is the help extended to the Central government's borrowing programme by the Reserve Bank of India.

Money

Money is any object or record that is generally accepted as payment for goods and services and repayment of debts in a given socio-economic context or country. The main functions of money are distinguished as: a medium of exchange; a unit of account; a store of value; and, occasionally in the past, a standard of deferred payment. Any kind of object or secure verifiable record that fulfils

these functions can be considered money. Money is historically an emergent market phenomenon establishing a commodity money, but nearly all contemporary money systems are based on fiat money.Fiat money, like any check or note of debt, is without intrinsic use value as a physical commodity. It derives its value by being declared by a government to be legal tender; that is, it must be accepted as a form of payment within the boundaries of the country, for "all debts, public and private". Such laws in practice cause fiat money to acquire the value of any of the goods and services that it may be traded for within the nation that issues it. The money supply of a country consists of currency (banknotes and coins) and bank money (the balance held in checking accounts and savings accounts). Bank money, which consists only of records (mostly computerized in modern banking), forms by far the largest part of the money supply in developed nations.

Money Income

Income of the consumer measured in actual dollar amounts per period of time.

Money Market

The money market became a component of the financial markets for assets involved in short-term borrowing, lending, buying and selling with original maturities of one year or less. Trading in the money markets is done over the counter, is wholesale. Various instruments exist, such as Treasury bills, commercial paper, bankers' acceptances, deposits, certificates of deposit, bills of exchange, repurchase agreements, federal funds, and short-lived mortgage-, and asset-backed securities. It provides liquidity funding for the global financial system. Money markets and capital markets are parts of financial markets. The instruments bear differing maturities, currencies, credit risks, and structure. Therefore, they may be used to distribute the exposure.

Money Supply

The total stock of money in the economy; currency held by the public plus money in accounts in banks. It consists primarily currency in circulation and deposits in savings and checking accounts. Too much money in relation to the output of goods tends to push interest rates down and push inflation up; too little money tends to push rates up and prices down, causing unemployment and idle plant capacity. The central bank manages the money supply by raising and lowering the reserves banks are required to hold and the discount rate at which they can borrow money from the central bank. The central bank also trades government securities (called repurchase agreements) to take money out of the system or put it in. There are various measures of money supply, including M1, M2, M3 and L; these are referred to as monetary aggregates.

Monopolistic Competition

Monopolistic competition is a type of imperfect competition such that many producers sell products that are differentiated from one another as goods but not perfect substitutes (such as from branding, quality, or location). In monopolistic competition, a firm takes the prices charged by its rivals as given and ignores the impact of its own prices on the prices of other firms.

There are six characteristics of monopolistic competition (MC):
1. Product differentiation
2. Many firms
3. Free entry and exit in the long run
4. Independent decision making
5. Market Power
6. Buyers and Sellers do not have perfect information (Imperfect Information)

Monopoly

A monopoly exists when a specific person or enterprise is the only supplier of a particular commodity (this contrasts with a monopsony which relates to a single entity's control of a market to purchase a good or service, and with oligopoly which consists of a few entities dominating an industry). Monopolies are thus characterized by a lack of economic competition to produce the good or service and a lack of viable substitute goods. The verb "monopolize" refers to the process by which a company gains the ability to raise prices or exclude competitors. In economics, a monopoly is a single seller. In law, a monopoly is a business entity that has significant market power, that is, the power, to charge high prices. Although monopolies may be big businesses, size is not a characteristic of a monopoly. A small business may still have the power to raise prices in a small industry (or market).

Monopsonistic Firm

A firm which is the sole buyer of a good or service, most likely of labour in a particular market.

Monopsony

A market structure in which there is only a single buyer.

Moral Hazard

Phenomenon by which a person's or firm's behaviour may change after buying insurance so as to increase the probability of theft, fire, or other loss covered by the insurance.

Multicollinearity

A term that refers to correlation among the independent variables in a multiple regression model; it is usually invoked when some correlations are "large," but an actual magnitude is not well-defined.

Multi-Fibre Arrangement (MFA)

A set of nontariff bilateral quotas established by developed countries on imports of cotton, wool, and synthetic textiles and clothing from individual LDCs.

Multinational Corporation (MNC)

An international or transnational corporation with headquarters in one country but branch offices in a wide range of both developed and developing countries. Examples include General Motors, Coca-Cola, Firestone, Philips, Volkswagen, British Petroleum, Exxon, and ITT. Firms become multinational corporations when they perceive advantages to establishing production and other activities in foreign locations. Firms globalize their activities both to supply their home-country market more cheaply and to serve foreign markets more directly. Keeping foreign activities within the corporate structure lets firms avoid the costs inherent in arm's-length dealings with separate entities while utilizing their own firm-specific knowledge such as advanced production techniques.

Multinational Firm

A firm that invests in other countries and produces and markets its products abroad.

Multiplant Monopoly

A monopolist that owns and operates more than one plant and that must determine the output of each of its plants.

Multiple Hypothesis Test

A test of a null hypothesis involving more than one restriction on the parameters.

Multiple Regression Analysis

A type of analysis that is used to describe estimation of and inference in the multiple linear regression model.

Multiple Restrictions

More than one restriction on the parameters in an econometric model.

Multiple Step-Ahead Forecast

A time series fore cast of more than one period into the future.

Multiplicative Measurement Error

Measurement error where the observed variable is the product of the true unobserved variable and a positive measurement error.

Multiplier

A multiplier is a factor of proportionality that measures how much an endogenous variable changes in response to a change in some exogenous variable. For example, suppose a one-unit change in some variable x causes another variable y to change by M units. Then the multiplier is M.

Multiplier Effect

The tendency for a change in aggregate spending to cause a more than proportionate change in the level of real national income.

Multiproduct Firm

A firm that produces more than one product.

N

NAMEA

The national accounting matrix including environmental accounts developed by the Netherlands and used in their national income accounting reports. It contains figures on environmental burdens related to economic activity as reflected in the national accounts.

Nash Equilibrium

An equilibrium in game theory where, given every other player's chosen strategies, each player has no reason to change his or her own strategy.

National Association Of Securities Dealers Automated Quotations

The largest U.S. electronic stock market with approximately 3,300 companies listed on it. Now known as NASDAQ only.

National Council Of Applied Economic Research

One of India's premier economic research institutions - www.ncaer.org

National Debt

The term national debt is the amount borrowed the central government. This debt is a taken in order to finance the budget deficits. Government debt (also known as public debt, national debt) is the debt owed by a central government. (In the U.S. and other federal states, "government debt" may also refer to the debt of a state or provincial government, municipal or local government.) By contrast, the annual "government deficit" refers to the difference between government receipts and spending in a single year, that is, the increase of debt over a particular year.

National Income

The general term used to refer to the total value of a country's output of goods and services in some accounting period without specifying the formal accounting concept such as Gross Domestic Product. A variety of measures of national income and output are used in economics to estimate total economic activity in a country or region, including gross domestic product (GDP), gross national product (GNP), net national income (NNI), and adjusted national income (NNI* adjusted for natural resource depletion). All are specially concerned with counting the total amount of goods and services produced within some "boundary". The boundary is usually defined by geography or citizenship, and may also restrict the goods and services that are counted. For instance, some measures count only goods and services that are exchanged for money, excluding bartered goods, while other measures may attempt to include bartered goods by imputing monetary values to them.

National Income (GDP) Deflator

A general way of referring to the price index which measures the average level of the prices of all the goods and services comprising the national income or GDP.

Natural Increase

Growth of the population due to an excess of births over deaths.

Natural Monopoly

One producer supplying all of the market at lower costs than many producers could. A monopoly describes a situation where all (or most) sales in a market are undertaken by a single firm. A natural monopoly by contrast is a condition on the cost-technology of an industry whereby it is most efficient (involving the lowest long-run average cost) for production to be concentrated in a single firm. In some cases, this gives the largest supplier in an industry, often the first supplier in a market, an overwhelming cost advantage over other actual and potential competitors. This tends to be the case in industries where capital costs predominate, creating economies of scale that are large in relation to the size of the market, and hence high barriers to entry; examples include public utilities such as water services and electricity.

Natural Rate Of Unemployment

The rate of unemployment that would exist when the economy is operating at full capacity. It would be equal to the amount of frictional unemployment in the system.

Natural Resources

Natural resources occur naturally within environments that exist relatively undisturbed by mankind, in a natural form. A natural resource is often characterized by amounts of biodiversity and geodiversity existent in various ecosystems. Natural resources are derived from the environment. Some of them are essential for our survival while most are used for satisfying our wants. Natural resources may be further classified in different ways. Natural resources are materials and components (something that can be used) that can be found within the environment. Every man-made product is composed of natural resources (at its fundamental level). A natural resource may exist as a separate entity such as fresh water, and air, as well as a living organism such as a fish, or it may exist in an alternate form which must be processed to obtain the resource such as metal ores, oil, and most forms of energy.

Natural Unemployment Rate

An economy's civilian unemployment rate when supply and demand for labour are equal. The natural rate is the percentage of the civilian labour force unemployed at one time or another during any given year multiplied by the average time people spend searching for jobs.

Need

A need is something that is necessary for organisms to live a healthy life. Needs are distinguished from wants because a deficiency would cause a clear negative outcome, such as dysfunction or death. Needs can be objective and physical, such as food, or they can be subjective and psychological, such as the need for self-esteem. On a social level, needs are sometimes controversial. Understanding needs and wants is an issue in the fields of politics, social science, and philosophy.

Net Exports

The total value of goods and services exported during the accounting period minus the total value of goods and services imported.

Net Immigration

The total number of people leaving the country to take up permanent residence abroad minus the number of people entering the country for the purpose of taking up permanent residence.

Net Investment

Net investment refers to an activity of spending which increases the availability of fixed capital goods or means of production. It is the total spending on new fixed investment minus replacement investment, which simply replaces depreciated capital goods.

Net Worth

Net worth (sometimes called net assets) is the total assets minus total outside liabilities of an individual or a company. For a company, this is called shareholders' preference and may be referred to as book value. Net worth is stated as at a particular year in time. In the case of an individual, the term estate is used in relation to deceased individuals in probate. For businesses, the term is used in the context of fraudulent law and on the dissolution of the company. Net worth in business is generally based on the value of all assets and liabilities at the carrying value which is the value as expressed on the financial statements. To the extent items on the balance sheet do not express their true (market) value, the net worth will also be inaccurate.

Net Worth Tax

A tax is generally conceived of as a levy based on the aggregate value of all household assets, including owner-occupied housing; cash, bank deposits, money funds, and savings in insurance and pension plans; investment in real estate and unincorporated businesses; and corporate stock, financial securities, and personal trusts. A wealth tax is a tax on the accumulated stock of purchasing power, in contrast to income taxes which is a tax on the flow of assets (a change in stock). In France, the net worth tax on "natural persons" is called the "solidarity tax on wealth". In other places, the tax may be called, or be known as, a "Capital Tax", an "Equity Tax", a "Net Worth Tax", a "Net Wealth Tax", or just a "Wealth Tax".

Net Present Value Rule

The rule that a firm should carry out any investment project with a positive net present value. An investment's net present value is the present value of its fixture cash flows minus its cost.

Newly Industrializing Countries (NICS)

A small group of countries at a relatively advanced level of economic development with a substantial and dynamic industrial sector and with close links to the international trade, finance, and investment system (Argentina, Brazil, Greece, Mexico, Portugal, Singapore, South Korea, Spain, India and China).

NGOs

A non-governmental organization (NGO) is a legally constituted organization created by natural or legal persons that operates independently from any form of government. The term originated from the United Nations (UN), and is normally used to refer to organizations that are not a part of the government and are not conventional for-profit business. In the cases in which NGOs are funded totally or partially by governments, the NGO maintains its non-governmental status by excluding government representatives from membership in the organization. The term is usually applied only to organizations that pursue wider social aims that have political aspects, but are not openly political organizations such as political parties. The number of NGOs operating in the United States is estimated at 40,000. International numbers are even higher: Russia has 277,000 NGOs; India is estimated to have around 3.3 million NGOs in year 2009, which is just over one NGO per 400 Indians, and many times the number of primary schools and primary health centres in India.

Niskanen, William Arthur (1933-2011)

An American economist born in Oregon who studied economics at both Harvard and Chicago. Niskanen has held various posts in government (US Department of Defence) and business (Ford Motor Co.) He was a pioneer in the economic theory of bureaucracy. His best-known book is *Bureaucracy and Representative Government*, 1971.

No Regrets Strategy

A strategy in response to the threat of climate change which argues that energy-saving measures should be undertaken immediately to help reduce global warming and climate change. Even if the threat of climate change is not as pronounced as we now fear, the supporters of this strategy say would not need to be any regrets because we would have benefited from saving the energy.

Nominal GNP

GNP measured in current prices (see Real GNP).

Nominal Interest Rate

Nominal interest rate or nominal rate of interest refers to two distinct things: the rate of interest before adjustment for inflation (in contrast with the real interest rate); or, for interest rates "as stated" without adjustment for the full effect of compounding (also referred to as the nominal annual rate). An interest rate is called nominal if the frequency of compounding (e.g. a month) is not identical to the basic time unit (normally a year).

Nominal Variable

A variable measured in nominal or current euros.

Nondiversifiable Risk

Risk that cannot be reduced by diversification.

Non-Durables

Consumer goods expected to last less than three years.

Nonexperimental Data

Data that have not been obtained through a controlled experiment.

Nonlinear Function

A function whose slope is not constant.

Non-Plan Expenditure

This expenditure is a combination of expenses like capital expenditure, revenue expenditure on interest payments, postal deficit, pensions, economic services, defence expenditure and subsidies. Non-plan expenditure also includes expenditure on police, loans & grants to public sector, governments whether State or foreign and Union territories.

Non-price Competition

Non-price competition is a marketing strategy "in which one firm tries to distinguish its product or service from competing products on the basis of attributes like design and workmanship" (McConnell-Brue, 2002, p. 43.7-43.8). The firm can also distinguish its product offering through quality of service, extensive distribution, customer focus, or any other sustainable competitive advantage than price. It can be contrasted with price competition, which is where a company tries to distinguish its product or service from competing products on the basis of low price. Non-price competition typically involves promotional expenditures (such as advertising, selling staff, the locations convenience, sales promotions, coupons, special orders, or free gifts), marketing research, new product development, and brand management costs.

Non-Price Determinants Of Supply

The factors that influence the amount a producer will supply of a product at each possible price. The non-price determinants of supply are the factors that can change the entire supply schedule and curve.

Non-Resident Indian (NRI)

A non-resident Indian (NRI) is a citizen of India who holds an Indian passport and has temporarily emigrated to another country for six months or more for work, residence or any other purpose. NRI refers only to the tax status of an Indian citizen who, as per section 6 of the Income-tax Act of 1961, has not resided in India for a specified period for the purposes of the Income Tax Act. The rates of income tax are different for persons who are "resident in India" and for NRIs. For the purposes of the Income-tax Act, "residence in India" requires stay in India of at least 182 days in a calendar year or 365 days spread out

over four consecutive years. According to the act, any Indian citizen who does not meet the criteria as a "resident of India" is a non-resident of India and is treated as NRI for paying income tax.

Nontariff Trade Barrier

A barrier to free trade that takes a form other than a tariff, such as quotas or sanitary requirements for imported meats and dairy products.

Normal Distribution

A probability distribution commonly used in statistics and econometrics for modelling a population. Its probability distribution function has a bell shape.

Normal Good

Normal goods are any goods for which demand increases when income increases and falls when income decreases but price remains constant, i.e. with a positive income elasticity of demand. The term does not necessarily refer to the quality of the good, but an abnormal good would clearly not be in demand, except for possibly lower socioeconomic groups.

Normal Profit

Normal profit represents the total opportunity costs (both explicit and implicit) of a venture to an investor, whereas economic profit (also abnormal, pure, supernormal, or excess profit, as the case may be monopoly or oligopoly profit) is the difference between a firm's total revenue and all costs (including normal profit). A related concept, sometimes considered synonymous to profit in certain contexts, is that of economic rent. Normal profit is a component of (implicit) costs, and so not a component of business profit at all. It represents the opportunity cost for enterprise, since the time that the owner spends running the firm could be spent on running another firm. The enterprise component of normal profit is thus the profit that a business owner considers necessary to make running the business worth his while i.e. it is comparable to the next best amount the entrepreneur could earn doing another job.

Normality Assumption

The classical linear model assumption which states that the error (or dependent variable) has a normal distribution, conditional on the explanatory variables.

Normative Economics

Normative economics (as opposed to positive economics) is that part of economics that expresses value judgments (normative judgments) about economic fairness or what the economy ought to be like or what goals of public policy ought to be. It is common to distinguish normative economics ("what ought to be" in economic matters) from positive economics ("what is"). But many normative (value) judgments are held conditionally, to be given up if facts or knowledge of facts changes, so that a change of values may be purely scientific. But welfare economist Amartya Sen distinguishes basic (normative) judgments, which do not depend on such knowledge, from nonbasic judgments, which do. He finds it interesting to note that "no judgments are demonstrably basic" while some value judgments may be shown to be nonbasic. This leaves open the possibility of fruitful scientific discussion of value judgments.

Null Hypothesis

In classical hypothesis testing, we take this hypothesis as true and require the data to provide substantial evidence against it.

O

Object Gap
Notion that LDCs suffer from a lack of material items including roads, buildings, machinery, etc., in comparison with developed countries.

Official Development Assistance (ODA)
Flows of official financing administered with the promotion of the economic development and welfare of developing countries as the main objective, and which are concessional in character with a grant element of at least 25 percent (using a fixed 10 percent rate of discount). By convention, ODA flows comprise contributions of donor government agencies, at all levels, to developing countries ("bilateral ODA") and to multilateral institutions. ODA receipts comprise disbursements by bilateral donors and multilateral institutions. Net disbursements of loans or grants made on concessional terms by official agencies of member countries of the Organization for Economic Cooperation and Development (OECD). In other words, ODA needs to contain the three elements:

1. undertaken by the official sector;
2. With promotion of economic development and welfare as the main objective; and
3. At concessional financial terms (if

a loan, having a grant element of at least 25 per cent).

Official Exchange Rate
Rate at which the central bank will buy and sell the domestic currency in terms of a foreign currency such as the U.S. dollar.

Official Settlements Account
A record of the net increase or decrease in a country's official foreign exchange reserves.

Oligopoly
An oligopoly is a market form in which a market or industry is dominated by a small number of sellers (oligopolists). A general lack of competition can lead to higher costs for consumers. Because there are few sellers, each oligopolist is likely to be aware of the actions of the others. The decisions of one firm influence, and are influenced by, the decisions of other firms. Strategic planning by oligopolists needs to take into account the likely responses of the other market participants. Oligopoly is a common market form. As a quantitative description of oligopoly, the four-firm concentration ratio is often utilized. This measure expresses the market share of the four largest firms in an industry as a percentage.

Oligopsony

An oligopsony is a market form in which the number of buyers is small while the number of sellers in theory could be large. This typically happens in a market for inputs where numerous suppliers are competing to sell their product to a small number of (often large and powerful) buyers. It contrasts with an oligopoly, where there are many buyers but few sellers. An oligopsony is a form of imperfect competition. The terms monopoly (one seller), monopsony (one buyer), and bilateral monopoly have a similar relationship.

OLS Intercept Estimate

The intercept in an OLS regression line.

OLS Regression Line

The equation relating the predicted value of the dependent variable to the independent variables, where the parameter estimates have been obtained by OLS.

OLS Slope Estimate

A slope in an OLS regression line.

Omitted Variable Bias

Omitted-variable bias (OVB) occurs when a model is created which incorrectly leaves out one or more important causal factors. The 'bias' is created when the model compensates for the missing factor by over- or underestimating the effect of one of the other factors. More specifically, OVB is the bias that appears in the estimates of parameters in a regression analysis, when the assumed specification is incorrect in that it omits an independent variable that is correlated with both the dependent variable and one or more included independent variables.

Omitted Variables

One or more variables, which we would like to control for, have been omitted in estimating a regression model.

One-Sided Alternative

An alternative hypothesis which states that the parameter is greater than (or less than) the value hypothesised under the null.

One-Step-Ahead Forecast

A time series forecast one period into the future.

One-Tailed Test

A hypothesis test against a one sided alternative.

Open Access Resource

An open access resource is one where it is impossible to control the access of individuals who want to use it. Common examples are a fishery, or (in the classic example of the tragedy of the commons) a common pasture.

Open Economy

An open economy is an economy in which there are economic activities between domestic community and outside, e.g. people, including businesses, can trade in goods and services with other people and businesses in the international community, and flow of funds as investment across the border. Trade can be in the form of managerial exchange, technology transfers, all kinds of goods and services. Although, there are certain exceptions that cannot be exchanged, like, railway services of a country cannot be traded with another to avail this service, a country has to produce its own. This contrasts with a closed economy in which international trade and finance cannot take place.

The act of selling goods or services to a foreign country is called exporting. The act of buying goods or services from a foreign country is called importing. Together exporting and importing are collectively called international trade. In an open economy, a country's spending in any given year need not to equal its output of goods and services. A country can spend more money than it produces by borrowing from abroad, or it can spend less than it produces and lend the difference to foreigners. There is no closed economy in today's world.

Open Market Operations

An open market operation (also known as OMO) is an activity by a central bank to buy or sell government bonds on the open market. A central bank uses them as the primary means of implementing monetary policy. The usual aim of open market operations is to control the short term interest rate and the supply of base money in an economy, and thus indirectly control the total money supply. This involves meeting the demand of base money at the target interest rate by buying and selling government securities, or other financial instruments. Monetary targets, such as inflation, interest rates, or exchange rates, are used to guide this implementation.

Opportunity Cost

Opportunity cost is the cost of any activity measured in terms of the value of the next best alternative forgone (that is not chosen). It is the sacrifice related to the second best choice available to someone, or group, who has picked among several mutually exclusive choices. The opportunity cost is also the "cost" (as a lost benefit) of the forgone products after making a choice. Opportunity cost is a key concept in economics, and has been described as expressing "the basic relationship between scarcity and choice". The notion of opportunity cost plays a crucial part in ensuring that scarce resources are used efficiently. Thus, opportunity costs are not restricted to monetary or financial costs: the real cost of output forgone, lost time, pleasure or any other benefit that provides utility should also be considered opportunity costs. Opportunity cost is assessed in not only monetary or material terms, but also in terms of anything which is of value. For example, a person who desires to watch each of two television programmes being broadcast simultaneously, and does not have the means to make a recording of one, can watch only one of the desired programmes.

Opportunity Cost Of Capital

The opportunity cost of capital is the expected rate of return forgone by bypassing of other potential investment activities for a given capital. It is a rate of return that investors could earn in financial markets.

Optimal Input Combination

The combination of inputs that is economically efficient or that maximizes profit (that is, is optimal from a profit maximizing firm's point of view), or both.

Option

An option is a contract which gives the owner the right, but not the obligation, to buy or sell an underlying asset or instrument at a specified strike price on or before a specified date. The seller incurs a corresponding obligation to fulfil the transaction, that is to sell or buy, if the long holder elects to "exercise" the option prior to expiration. The buyer pays a premium to the seller for this right. An option which conveys the right to buy something at a specific price is called a call; an option which conveys the right to sell something at a specific price is called a put. Both are commonly traded, though in basic finance for clarity the call option is more frequently discussed, as it moves in the same direction as the underlying asset, rather than opposite, as does the put.

Option Value

Potential benefits of the environment not derived from actual use. This expresses the preference or willingness to pay for the preservation of an environment against some probability that the individual will make use of it at some later date. If we lose a species in the wild, such as the Bengal tiger, very few of us will have our welfare directly affected by not being able to see it, photograph it or hear it. That "use value" is very small. But many people will lose the option to do that in the future, should they care to. Economists call that "option value." Further, many people around the world derive some benefit just from knowing that Bengal tigers exist in the wild. That is "existence value.".

Option Value (Cost Benefit Analysis)

In cost benefit analysis and social welfare economics, the term option value refers to the value that is placed on private willingness to pay for maintaining or preserving a public asset or service even if there is little or no likelihood of the individual actually ever using it. The concept is most commonly used in public policy assessment to justify continuing investment in parks, wildlife refuges and land conservation, as well as rail transportation facilities and services. It is also recognized as an element of the total economic value of environmental resources. This concept of "option value" in cost-benefit analysis is different from the concept used in finance, where the term refers to the valuation of a financial instrument that provides for a future purchase of an asset. (See Option time value.) However, the two can be related insofar as both can be interpreted as a valuation of risk factors.

Ordinal Data

Ordinal data is a statistical data type describing data consisting of numeric scores that exist on an ordinal scale, i.e. an arbitrary numeric scale where the exact numeric quantity of a particular value has no significance beyond its ability to establish a ranking over a set of data points. A variable containing a single piece of ordinal data is known as an ordinal variable. In regression analysis, outcomes that are ordinal variables can be predicted using a variant of ordinal regression, such as ordered logit or ordered probit.

Ordinal Utility

Ordinal utility theory states that while the utility of a particular good or service cannot be measured using a numerical scale bearing economic meaning in and of itself, pairs of alternative bundles (combinations) of goods can be ordered such that one is considered by an individual to be worse than, equal to, or better than the other. This contrasts with cardinal utility theory, which generally treats utility as something whose numerical value is meaningful in its own right. The concept has been introduced first by Pareto in 1906.

Ordinal Variable

A variable where the ordering of the values conveys information but the magnitude of the values does not.

Ordinary Least Squares (OLS)

A method for estimating the parameters of a multiple linear regression model. The ordinary least squares estimates are obtained by minimising the sum of squared residuals.

Organization For Economic Cooperation And Development (OECD)

An organization of 20 countries from the Western world including all of those in Europe and North America. Its major objective is to assist the economic growth of its member nations by promoting cooperation and technical analysis of national and international economic trends.

Organization of Petroleum Exporting Countries (OPEC)

The Organization of the Petroleum Exporting Countries is an intergovernmental organization of twelve oil-producing countries made up of Algeria, Angola, Ecuador, Iran, Iraq, Kuwait, Libya, Nigeria, Qatar, Saudi Arabia, the United Arab Emirates and Venezuela. OPEC has had its headquarters in Vienna since 1965, and hosts regular meetings among the oil ministers of its member countries. Indonesia withdrew in 2008 after it became a net importer of oil, but stated it would likely return if it became a net exporter again. OPEC's influence on the market has been widely criticized, since it became effective in determining production and prices. Arab members of OPEC alarmed the developed world when they used the "oil weapon" during the Yom Kippur War by implementing oil embargoes and initiating the 1973 oil crisis. Although largely political explanations for the timing and extent of the OPEC price increases are also valid, from OPEC's point of view, these changes were triggered largely by previous unilateral changes in the world financial system and the ensuing period of high inflation in both the developed and developing world.

Outliers

Outliers can occur by chance in any distribution, but they are often indicative either of measurement error or that the population has a heavy-tailed distribution. In the former case one wishes to discard them or use statistics that are robust to outliers, while in the latter case they indicate that the distribution has high kurtosis and that one should be very cautious in using tools or intuitions that assume a normal distribution. A frequent cause of outliers is a mixture of two distributions, which may be two distinct sub-populations, or may indicate 'correct trial' versus 'measurement error'; this is modeled by a mixture model.

Out-of-Sample Criteria

Criteria used for choosing forecasting models that are based on a part of the sample that was not used in obtaining parameter estimates.

Output

Output in economics is the "quantity of goods or services produced in a given time period, by a firm, industry, or country," whether consumed or used for further production. The concept of national output is absolutely essential in the field of macroeconomics. It is national output that makes a country rich, not large amounts of money. The result of an economic process that has used inputs to produce a product or service that is available for sale or use somewhere else. Net output,

182

sometimes called netput is a quantity, in the context of production, that is positive if the quantity is output by the production process and negative if it is an input to the production process.

Overall Significance Of A Regression

A test of the joint significance of all explanatory variables appearing in a multiple regression equation.

Overvalued Exchange Rate

An official exchange rate set at a level higher than its real or shadow value—for example, 7 Kenyan shillings per dollar instead of, say, 10 shillings per dollar. Overvalued rates cheapen the real cost of imports while raising the real cost of exports. They often lead to a need for exchange control.

P

Pairwise Uncorrelated Random Variables

A set of two or more random variables where each pair is uncorrelated.

Panel Data

A data set constructed from repeated cross sections over time. With a balanced panel, the same units appear in each time period. With an unbalanced panel, some units do not appear in each time period, often due to attrition.

Parameter

An unknown value that describes a population relationship.

Pareto Ananlysis

Pareto analysis is a statistical technique in decision making that is used for selection of a limited number of tasks that produce significant overall effect. It uses the Pareto principle – the idea that by doing 20% of work, 80% of the advantage of doing the entire job can be generated. Or in terms of quality improvement, a large majority of problems (80%) are produced by a few key causes (20%). Pareto analysis is a formal technique useful where many possible courses of action are competing for attention. In essence, the problem-solver estimates the benefit delivered by each action, then selects a number of the most effective actions that deliver a total benefit reasonably close to the maximal possible one. Pareto analysis is a creative way of looking at causes of problems because it helps stimulate thinking and organize thoughts. However, it can be limited by its exclusion of possibly important problems which may be small initially, but which grow with time. It should be combined with other analytical tools such as failure mode and effects analysis and fault tree analysis for example.

Pareto Criterion

Pareto efficiency, or Pareto optimality, is a concept in economics with applications in engineering. The term is named after Vilfredo Pareto (1848–1923), an Italian economist who used the concept in his studies of economic efficiency and income distribution. In a Pareto efficient economic allocation, no one can be made better off without making at least one individual worse off. Given an initial allocation of goods among a set of individuals, a change to a different allocation that makes at least one individual better off without making any other individual worse off is called a Pareto improvement. An allocation is defined as "Pareto efficient" or "Pareto optimal" when no further Pareto improvements can be made. Pareto efficiency is a minimal notion of efficiency and does not necessarily result in a socially desirable distribution of resources: it makes no statement about equality, or the overall well-being of a society. The notion of Pareto efficiency can also be applied to the selection of alternatives in engineering and similar fields. Each option is first assessed under multiple criteria and then a subset of options is identified with the property that no other option can categorically outperform any of its members.

Pareto Distribution

The Pareto distribution, named after the Italian economist Vilfredo Pareto, is a power law probability distribution that coincides with social, scientific, geophysical, actuarial, and many other types of observable phenomena.

Pareto Index

In economics the Pareto index, named after the Italian economist and sociologist Vilfredo Pareto, is a measure of the breadth of income or wealth distribution. It is one of the parameters specifying a Pareto distribution and embodies the Pareto principle. As applied to income, the Pareto principle is sometimes stated in popular expositions by saying 20% of the population has 80% of the income. In fact, Pareto's data on British income taxes in his Cours d'économie politique indicates that about 20% of the population had about 80% of the income.

Pareto Optimality

The condition which exists when it is impossible to make any individual better off without making any other individual worse off.

Pareto Optimum

Situation in which it is impossible to make any individual better off without making someone else worse off, where better off means more preferred

and worse off means less preferred. Every competitive market equilibrium is a Pareto optimum and every Pareto optimum is a competitive equilibrium if a set of assumptions (e.g. perfect information, absence of externalities, etc.) holds true.

Pareto, Vilfredo (1848-1923)

Born in Paris of French and Italian parents, Pareto was educated in Italy where he was trained in mathematics and engineering. After working as an engineer for some years, he inherited a fortune and devoted himself to his broad-ranging interests in mathematics, sociology and religion. He was active in the turbulent politics of turn-of-the-century Europe. He also held an academic appointment at Lausanne where he lectured in economics and sociology. In 1906 he retired to his estate near Celigny on Lake Geneva and occupied himself developing a rather peculiar system of sociology. When the fascists came to power in Italy Mussolini appointed him a Senator, presumably because of his professed hatred of democrats. His major contributions to economics were the indifference curve analysis which he had adapted from the work of Francis Edgeworth, a British economist, and which was in turn picked up and developed by J.R. Hicks; various elements of general equilibrium theory, most notably the concept of what has come to be known as "Pareto optimality" and a theory of income distribution which held that the pattern of income distribution was essentially the same in all economies and at all times.

Parsimonious Model

A model with as few parameters as possible for capturing any desired features.

Partial Effect

The effect of an explanatory variable on the dependent variable, holding other factors in the regression model fixed.

Partial Equilibrium Analysis

An analysis assuming (in contrast to a general equilibrium analysis) that changes in price in a particular market can occur without causing significant changes in price in other markets.

Partnership

A partnership is a nominate contract between individuals who, in a spirit of cooperation, agree to carry on an enterprise; contribute to it by combining property, knowledge or activities; and share its profit. Partners may have a partnership agreement, or declaration of partnership and in some jurisdictions such agreements may be registered and available for public inspection. In many countries, a partnership is also considered to be a legal entity, although different legal systems reach different conclusions on this point.

Patents

The word patent originates from the Latin patere, which means "to lay open" (i.e., to make available for public inspection). More directly, it is a shortened version of the term letters patent, which was a royal decree granting exclusive rights to a person, predating the modern patent system. Similar grants included land patents, which were land grants by early state governments in the USA, and printing patents, a precursor of modern copyright. In modern usage, the term patent usually refers to the right granted to anyone who invents any new, useful, and non-obvious process, machine, article of manufacture, or composition of matter. Some other types of intellectual property rights are also called patents in some jurisdictions: industrial design rights are called design patents in the US, plant breeders' rights are sometimes called plant patents, and utility models and Gebrauchsmuster are sometimes called petty patents or innovation patents.

Peak Rate

The term peak rate is common in Indian Budget and refers to the maximum rate of customs duty which is applied on any item.

Pecuniary Benefits

Benefits arising because of changes in relative prices that come about as the economy adjusts to a project (as distinguished from real benefits, which augment society's welfare).

Per Capita Income

Per capita income is often used as average income, a measure of the wealth of the population of a nation, particularly in comparison to other nations. It is usually expressed in terms of a commonly used international currency such as the Euro or United States dollar, and is useful because it is widely known, easily calculated from readily-available GDP and population estimates, and produces a useful statistic for comparison of wealth between sovereign territories.

Critics claim that per capita income has several weaknesses as an accurate measurement of prosperity:

1. Comparisons of per capita income over time need to take into account changes in prices. Without using measures of income adjusted for inflation, they will tend to overstate the effects of economic growth.

2. International comparisons can be distorted by differences in the costs of living between countries that aren't reflected in exchange rates. Where the objective of the comparison is to look at differences in living standards between countries, using a measure of per capita income adjusted for differences in purchasing power parity more accurately reflects the differences in what people are actually able to buy with their money.

Percentage Change

The proportionate change in a variable, multiplied by 100.

Percentage Point Change

The change in a variable that is measured as a percent.

Perfect Collinearity

In multiple regression, one independent variable is an exact linear function of one or more other independent variables.

Perfect Competition

In economic theory, perfect competition (sometimes called pure competition) describes markets such that no participants are large enough to have the market power to set the price of a homogeneous product. Because the conditions for perfect competition are strict, there are few if any perfectly competitive markets. Still, buyers and sellers in some auction-type markets, say for commodities or some financial assets, may approximate the concept. Perfect competition serves as a benchmark against which to measure real-life and imperfectly competitive markets. In perfect competition, any profit-maximizing producer faces a market price equal to its marginal cost (P=MC). This implies that a factor's price equals the factor's marginal revenue product. It allows for derivation of the supply curve on which the neoclassical approach is based. This is also the reason why "a monopoly does not have a supply curve". The abandonment of price taking creates considerable difficulties for the demonstration of a general equilibrium except under other, very specific conditions such as that of monopolistic competition.

Performance Budget

A budget format that relates the input of resources and the output of services for each organizational unit individually. Sometimes used synonymously with programme budget. It is a budget wherein expenditures are based primarily upon measurable performance of activities.

Perpetuity

A perpetuity is an annuity in which the periodic payments begin on a fixed date and continue indefinitely. It is sometimes referred to as a perpetual annuity. Fixed coupon payments on permanently invested (irredeemable) sums of money are prime examples of perpetuities. Scholarships paid perpetually from an endowment fit the definition of perpetuity. The value of the perpetuity is finite because receipts that are anticipated far in the future have extremely low present value (present value of the future cash flows). Unlike a typical bond, because the principal is never repaid, there is no present value for the principal.

Personal Distribution

The distribution of income on the basis of income groups. For example, by dividing all income recipients into ten groups (deciles) and showing the share each of these groups had of the total income.

Personal Saving

The difference between household income (after taxes) and consumption expenditures.

Physical Capital

In economics, physical capital or just 'capital' refers to a factor of production (or input into the process of production), such as machinery, buildings, or computers. The production function takes the general form Y = f(K, L), where Y is output, K is capital stock and L is labour. In economic theory, physical capital is one of the three primary factors of production, also known as inputs in the production function. The others are natural resources (including land), and labour — the stock of competences embodied in the labour force. "Physical" is used to distinguish physical capital from human capital (a result of investment in the human agent)) and financial capital. "Physical capital" may also refer to fixed capital, any kind of real or physical asset that is not used up in the production of a product, as distinguished from circulating capital.

Plan Expenditure

Money provided for the execution of Central Plan. This monetary aid is given from the government's account and consists of expenditure both capital & revenue and Central assistance to Union territories & States.

Planning

Planning (also called forethought) is the process of thinking about and organizing the activities required to achieve a desired goal. Planning involves the creation and maintenance of a plan. As such, planning is a fundamental property of intelligent behaviour. This thought process is essential to the creation and refinement of a plan, or integration of it with other plans; that is, it combines forecasting of developments with the preparation of scenarios of how to react to them.

Planning Curve

The long run average cost curve.

Plug-In Solution To The Omitted Variables Problem

A proxy variable is substituted for an unobserved omitted variable in an OLS regression.

Point Forecast

The forecasted value of a future outcome.

Policy Analysis

An empirical analysis that uses econometric methods to evaluate the effects of a certain policy.

Political Economy

Political economy was the original term used for studying production, buying, and selling, and their relations with law, custom, and government, as well as with the distribution of national income and wealth. Political economy originated in moral philosophy. It developed in the 18th century as the study of the economies of states, polities, hence the term political economy. political economy meant the study of the conditions under which production or consumption within limited parameters was organized in the nation-states. In that way, political economy expanded the emphasis of economics, which comes from the Greek oikos (meaning "home") and nomos (meaning "law" or "order"); thus political economy was meant to express the laws of production of wealth at the state level, just as economics was the ordering of the home.

Polluter Pays Principal

Policies that emphasize the interaction between politics and economics and that have political and economic effects.

Pollution Fee Or Tax

Charge for the amount of waste or pollution. Examples include the BTU tax that was an early casualty in the President's budget bill. Several European nations have air and water pollution charges; Unit pricing for trash pickup, charging by the amount of trash collected (or the size of the container). The charge makes it worthwhile for a producer to cut back, right up to the point where it begins to cost more to reduce pollution than to pay the tax. A system like this also raises money for government, allowing government, if it chooses, to reduce taxes in other areas while collecting the same amount of total revenue.

Pooled Cross Section

A data configuration where independent cross sections, usually collected at different points in time, are combined to produce a single data set.

Population

A population is all the organisms of the same group or species who live in the same geographical area and are capable of interbreeding. In ecology the population of a certain species in a certain area is estimated using the Lincoln Index. The area that is used to define a sexual population is such that inter-breeding is possible between any pair within the area and more probable than cross-breeding with individuals from other areas. Normally breeding is substantially more common within the area than across the border.

In sociology, population refers to a collection of human beings. Demography is a social science which entails the statistical study of human populations. This article refers mainly to human population.

Population Model

A population model is a type of mathematical model that is applied to the study of population dynamics. Models allow a better understanding of how complex interactions and processes work. Modelling of dynamic interactions in nature can provide a manageable way of understanding how numbers change over time or in relation to each other. Ecological population modelling is concerned with the changes in population size and age distribution within a population as a consequence of interactions of organisms with the physical environment, with individuals of their own species, and with organisms of other species. The world is full of interactions that range from simple to dynamic.

Population R-Squared

In the population, the fraction of the variation in the dependent variable that is explained by the explanatory variables.

Portfolio Investment

Financial investments by private individuals, corporations, pension funds, and mutual funds in stocks, bonds, certificates of deposit, and notes issued by private companies and the public agencies of LDCs.

Portfolio Theory

The analysis of how an investor can maximize the expected return from a "portfolio" of various kinds of financial assets having given degrees of risk and uncertainty associated with them (or minimize the risk involved in realizing some given expected return).

Positional Goods

In economics, positional goods are products and services whose value is mostly (if not exclusively) a function of their ranking in desirability by others, in comparison to substitutes. The extent to which a good's value depends on such a ranking is referred to as its positionality. The term was coined by Fred Hirsch in 1976. Positional goods often earn economic rents or quasi-rents. Examples of positional goods include high social status, exclusive real estate, a spot in the freshman class of a prestigious university, a reservation at the "hottest" new restaurant, and fame. The measure of satisfaction derived from a positional good depends on how much one has in relation to everyone else. Competitions for positional goods are zero-sum games because such goods are inherently scarce, at least in the short run. Attempts to acquire them can only benefit one player at the expense of others. By definition, every person cannot be the most popular, cool, or elite, in the same way that every person cannot be a star athlete – all of those terms imply a separation or superiority over other people.

Posner, Richard A. (1939-)

An American lawyer, economist and jurist, educated at Yale and Harvard. Posner lectured at the University of Chicago Law School in the 1980s, and was appointed to the US Court of Appeals during the Reagan administration. His major work in economics has been concerned with the economic analysis of law. He has published several important articles and three major books, *Economic Analysis of Law*, 1973; *Antitrust Law: An Economic Perspective*, 1976; and *The Economics of Justice*, 1981.

Potential Pareto Improvement Criterion

The policy objective that gainers from a policy change (or project) could compensate the losers from the change and still be better off. In particular note that a policy that passes this criterion does not need to include the compensation, the compensation merely has to be possible.

Poverty

Poverty is the state of one who lacks a certain amount of material possessions or money. Absolute poverty or destitution refers to the deprivation of basic human needs, which commonly includes food, water, sanitation, clothing, shelter, health care and education. Relative poverty is defined contextually as economic inequality in the location or society in which people live.

Poverty Gap

The sum of the difference between the poverty line and actual income levels of all people living below that line.

Poverty Gap Index

Poverty gap index is a measure of the intensity of poverty. It is defined as the average poverty gap in the population as a proportion of the poverty line. The poverty gap index is an improvement over the poverty measure headcount ratio which simply counts all the people below a poverty line, in a given population, and considers them equally poor. Poverty gap index estimates the depth of poverty by considering how far, on the average, the poor are from that poverty line.

Poverty Line

A level of income below, which people are deemed poor. A global poverty line of $1.25 per person per day was suggested in 2005 by World Bank 1990. This line facilitates comparison of how many poor people there are in different countries. But, it is only a crude estimate because the line does not recognize differences in the buying power of money in different countries, and, more significantly, because it does not recognize other aspects of poverty than the material, or income poverty.

Poverty Threshold

The poverty threshold, or poverty line, is the minimum level of income deemed adequate in a given country. In practice, like the definition of poverty, the official or common understanding of the poverty line is significantly higher in developed countries than in developing countries.

Power Of A Test

The probability of rejecting the null hypothesis when it is false; the power depends on the values of the population parameters under the alternative.

Practical Significance

The practical or economic importance of an estimate, which is measured by its sign and magnitude, as opposed to its statistical significance.

Predatory Pricing

The practice of setting price at a low level in order to drive a rival firm out of business.

Prediction

The estimate of an outcome obtained by plugging specific values of the explanatory variables into an estimated model, usually a multiple regression model.

Prediction Error

The difference between the actual outcome and a prediction of that outcome.

Prediction Error Variance

The variance in the error that arises when predicting a future value of the dependent variable based on an estimated multiple regression equation.

Prediction Interval

A confidence interval for an unknown outcome on a dependent variable in a multiple regression model.

Preference Shares

These are the shares entitled to a fixed dividend before any distribution of profits can be made amongst the holders of ordinary shares or stock.

Present Value

Present value, also known as present discounted value, is the value on a given date of a payment or series of payments made at other times. If the payments are in the future, they are discounted to reflect the time value of money and other factors such as investment risk. If they are in the past, their value is correspondingly enhanced to reflect that those payments have been (or could have been) earning interest in the intervening time. Present value calculations are widely used in business and economics to provide a means to compare cash flows at different times on a meaningful "like to like" basis.

Price

Price is the quantity of payment or compensation given by one party to another in return for goods or services. In modern economies, prices are generally expressed in units of some form of currency. (For commodities, they are expressed as currency per unit weight of the commodity, e.g. euros per kilogram.) Although prices could be quoted as quantities of other goods or services this sort of barter exchange is rarely seen. Prices are sometimes quoted in terms of vouchers such as trading stamps and air miles. In some circumstances, cigarettes have been used as currency, for example in prisons, in times of hyperinflation, and in some places during World War 2. In the black economy, barter is also relatively common.

Price Ceiling

A price ceiling is a government-imposed limit on the price charged for a product. Governments intend price ceilings to protect consumers from conditions that could make necessary commodities unattainable. However, a price ceiling can cause problems if imposed for a long period without controlled rationing. Price ceilings can produce negative results when the correct solution would have been to increase supply. Misuse occurs when a government misdiagnoses a price as too high when the real problem is that the supply is too low. In an unregulated market economy price ceilings do not exist.

Price Discrimination

Price discrimination or price differentiation exists when sales of identical goods or services are transacted at different prices from the same provider. In a theoretical market with perfect information, perfect substitutes, and no transaction costs or prohibition on secondary exchange (or re-selling) to prevent arbitrage, price discrimination can only be a feature of monopolistic and oligopolistic markets, where market power can be exercised. Otherwise, the moment the seller tries to sell the same good at different prices, the buyer at the lower price can arbitrage by selling to the consumer buying at the higher price but with a tiny discount. However, product heterogeneity, market frictions or high fixed costs (which make marginal-cost pricing unsustainable in the long run) can allow for some degree of differential pricing to different consumers, even in fully competitive retail or industrial markets. Price discrimination also occurs when the same price is charged to customers which have different supply costs.

Price Elastic

Description of the demand for a product if its price elasticity of demand exceeds 1.

Price Elasticity Of Demand

Price elasticity of demand (PED or Ed) is a measure used in economics to show the responsiveness, or elasticity, of the quantity demanded of a good or service to a change in its price. More precisely, it gives the percentage change in quantity demanded in response to a one percent change in price (ceteris paribus, i.e. holding constant all the other determinants of demand, such as income). It was devised by Alfred Marshall. Price elasticities are almost always negative, although analysts tend to ignore the sign even though this can lead to ambiguity. Only goods which do not conform to the law of demand, such as Veblen and Giffen goods, have a positive PED. In general, the demand for a good is said to be inelastic (or relatively inelastic) when the PED is less than one (in absolute value): that is, changes in price have a relatively small effect on the quantity of the good demanded. The demand for a good is said to be elastic (or relatively elastic) when its PED is greater than one (in absolute value): that is, changes in price have a relatively large effect on the quantity of a good demanded.

Price Elasticity Of Supply

The responsiveness of the quantity of a commodity supplied to a change in its price, expressed as the percentage change in quantity supplied divided by the percentage change in price.

Price Floor

A price floor is a government- or group-imposed limit on how low a price can be charged for a product. A price floor must be greater than the equilibrium price in order to be effective. A price floor can be set below the free-market equilibrium price. In the first graph at right, the dashed green line represents a price floor set below the free-market price. In this case, the floor has no practical effect. The government has mandated a minimum price, but the market already bears a higher price.

Price Inelastic

Description of the demand for a product if its price elasticity of demand is less than 1.

Price Leader

A firm in an oligopolistic industry that sets a price that other firms are willing to follow.

Price System

A system in which each good and service has a price and that, in a purely capitalistic economy, carries out the basic functions of an economic system (determining what will be produced, how it will be produced, how much of it each person will get, and what the country's growth of per capita output will be).

Price-Consumption Curve

A curve connecting the various equilibrium points corresponding to market baskets chosen by the consumer at various prices of a commodity.

Prices

The amounts that people pay for units of particular goods or services.

Primary Deficit

A primary deficit is the deficit which is derived after deducting the interest payments component from the total deficit of any budget. the total of primary deficit and interest payments makes up the total or fiscal deficit. The opposite of a primary deficit is a primary surplus.

Principal-Agent Problem

The problem that arises because managers or workers may pursue their own objectives, even though this reduces the profits of the owners of the firm. The managers or workers are agents who work for the owners the principals.

Principle Of Diminishing Marginal Utility

The proposition that the satisfaction derived from consuming an additional unit of a good or service declines as additional units are acquired.

Principle Of Diminishing Returns

The proposition that the marginal product of the last unit of labour employed declines as additional units of labour are employed.

Prisoners' Dilemma

A situation in which two persons (or firms) would both do better to cooperate than not to cooperate, but in which each feels it is in his or her interests not to do so; therefore each fares worse than if they cooperated.

Private Cost

The expense incurred by the individual user to obtain the use of a resource.

Private Good

A private good is defined in economics as "an item that yields positive benefits to people" that is excludable, i.e. its owners can exercise private property rights, preventing those who have not paid for it from using the good or consuming its benefits; and rivalrous, i.e. consumption by one necessarily prevents that of another. A private good, as an economic resource is scarce, which can cause competition for it. The market demand curve for a private good is a horizontal summation of individual demand curves. Unlike public goods, private goods are less likely to have the free rider problem. Assuming a private good is valued positively by everyone, the efficiency of obtaining the good is obstructed by its rivalry, that is simultaneous consumption of a rivalrous good is theoretically impossible; the feasibility of obtaining the good is made difficult by its excludability, that is people have to pay for it to enjoy its benefits.

Privatization

The selling-off of publicly owned enterprises to private owners.

Probability

Probability is a measure of the expectation that an event will occur or a statement is true. Probabilities are given a value between 0 (will not occur) and 1 (will occur). The higher the probability of an event, the more certain we are that the event will occur.

Probability Density Function (PDF)

A function that, for discrete random variables, gives the probability that the random variable takes on each value; for continuous random variables, the area under the pdf gives the probability of various events.

Probability Limit

The value to which an estimator converges as the sample size grows without bound.

Producer Surplus

The aggregate profits of firms making a good plus the amount that owners of inputs (used to make the good) are compensated above and beyond the minimum they would insist on. Geometrically, it equals the area above the supply curve and below the price.

Producers

People who use resources to make goods and services (also called workers).

Product Differentiation

Causing buyers to believe that a particular version of a product is superior to that being offered by competitors.

Production

In economics, production is the act of creating output, a good or service which has value and contributes to the utility of individuals. The act may or may not include factors of production other than labour. Any effort directed toward the realization of a desired product or service is a "productive" effort and the performance of such act is production. The relation between the amount of inputs used in production and the resulting amount of output is called the production function.

Production Function

The relationship between the quantities of various inputs used per period of time and the maximum amount of output that can be produced per period of time.

Production Possibilities

Levels of output which are within the range of possibilities for a particular economy.

Production Possibilities Curve

All combinations of the maximum amounts of goods that a society can produce with the available resources and technology.

Productive Resources

All natural resources (land), human resources (labour), and human-made resources (capital) used in the production of goods and services.

Productivity

Productivity is a measure of the efficiency of production. Productivity is a ratio of production output to what is required to produce it (inputs). The measure of productivity is defined as a total output per one unit of a total input. These definitions are short but too general and insufficient to make the phenomenon productivity understandable. A more detailed theory of productivity is needed, which explains the phenomenon productivity and makes it comprehensible. In order to obtain a measurable form of productivity, operationalization of the concept is necessary. In explaining and operationalizing a set of production models are used. A production model is a numerical expression of the production process that is based on production data, i.e. measured data in the form of prices and quantities of inputs and outputs.

Profit

The difference between total revenues and the full costs involved in producing or selling a good or service; it is a return for risk taking.

Programme Evaluation

Programme evaluation is a systematic method for collecting, analyzing, and using information to answer questions about projects, policies and programmes, particularly about their effectiveness and efficiency. In both the public and private sectors, stakeholders will want to know if the programmes they are funding, implementing, voting for, receiving or objecting to are actually having the intended effect (and to what cost). This definition focuses on the question of whether the programme, policy or project has, as indicated, the intended effect.

Progressive Tax

Progressive tax is a tax where the wealthy have to give more income tax as compared to the poor.

Property Rights

Property rights are a controversial, theoretical construct in economics for determining how a resource is used, and who owns that resource - government, collective bodies, or by individuals. Property rights can be viewed as an attribute of an economic good. This attribute has four broad components and is often referred to as a bundle of rights:
1. the right to use the good
2. the right to earn income from the good
3. the right to transfer the good to others
4. the right to enforcement of property rights.

In economics, property usually refers to ownership (rights to the proceeds of output generated) and control over the use of the means of production. They may be owned privately, by the state, by those who use it, or held in common by society. The concept of property rights as used by economists and legal scholars (see property for the legal concept) are related but distinct. The distinction is largely seen in the economists' focus on the ability of an individual or collective to control the use of the good.

Property Tax

A property tax (or millage tax) is a levy on property that the owner is required to pay. The tax is levied by the governing authority of the jurisdiction in which the property is located; it may be paid to a national government, a federated state, a county/region, or a municipality. Multiple jurisdictions may tax the same property. There are four broad types of property: land, improvements to land (immovable man-made objects, such as buildings), personal property (movable man-made objects), and intangible property. Real property (also called real estate or realty) means the combination of land and improvements. Under a property tax system, the government requires and/or performs an appraisal of the monetary value of each property, and tax is assessed in proportion to that value. Forms of property tax used vary among countries and jurisdictions.

Proportionate Change

The change in a variable relative to its initial value; mathematically, the change divided by the initial value.

Prospect Theory

States that individual values with respect to gains and losses are in comparison to a reference point. Derived from psychology helps explain some anomalies including differences with respect to willingness to pay and willingness to accept. This contrasts with the economic assumption that individuals maximize utility. What matters is the point from which gains and losses are measured. It also suggests that values for negative deviations from the reference point will be greater than values place on positive deviations. Gains are valued less than losses. Third, the manner in which the gains and losses are to be secured matters a great deal.

Prospect Theory

States that individual values with respect to gains and losses are in comparison to a reference point. Derived from psychology helps explain some anomalies including differences with respect to willingness to pay and willingness to accept. This contrasts with the economic assumption that individuals maximize utility. What matters is the point from which gains and losses are measured. It also suggests that values for negative deviations from the reference point will be greater than values place on positive deviations. Gains are valued less than losses. Third, the manner in which the gains and losses are to be secured matters a great deal.

Proxy Variable

An observed variable that is related but not identical to an unobserved explanatory variable in multiple regression analysis.

Public Good

In economics, a public good is a good that is both non-excludable and non-rivalrous in that individuals cannot be effectively excluded from use and where use by one individual does not reduce availability to others. Examples of public goods include fresh air, knowledge, lighthouses, national defence, flood control systems and street lighting. Public goods that are available everywhere are sometimes referred to as global public goods. Many public goods may at times be subject to excessive use resulting in negative externalities affecting all users; for example air pollution and traffic congestion. Public goods problems are often closely related to the "free-rider" problem or the tragedy of the commons, in which people not paying for the good may continue to access it. Thus, the good may be under-produced, overused or degraded. Public goods may also become subject to restrictions on access and may then be considered to be club goods or private goods; exclusion mechanisms include copyright, patents, congestion pricing, and pay television. The opposite of a public good is a private good, which does not possess these properties. A loaf of bread, for example, is a private good: its owner can exclude others from using it, and once it has been consumed, it cannot be used again.

Public Interest

The public interest refers to the "common well-being" or "general welfare". The public interest is central to policy debates, politics, democracy and the nature of government itself. While nearly everyone claims that aiding the common well-being or general welfare is positive, there is little, if any, consensus on what exactly constitutes the public interest, or whether the concept itself is a coherent one.

Public Sector

A term which is generally applied to state enterprises, i.e., those companies which are nationalized and run by the government.

Public Sector Undertaking

A company (majority) owned, managed and run by the Government of India.

Purchasing Power Parity

A concept in which a given amount of U.S. dollars will purchase the same bundle of goods in all economies. In calculating purchasing power parity, adjustments are made to exchange rates to raise or lower the relative value of currencies to equilibrate purchasing power.

Pure Competition

A situation where many sellers sell the same product and no seller can set the price.

P-Value

The smallest significance level at which the null hypothesis can be rejected. Equivalently, the largest significance level at which the null hypothesis cannot be rejected.

Q

Quadratic Functions

Functions that contain squares of one or more explanatory variables; they capture diminishing or increasing effects on the dependent variable.

Qualitative Variable

A variable describing a nonquantitative feature of an individual, a firm, a city, and so on.

Quantity Demanded

The amount of product consumers will purchase at a specific price.

Quantity Supplied

The amount of a product producers will produce and sell at a specific price.

Quantity Theory Of Money

The idea that there is a direct link between the quantity of money in the economy and the price level.

Quasi-Rent

Quasi-rent is an analytical term in economics, for the income earned, in excess of post-investment opportunity cost, by a sunk cost investment. Alfred Marshall (1842-1924) was the first to observe quasi-rents. In general, an economic rent is the difference between the income from a factor of production in a particular use, and either the cost of bringing the factor into economic use (classical factor rent), or the opportunity cost of using the factor, where opportunity cost is defined as the current income minus the income available in the next best use (Paretian factor rent). In other words, economic rent is the difference between the income in the current use of the factor and the absolute minimum required to draw a factor into a particular use (from no use at all, or from the next best use), (see economic rent.)

Quota

A quota is a physical limitation on the quantity of any item that can be imported into a country, such as so many automobiles per year. Also a method for allocating limited school places by noncompetitive means—for example, by income or ethnicity.

R

Random Sampling

A sampling scheme whereby each observation is drawn at random from the population. In particular, no unit is more likely to be selected than any other unit, and each draw is independent of all other draws. In a simple random sample (SRS) of a given size, all such subsets of the frame are given an equal probability. Each element of the frame thus has an equal probability of selection: the frame is not subdivided or partitioned. Furthermore, any given pair of elements has the same chance of selection as any other such pair (and similarly for triples, and so on). This minimises bias and simplifies analysis of results. In particular, the variance between individual results within the sample is a good indicator of variance in the overall population, which makes it relatively easy to estimate the accuracy of results. However, SRS can be vulnerable to sampling error because the randomness of the selection may result in a sample that doesn't reflect the makeup of the population. For instance, a simple random sample of ten people from a given country will on average produce five men and five women, but any given trial is likely to overrepresent one sex and underrepresent the other. Systematic and stratified techniques, discussed below, attempt to overcome this problem by using information about the population to choose a more representative sample.

Random Variable

A random variable or stochastic variable is a variable whose value is subject to variations due to chance (i.e. randomness, in a mathematical sense). As opposed to other mathematical variables, a random variable conceptually does not have a single, fixed value (even if unknown); rather, it can take on a set of possible different values, each with an associated probability. A random variable's possible values might represent the possible outcomes of a yet-to-be-performed experiment or an event that has not happened yet, or the potential values of a past experiment or event whose already-existing value is uncertain (e.g. as a result of incomplete information or imprecise measurements). They may also conceptually represent either the results of an "objectively" random process (e.g. rolling a die), or the "subjective" randomness that results from incomplete knowledge of a quantity.

Random Walk

A time series process where next period's value is obtained as this period's value, plus an independent (or at least an uncorrelated) error term.

Random Walk With Drift

A random walk that has a constant (or drift) added in each period.

Rational Behaviour

Behaviour that is consistent with the attainment of an individual's perception of his or her own best interest.

Rational Expectations

Rational expectations is a hypothesis in economics which states that agents' predictions of the future value of economically relevant variables are not systematically wrong in that all errors are random. Equivalently, this is to say that agents' expectations equal true statistical expected values. An alternative formulation is that rational expectations are model-consistent expectations, in that the agents inside the model assume the model's predictions are valid. The rational expectations assumption is used in many contemporary macroeconomic models, game theory and applications of rational choice theory.

Ray

A line that starts from some point and goes off into space. If capital is on one axis and labour is on the other, a ray from the origin describes all input combinations where the capital-labour ratio is constant.

Reaction Curve

A curve showing how much one duopolist will produce and sell, depending on how much it thinks the other duopolist will produce and sell.

Real Balance Effect

The influence a change the quantity of real money has on the quantity of real national income demanded.

Real Benefits

Benefits that augment society's welfare (as distinguished from pecuniary benefits, which arise because of changes in relative prices that come about as the economy adjusts to a project).

Real Federal Funds Rate

The nominal federal funds rate minus the near-term expected rate of inflation. The federal funds rate is the rate that one depository institution charges another on borrowings of funds held at Federal Reserve Banks. The Federal Reserve targets the federal funds rate and sets the discount rate, the rate the Federal Reserve charges on Federal Reserve lending to depository institutions.

Real GNP

The GNP of any year measured in the prices of a base year. Real GNP is nominal GNP adjusted for inflation.

Real Rate Of Interest

The dollar interest rate corrected for inflation; equal to the nominal rate minus the inflation rate.

Real Variable

A monetary value measured in terms of a base period.

Real Wage

The term real wages refers to wages that have been adjusted for inflation. This term is used in contrast to nominal wages or unadjusted wages. Real wages provide a clearer representation of an individual's wages, but suffer the disadvantage of not being well defined, since the amount of inflation, based on different goods and services, is itself not well defined. Real wages are a useful economic measure, as opposed to nominal wages, which simply show the monetary value of wages in that year. However, real wages does not take into account other compensation like benefits or old age pensions.

Recession

In economics, a recession is a business cycle contraction, a general slowdown in economic activity. Macroeconomic indicators such as GDP, employment, investment spending, capacity utilization, household income, business profits, and inflation fall, while bankruptcies and the unemployment rate rise. Recessions generally occur when there is a widespread drop in spending (an adverse demand shock). This may be triggered by various events, such as a financial crisis, an external trade shock, an adverse supply shock or the bursting of an economic bubble. Governments usually respond to recessions by adopting expansionary macroeconomic policies, such as increasing money supply, increasing government spending and decreasing taxation.

Redistribution Policy

Measures taken by government to transfer income from some individuals to others.

Regression Through The Origin

Regression analysis where the intercept is set to zero; the slopes are obtained by minimising the sum of squared residuals, as usual.

Regressive Taxes

A regressive tax is a tax imposed in such a manner that the tax rate decreases as the amount subject to taxation increases. "Regressive" describes a distribution effect on income or expenditure, referring to the way the rate progresses from high to low, where the average tax rate exceeds the marginal tax rate. In terms of individual income and wealth, a regressive tax imposes a greater burden (relative to resources) on the poor than on the rich — there is an inverse relationship between the tax rate and the taxpayer's ability to pay as measured by assets, consumption, or income.

Rejection Region

The set of values of a test statistic that leads to rejecting the null hypothesis.

Rejection Rule

In hypothesis testing, the rule that determines when the null hypothesis is rejected in favour of the alternative hypothesis.

Relative Prices

The relationship between the prices of different goods and services. May be thought of in terms of the amount of one good which can be had for a certain expenditure compared to the amount of another good which can be had for the same expenditure.

Rent

The return paid to an input that is fixed in supply.

Rent Controls

Fixed limits on rents that can be charged to tenants by owners according to a legal restriction.

Rent-Seeking

The activities of individuals or firms to obtain special privileges, such as monopoly power, which will enable them to increase their incomes. Using up resources to win such privileges from governments or their agencies.

Repo Rate

This is one of the credit management tools used by the Reserve Bank to regulate liquidity. South Africa (customer spending). The bank borrows money from the Reserve Bank to cover its shortfall. The Reserve

Bank only makes a certain amount of money available and this determines the repo rate. If the bank requires more money than what is available, this will increase the repo rate and vice versa.

Residual

The difference between the actual value and the fitted (or predicted) value; there is a residual for each observation in the sample used to obtain an OLS regression line.

Residual Analysis

A type of analysis that studies the sign and size of residuals for particular observations after a multiple regression model has been estimated.

Residual Sum Of Squares (RSS)

In multiple regression analysis, the sum of the squared OLS residuals across all observations.

Resources

A resource is a source or supply from which benefit is produced. Typically resources are materials or other assets that are transformed to produce benefit and in the process may be consumed or made unavailable. From a human perspective a natural resource is anything obtained from the environment to satisfy human needs and wants. From a broader biological or ecological perspective a resource satisfies the needs of a living organism. Resources have three main characteristics: utility, limited availability, and potential for depletion or consumption. Resources have been variously categorized as biotic versus abiotic, renewable versus non-renewable, and potential versus actual, along with more elabourate classifications.

Restricted Model

In hypothesis testing, the model obtained after imposing all of the restrictions required under the null.

Retained Earnings

Business profits which are held by firms and not paid to the stockholders of the firm; the earnings are usually reinvested by the firms.

Revenue

Revenue or turnover is income that a company receives from its normal business activities, usually from the sale of goods and services to customers. In many countries, such as the United Kingdom, revenue is referred to as turnover. Some companies receive revenue from interest, royalties, or other fees. Revenue may refer to business income in general, or it may refer to the amount, in a monetary unit, received during a period of time, as in "Last year, Company X had a revenue of $42 million." Profits or net income generally imply total revenue minus total expenses in a given period.

Revenue Deficit

This budget related term is the difference between revenue expenditure and revenue receipts.

Revenue Expenditure

This is expenditure on recurring items, including the running of services and financing capital spending that is paid for by borrowing. This is meant for normal running of governments' maintenance expenditures, interest payments, subsidies and transfers etc. It is current expenditure which does not result in the creation of assets. Grants given to State governments or other parties are also treated as revenue expenditure even if some of the grants may be meant for creating assets.

Revenue Receipts

Additions to assets that do not incur an obligation that must be met at some future date and do not represent exchanges of property for money. Assets must be available for expenditures. These include proceeds of taxes and duties levied by the government, interest and dividend on investments made by the government, fees and other receipts for services rendered by the government.

Revenues

Total gross earnings of a firm before subtracting costs.

Ricardo, David (1772-1823)

Born in London, Ricardo had a successful financial career. He developed a strong interest in the work of Adam Smith and other early contributors to economics such as Jeremy Bentham and Thomas Malthus. He had a life-long friendship with the latter, although their ideas were usually sharply conflicting. Ricardo wrote several influential pamphlets on economic issues of his day, particularly on taxation and commercial policy. In 1817 he published his major work, *Principles of Political Economy and Taxation*. Smith, Malthus and Ricardo are generally regarded as the main members of the classical school of economics.

Risk

Those undertaking investments or the production of goods and services for sale cannot know with certainty whether they will recover the outlays needed to conduct these activities. Although some risks can be insured against (the risk of fire losses for example) there is no way of insuring against the possibility of business losses due to the uncertainty of the market place.

Risk Averters

When confronted with gambles with equal expected monetary values, risk averters prefer a gamble with a more-certain outcome to one with a less-certain outcome.

Risk Lovers

When confronted with gambles with equal expected monetary values, risk lovers prefer a gamble with a less-certain outcome to one witha more-certain outcome.

Risk Neutral

Risk-neutral individuals do not care whether a gamble has a less-certain or more-certain outcome. They choose among gambles on the basis of expected monetary value alone; specifically, they maximize expected monetary value.

Robinson, Joan (1903-83)

Born in Surrey, England. A prominent Cambridge economist, Joan Robinson first attracted attention with her work on imperfect competition which became the basis of standard expositions in university textbooks on economic theory, but which she subsequently repudiated. She was a powerful advocate of Keynesian economics in the 1930s and 40s. After World War II she sought to develop a dynamic version of the Keynesian model and her work was the basis for what is sometimes called "neo-Keynesianism", a radical form of Keynesianism associated with a small group of economists at Cambridge. She was one of the few mainstream academic economists to take Marxian economics seriously and incorporated elements of it into her own work. In the 1960s and 1970s she engaged in a vigorous intellectual controversy with Paul Samuelson and other dominant American theorists (based at the Massachusetts Institute of Technology) over the theory of capital and the marginal productivity theory of income distribution.

Root Mean Squared Deviation

The root-mean-square deviation (RMSD) or root-mean-square error (RMSE) is a frequently used measure of the differences between values predicted by a model or an estimator and the values actually observed. RMSD is a good measure of accuracy, but only to compare different forecasting errors within a dataset and not between different ones, as it is scale-dependent. These individual differences are also called residuals, and the RMSD serves to aggregate them into a single measure of predictive power.

R-Squared

In a multiple regression model, the proportion of the total sample variation in the dependent variable that is explained by the independent variable.

R-Squared Form Of The F Statistic

The F statistic for testing exclusion restrictions expressed in terms of the R-squareds from the restricted and unrestricted models.

S

Sales Tax

A sales tax is a tax paid to a governing body by a seller for the sales of certain goods and services. Usually laws allow (or require) the seller to collect funds for the tax from the consumer at the point of purchase. Laws may allow sellers to itemized the tax separately from the price of the goods or services, or require it to be included in the price (tax-inclusive). The tax amount is usually calculated by applying a percentage rate to the taxable price of a sale. When a tax on goods or services is paid to a governing body directly by a consumer, it is usually called a use tax.

Sample Average

The sum of n numbers divided by n; a measure of central tendency.

Sample Correlation

For outcomes on two random variables, the sample covariance divided by the product of the sample standard deviations.

Sample Covariance

An unbiased estimator of the population covariance between two random variables.

Sample Standard Deviation

A consistent estimator of the population standard deviation.

Sample Variance

An unbiased, consistent estimator of the population variance.

Sampling Distribution

A sampling distribution or finite-sample distribution is the probability distribution of a given statistic based on a random sample. Sampling distributions are important in statistics because they provide a major simplification on the route to statistical inference. More specifically, they allow analytical considerations to be based on the sampling distribution of a statistic, rather than on the joint probability distribution of all the individual sample values.

Sampling Variance

The variance in the sampling distribution of an estimator; it measures the spread in the sampling distribution.

Save

Set aside earnings (income) for a future use.

Saving

Saving is income not spent, or deferred consumption. Methods of saving include putting money aside in a bank or pension plan. Saving also includes reducing expenditures, such as recurring costs. In terms of personal finance, saving specifies low-risk preservation of money, as in a deposit account, versus investment, wherein risk is higher. In a primitive agricultural economy savings might take the form of holding back the best of the corn harvest as seed corn for the next planting season. If the whole crop were consumed the economy would deteriorate to hunting and gathering the next season.

Saving Function

The relationship between saving and national income.

Scarce Good

A good which people want more of and which is costly to obtain.

Scarcity

Scarcity is the fundamental economic problem of having humans who have unlimited wants and needs in a world of limited resources. It states that society has insufficient productive resources to fulfill all human wants and needs. Alternatively, scarcity implies that not all of society's goals can be pursued at the same time; trade-offs are made of one good against others. In an influential 1932 essay, Lionel Robbins defined economics as "the science which studies human behaviour as a relationship between ends and scarce means which have alternative uses."

Scarcity Shortage

A term used when the quantity of a good demanded exceeds the quantity supplied at the existing price.

Schedule

A table or list of values.

Schumpeter, Joseph (1883-1950)

An Austrian-born economist who had a broad-based career as a lawyer, banker, teacher and senior civil servant in Austria before migrating to the US where he became a professor economics at Harvard in 1932. His scholarly writing ranges over topics as diverse as business cycles and the historical evolution of capitalism. He is perhaps best known today for his defence of monopoly, which he developed in conjunction with his view that the success of capitalism was largely attributable to the freedom it allowed for innovation and entrepreneurial activity.

Seasonal Dummy Variables

A set of dummy variables used to denote the quarters or months of the year.

Seasonal Unemployment

Unemployment which occurs regularly because of seasonal changes in the demand for certain kinds of labour.

Seasonality

A feature of monthly or quarterly time series where the average value differs systematically by season of the year.

Seasonally Adjusted

Monthly or quarterly time series data where some statistical procedure possibly regression on seasonal dummy variables-has been used to remove the seasonal component.

SEBI

Securities and Exchange Board of India is a regulatory body appointed by the Government of India, which supervises the Indian debt and equity markets. It was formed officially by the Government of India in 1992 with SEBI Act 1992 being passed by the Indian Parliament. SEBI is headquartered in the business district of Bandra Kurla Complex in Mumbai, and has Northern, Eastern,

Southern and Western regional offices in New Delhi, Kolkata, Chennai and Ahmedabad. Controller of Capital Issues was the regulatory authority before SEBI came into existence; it derived authority from the Capital Issues (Control) Act, 1947. Initially SEBI was a non statutory body without any statutory power. However in 1995, the SEBI was given additional statutory power by the Government of India through an amendment to the Securities and Exchange Board of India Act 1992. In April, 1998 the SEBI was constituted as the regulator of capital markets in India under a resolution of the Government of India.

Second-Degree Price Discrimination

Strategy by which a monopolist charges a different price depending on how much the consumer purchases, thus increasing the monopolist's revenues and profit.

Secular Change

Change over a long period of time, such as a decade or more. Distinguished from cyclical change which occurs in shorter time periods such as a year.

Selling Expenses

The expenses of advertising and distributing a product and of trying to convince potential customers that they should buy it.

Semi-Elasticity

The percentage change in the dependent variable given a one-unit increase in an independent variable.

Sensitivity Analysis

The process of checking whether the estimated effects and statistical significance of key explanatory variables are sensitive to inclusion of other explanatory variables, functional form, dropping of potentially outlying observations, or different methods of estimation.

Serial Correlation

In a time series or panel data model, correlation between the errors in different time periods.

Serially Uncorrelated

The errors in a time series or panel data model are pairwise uncorrelated across time.

Services

In economics, a service is an intangible commodity. More specifically, services are an intangible equivalent of economic goods. Service provision is often an economic activity where the buyer does not generally, except by exclusive contract, obtain exclusive ownership of the thing purchased. The benefits of such a service, if priced, are held to be self-evident in the buyer's willingness to pay for it. Public services are those society as a whole pays for through taxes and other means.

Shadow Prices

The shadow price is the instantaneous change per unit of the constraint in the objective value of the optimal solution of an optimization problem obtained by relaxing the constraint. In other words, it is the marginal utility of relaxing the constraint, or, equivalently, the marginal cost of strengthening the constraint. In a business application, a shadow price is the maximum price that management is willing to pay for an extra unit of a given limited resource. For example, if a production line is already operating at its maximum 40-hour limit, the shadow price would be the maximum price the manager would be willing to pay for operating it for an additional hour, based on the benefits he would get from this change. Unobserved hidden or implicit prices derived through inferences and such methods as Contingent Valuation and Hedonic Pricing. Reflect movements along efficient frontier and tradeoffs between attributes.

Shareholder

A shareholder or stockholder is an individual or institution (including a corporation) that legally owns a share of stock in a public or private corporation. Stockholders are granted special privileges depending on the class of stock. These rights may include:

1. The right to sell their shares,
2. The right to vote on the directors nominated by the board,
3. The right to nominate directors (although this is very difficult in practice because of minority protections) and propose shareholder resolutions,
4. The right to dividends if they are declared,
5. The right to purchase new shares issued by the company, and
6. The right to what assets remain after a liquidation.

Stockholders or shareholders are considered by some to be a subset of stakeholders, which may include anyone who has a direct or indirect interest in the business entity. For example, labour, suppliers, customers, the community, etc., are typically considered stakeholders because they contribute value and/or are impacted by the corporation. Shareholders in the primary market who buy IPOs provide capital to corporations; however, the vast majority of shareholders are in the secondary market and provide no capital directly to the corporation.

Short Run

The short run is the conceptual time period in which at least one factor of production is fixed in amount and others are variable in amount. Costs that are fixed, say from existing plant size, have no impact on a firm's short-run decisions, since only variable costs and revenues affect short-run profits. Such fixed costs raise the associated short-run average cost of an output leveong-run average cost if the amount of the fixed factor is better suited for a different output level. In the short run, a firm can raise output by increasing the amount of the variable factor(s), say labour through overtime.

Short-run Average Variable Cost Curve (SRAVC)

Average variable cost (which is a short-run concept) is the variable cost (typically labour cost) per unit of output: SRAVC = wL / Q where w is the wage rate, L is the quantity of labour used, and Q is the quantity of output produced. The SRAVC curve plots the short-run average variable cost against the level of output, and is typically drawn as U-shaped.

Short-run Average Total Cost Curve (SRATC or SRAC)

The average total cost curve is constructed to capture the relation between cost per unit of output and the level of output, ceteris paribus. A perfectly competitive and productively efficient firm organizes its factors of production in such a way that the average cost of production is at the lowest point. In the short run, when at least one factor of production is fixed, this occurs at the output level where it has enjoyed all possible average cost gains from increasing production. This is at the minimum point in the diagram on the right.

Shortage

The situation resulting when the quantity demanded exceeds the quantity supplied of a good or service, usually because the price is for some reason below the equilibrium price in the market.

Short-Run Elasticity

The impact propensity in a distributed lag model when the dependent and independent variables are in logarithmic form.

Significance Level

The probability of Type I error in hypothesis testing.

Simple Money Multiplier

The amount by which a change in the monetary base is multiplied to bring about the eventual change in the total money supply. It is called the simple money multiplier because it does not take into account possible offsets to the process, such as a rise in the amount of money individuals or households may choose to hold as cash when the money supply increases.

Simultaneous Equations Model (SEM)

A model that jointly determines two or more endogenous variables, where each endogenous variable can be a function of other endogenous variables as well as of exogenous variables and an error term.

Single (Simple) Linear Regression Model

A model where the dependent variable is a linear function of a single independent variable, plus an error term.

Single Proprietorship

A form of unincorporated business in which there is only one owner.

Size Distribution Of Income

The distribution of income among groups of income recipients defined on the basis of the size of their incomes.

Slope Parameter

The coefficient on an independent variable in a multiple regression model.

Small-Scale Industry

Unit is an industrial undertaking with an investment of less than Rs.10 million ($0.2 million) in plant and machinery and an annual turnover of Rs. 10 million to Rs. 100 million.

SME

Small and Medium Enterprise as defined by the Draft SME Bill is a company with an investment of less than Rs. 100 million ($2.2 million) for a manufacturing unit and Rs. 50 million (US$1.1 million) for services.

Smith, Adam (1723-90)

Generally regarded as the founder of modern economics, Adam Smith was born in 1723 in Kirkaldy, Scotland. Educated at Glasgow College and at Oxford, he eventually gained the chair of moral philosophy at the University of Edinburgh. He published his *Theory of Moral Sentiments* in 1759 and his great work, *An Inquiry into the Nature and Causes of the Wealth of Nations* in 1776. The latter was an immediate success and its influence is still felt today. Perhaps its most famous passage is that in which Smith elabourated on his notion that individuals are motivated not by altruism, but by self-interest. In pursing their own interests, however, they inadvertently advance the interest of society as a whole, led as it were by "an invisible hand."

Social Cost

Social cost in economics may be distinguished from "private cost". Economic theorists model individual decision-making as measurement of costs and benefits. Social cost is also considered to be the private cost plus external benefits. Rational choice theory often assumes that individuals consider only the costs they themselves bear when making decisions, not the costs that may be borne by others. The real cost to society of having a good or service produced, which may be greater than the private costs incorporated by the producer in its market price.

Social Darwinists

A disparate group of turn-of-the-century commentators on social issues who sought to utilize the Darwinian law of natural selection ("survival of the fittest") as a basis for social policy. The best-known of the social Darwinists was Herbert Spencer.

Special Economic Zone

A Special Economic Zone (SEZ) is a geographical region that has economic and other laws that are more free-market-oriented than a country's typical or national laws. "Nationwide" laws may be suspended inside a special economic zone. The category SEZ covers, including free trade zones (FTZ), export processing zones (EPZ), free zones (FZ), industrial parks or industrial estates (IE), free ports, free economic zones, urban enterprise zones and others.

Specialists

People who produce a narrower range of goods and services than they consume (also called specialized workers).

Specialists

People who produce a narrower range of goods and services than they consume (also called specialized workers).

Specialization

The act of producing more of a good than one consumes, the rest of that good being exchanged.

Spencer, Herbert (1820-1903)

A British philosopher and early sociologist. Spencer was trained mainly in engineering, but he developed an early interest in social science. He became involved with several radical social movements and tried to develop an ambitious, but never fully coherent philosophical system he called "Synthetic Philosophy." He published three major books: *Social Statics*, 1850; *The Man versus the State*, 1884; and *The Principles of Ethics*, 1892-3. His social theories were founded on the conviction that the evolution of society from a state of brutal barbarism to modern industrial civilization had depended on the subordination of the less capable members of society to their superiors. Any interventions which alleviated the circumstances of the less fit, Spencer contended, disrupted the operation of the benign natural processes which ensured progress by eliminating the idle, incompetent and unproductive members of society.

Spend

Use earnings (income) to buy goods and services.

Spreadsheet

A spreadsheet is an interactive computer application programme for organization and analysis of information in tabular form.

Spreadsheets developed as computerized simulations of paper accounting worksheets. The programme operates on data represented as cells of an array, organized in rows and columns. Each cell of the array is a model–view–controller element that can contain either numeric or text data, or the results of formulas that automatically calculate and display a value based on the contents of other cells. The user of the spreadsheet can make changes in any stored value and observe the effects on calculated values. This makes the spreadsheet useful for "what-if" analysis since many cases can be rapidly investigated without tedious manual recalculation. Modern spreadsheet software can have multiple interacting sheets, and can display data either as text and numerals, or in graphical form.

Spurious Correlation

A correlation between two variables that is not due to causality, but perhaps to the dependence of the two variables on another unobserved factor.

Spurious Regression Problem

A problem that arises when regression analysis indicates a relationship between two or more unrelated time series processes simply because each has a trend, is an integrated time series (such as a random walk), or both.

Stabilization Policies

A coordinated set of mostly restrictive fiscal and monetary policies aimed at reducing inflation, cutting budget deficits, and improving the balance of payments.

Stagflation

An economic condition characterized by simultaneous inflation, slow growth and high unemployment.

Stalin, Joseph Vissarianovich (Born J.V. Dzhugashvili) (1879-1953)

Lenin's disciple and successor as leader of the Soviet Union. Stalin reinforced the system of centralized state control after gaining power when Lenin died in 1924. Through systematic purging of dissenters from the Party apparatus, Stalin achieved supreme control and drove forward a massive programme of industrial development and forced collectivization of agriculture. As he once put it, "We lag behind the advanced countries by 50 to 100 years. We must make good this distance in ten years." Despite enormous losses due to famine in the 1930s and the devastation of World War II, by the time of his death Stalin had made the Soviet Union into a modern, industrial state capable of challenging the United States for international economic, political and technological leadership.

Standard Deviation

A common measure of spread in the distribution of a random variable. Standard deviation (represented by the symbol sigma, σ) shows how much variation or "dispersion" exists from the average (mean, or expected value). A low standard deviation indicates that the data points tend to be very close to the mean; high standard deviation indicates that the data points are spread out over a large range of values. The standard deviation of a random variable, statistical population, data set, or probability distribution is the square root of its variance. It is algebraically simpler though practically less robust than the average absolute deviation. A useful property of standard deviation is that, unlike variance, it is expressed in the same units as the data.

Standard Error Of The Regression (SER)

In multiple regression analysis, the estimate of the standard deviation of the population error, obtained as the square root of the sum of squared residuals over the degrees of freedom.

Standard Normal Distribution

The normal distribution with mean zero and variance one.

Standard Of Living

Standard of living refers to the level of wealth, comfort, material goods and necessities available to a certain socioeconomic class in a certain geographic area. The standard of living includes factors such as income, quality and availability of employment, class disparity, poverty rate, quality and affordability of housing, hours of work required to purchase necessities, gross domestic product, inflation rate, number of vacation days per year, affordable (or free) access to quality healthcare, quality and availability of education, life expectancy, incidence of disease, cost of goods and services, infrastructure, national economic growth, economic and political stability, political and religious freedom, environmental quality, climate and safety. The standard of living is closely related to quality of life.

Standard Of Value

One of the functions of money whereby the value of goods and services is expressed in money terms (prices).

Standardised Random Variable

A random variable transformed by subtracting off its expected value and dividing the result by its standard deviation; the new random variable has mean zero and standard deviation one.

Starting Point Bias

Because survey interviewers suggest the first bid this can influence the respondents answer and cause the respondent to agree too readily with bids in the vicinity of the initial bid .

Static Efficiency

Efficiency when technology and tastes are fixed. If departures from static efficiency result in a faster rate of technological change and productivity increase, they may lead to a higher level of consumer satisfaction than if the conditions for static efficiency are met.

Static Model

A time series model where only contemporaneous explanatory variables affect the dependent variable.

Stationary State

The economic condition envisioned by the classical writers once the growth of population had reached the point where output per capita was reduced to the subsistence level and the accumulation of capital had reduced the return to investment to zero. The economy would remain in equilibrium with no possibility of future increases in population or per capita incomes.

Statistical Inference

The act of testing hypotheses about population parameters.

Statistically Insignificant

Failure to reject the null hypothesis that a population parameter is equal to zero, at the chosen significance level.

Statistically Significant

Rejecting the null hypothesis that a parameter is equal to zero against the specified alternative, at the chosen significance level.

Statutory Liquidity Ratio (SLR)

It is the ratio of cash in hand, exclusive of cash balances maintained by banks to meet required CRR.

Stigler, George (1911-1991)

Stigler was born and grew up in the western US and studied at the University of Washington, at Northwestern, and Chicago. He subsequently taught at several universities in the American mid-west and at Columbia before settling down at the University of Chicago where he remained from 1958 until retirement in 1981. His published work covers a variety of topics in economic theory, including oligopoly, economies of scale and other aspects of industrial organization. Some of his most original contributions have to do with the economics of information, which he treated as a standard commodity subject to the usual influences of demand and supply, and the economic theory of regulation.

Stock

The capital stock (or stock) of an incorporated business constitutes the equity stake of its owners. It represents the residual assets of the company that would be due to stockholders after discharge of all senior claims such as secured and unsecured debt. Stockholders' equity cannot be withdrawn from the company in a way that is intended to be detrimental to the company's creditors

Store Of Value

One of the functions of money allowing people to save current purchasing power to buy goods and services in a future time period.

Store Of Value

One of the functions of money allowing people to save current purchasing power to buy goods and services in a future time period.

Strategic Bias

Causes survey results to differ from actual willingness to pay because individual have an incentive to not reveal the truth because they can secure a benefit in excess of the costs they have to pay. This arises from the free rider problem. For example, if individuals are told that a service will be provided if the total sum they are willing to pay exceeds the cost of provision and that each will be charged a price according to their maximum willingness to pay then individuals will have an incentive to understate his or her demand.

Strategic Move

A move that influences the other person's choice in a manner favourable to oneself by affecting the other person's expectations of how oneself will behave.

Stratified Sampling

A nonrandom sampling scheme whereby the population is first divided into several nonoverlapping, exhaustive strata, and then random samples are taken from within each stratum.

Strict Exogeneity

An assumption that holds in a time series or panel data model when the explanatory variables are strictly exogenous.

Strictly Exogenous

A feature of explanatory variables in a time series or panel data model where the error term at any time period has zero expectation, conditional on the explanatory variables in all time periods; a less restrictive version is stated in terms of zero correlations.

Structural Unemployment

Workers without jobs whose skills are no longer suitable for or do not match the types of jobs available.

Subsidies

The Central Government extends monetary aid either to a group of individuals or individual in order to enhance their business skills.

Subsidy

A payment by the government to producers or distributors in an industry to prevent the decline of that industry (e.g., as a result of continuous unprofitable operations) or an increase in the prices of its products or simply to encourage it to hire more labour (as in the case of a wage subsidy). Examples are export subsidies to encourage the sale of exports; subsidies on some foodstuffs to keep down the cost of living, especially in urban areas; and farm subsidies to encourage expansion of farm production and achieve self-reliance in food production.

Substitute Goods

In economics, one way two or more goods are classified is by examining the relationship of the demand schedules when the price of one good changes. This relationship between demand schedules leads to classification of goods as either substitutes or complements. Substitute goods are goods which, as a result of changed conditions, may replace each other in use (or consumption). A substitute good, in contrast to a complementary good, is a good with a positive cross elasticity of demand. This means a good's demand is increased when the price of another good is increased. Conversely, the demand for a good is decreased when the price of another good is decreased. If goods A and B are substitutes, an increase in the price of A will result in a leftward movement along the demand curve of A and cause the demand curve for B to shift out. A decrease in the price of A will result in a rightward movement along the demand curve of A and cause the demand curve for B to shift in.

Substitution Effect

1. The change in the quantity demanded of a good resulting from a price change when the level of satisfaction of the consumer is held constant.

2. measures how much less of a now more expensive commodity (x) will be consumed simply because of a price increase. It follows from the basic economic principle of substitution, i.e. consumers will tend to substitute a less expensive for a more expensive good or service.

Summation Operator

A notation, denoted by 'Σ', used to define the summing of a set of numbers.

Superfund Law

Comprehensive Environmental Response, Compensation and Liability Act (CERCLA), a .U.S. federal law enacted by Congress in 1980 for the purpose of cleaning up existing toxic sites.

Supply

In economics, supply is the amount of some product producers are willing and able to sell at a given price all other factors being held constant. Usually, supply is plotted as a supply curve showing the relationship of price to the amount of product businesses are willing to sell.

Supply And Demand

Supply and demand is an economic model of price determination in a market. It concludes that in a competitive market, the unit price for a particular good will vary until it settles at a point where the quantity demanded by consumers (at current price) will equal the quantity supplied by producers (at current price), resulting in an economic equilibrium for price and quantity.

Supply Chain

A supply chain is system of organizations, people, technology, activities, information and resources involved in moving a product or service from supplier to customer. Supply chain activities transform natural resources, raw materials and components into a finished product that is delivered to the end customer. In sophisticated supply chain systems, used products may re-enter the supply chain at any point where residual value is recyclable. Supply chains link value chains.

Supply Curve

A graphic representation of the relationship between quantities supplied at each price for a given time period.

Supply Curve Of Loanable Funds

The relationship between the quantity of loanable funds supplied and the interest rate.

Supply Decrease

A decrease in the quantity supplied at every price; a shift to the left of the supply curve.

Supply Increase

An increase in the quantity supplied at every price; a shift to the right of the supply curve.

Supply-Side Economics

Supply-side economics is a school of macroeconomic thought that argues that economic growth can be most effectively created by lowering barriers for people to produce (supply) goods and services, such as lowering income tax and capital gains tax rates, and by allowing greater flexibility by reducing regulation. According to supply-side economics, consumers will then benefit from a greater supply of goods and services at lower prices. Typical policy recommendations of supply-side economists are lower marginal tax rates and less regulation.

The term "supply-side economics" was thought, for some time, to have been coined by journalist Jude Wanniski in 1975, but according to Robert D. Atkinson's Supply-Side Follies, the term "supply side" ("supply-side fiscalists") was first used by Herbert Stein, a former economic adviser to President Nixon, in 1976, and only later that year was this term repeated by Jude Wanniski. Its use connotes the ideas of economists Robert Mundell and Arthur Laffer. Today, supply-side economics is likened by agreeable critics to "trickle-down economics". Supply-side economics is often used and referred to as overall term for "trickle-down economics" as it is not targeting specific tax cuts but is instead targeting general tax cuts and encouraging deregulation.

Surplus

The situation resulting when the quantity supplied exceeds the quantity demanded of a good or service, usually because the price is for some reason below the equilibrium price in the market.

Sustainable Development

A principle which states that a development plan must not compromise the welfare of future generations for the benefit of present generations.

Symmetric Distribution

A probability distribution characterised by a probability density function that is symmetric around its median value, which must also be the mean value (whenever the mean exists).

T

T Distribution

The distribution of the ratio of a standard normal random variable and the square root of an independent chi-square random variable, where the chi-square random variable is first divided by its df.

T Statistic

The statistic used to test a single hypothesis about the parameters in an econometric model.

Taking

Argument that government regulations can effectively take away or reduce the right of individuals or firms to use property to maximize their incomes or utilities.

Target Return

A desired rate of return that a firm hopes to achieve by means of markup pricing.

Tariff

A tax imposed by the government on imported goods (designed to cut down on import and thus protect domestic industry and workers from foreign competition).

Tariff (Ad Valorem)

A fixed percentage tax on the value of an imported commodity, levied at the point of entry into the importing country.

Tastes

The preferences of consumers.

Tata Strategic Management Group

One of the leading management consulting firms in South Asia.

Tax Avoidance

Tax avoidance is the legal usage of the tax regime to one's own advantage, to reduce the amount of tax that is payable by means that are within the law. The term tax mitigation is not however a synonym for tax avoidance. Its original use was by tax advisers as an alternative to the pejorative term tax avoidance. The term has also been used in the tax regulations of some jurisdictions to distinguish tax avoidance foreseen by the legislators from tax avoidance which exploits loopholes in the law. The United States Supreme Court has stated that "The legal right of an individual to decrease the amount of what would otherwise be his taxes or altogether avoid them, by means which the law permits, cannot be doubted." Tax evasion, on the other hand, is the general term for efforts by individuals, corporations, trusts and other entities to evade taxes by illegal means. Both tax avoidance and evasion can be viewed as forms of tax noncompliance, as they describe a range of activities that are unfavourable to a state's tax system.

Tax Base

The total property and resources subject to taxation.

Tax Evasion

Tax evasion is the general term for efforts by individuals, corporations, trusts and other entities to evade taxes by illegal means. Tax evasion usually entails taxpayers deliberately misrepresenting or concealing the true state of their affairs to the tax authorities to reduce their tax liability and includes in particular dishonest tax reporting, such as declaring less income, profits or gains than actually earned or overstating deductions. Tax evasion is an activity commonly associated with the informal economy and one measure of the extent of tax evasion is the amount of unreported income, namely the difference between the amount of income that should legally be reported to the tax authorities and the actual amount reported, which is also sometimes referred to as the tax gap.

Taxes

A tax is a financial charge or other levy imposed upon a taxpayer (an individual or legal entity) by a state or the functional equivalent of a state such that failure to pay is punishable by law. Taxes are also imposed by many administrative divisions. Taxes consist of direct or indirect taxes and may be paid in money or as its labour equivalent.

Technological Change

Technological change (TC) is a term that is used to describe the overall process of invention, innovation and diffusion of technology or processes. The term is synonymous with technological development, technological achievement, and technological progress. In essence TC is the invention of a technology (or a process), the continuous process of improving a technology (in which it often becomes cheaper) and its diffusion throughout industry or society. In short, technological change is based on both better and more technology.

Technology

Knowledge which permits or facilitates the transformation of resources into goods and services.

Terms Of Trade

The ratio of a country's average export price to its average import price; also known as the commodity terms of trade. A country's terms of trade are said to improve when this ratio increases and to worsen when it decreases, that is, when import prices rise at a relatively faster rate than export prices (the experience of most LDCs in recent decades).

Test Statistic

A rule used for testing hypotheses where each sample outcome produces a numerical value.

Text Editor

A text editor is a type of programme used for editing plain text files. Text editors are often provided with operating systems or software development packages, and can be used to change configuration files and programming language source code.

Text (ASCII) File

A universal file format that can be transported across numerous computer platforms.

The Confederation Of Indian Industry

Founded in 1895, CII is an Indian business association, with a direct membership of over 5300 companies from the private as well as public sectors, including SMEs and MNCs and indirect membership of over 80,000 companies from around 300 national and regional sectoral associations - www.ciionline.org

Third-Degree Price Discrimination

A situation in which a monopolist sells a good in more than one market, the good cannot be transferred from one market and resold in another, and the monopolist can set different prices in different markets.

Time Series Data

In statistics, signal processing, pattern recognition, econometrics, mathematical finance, weather forecasting, earthquake prediction, electroencephalography, control engineering and communications engineering a time series is a sequence of data points, measured typically at successive time instants spaced at uniform time intervals. Examples of time series are the daily closing value of the Dow Jones index or the annual flow volume of the Nile River at Aswan. Time series analysis comprises methods for analyzing time series data in order to extract meaningful statistics and other characteristics of the data. Time series forecasting is the use of a model to predict future values based on previously observed values. Time series are very frequently plotted via line charts.

Time Trend

A function of time that is the expected value of a trending time series process.

Time-Demeaned Data

Panel data where, for each cross-sectional unit, the average over time

is subtracted from the data in each time period.

Tit For Tat

A strategy in game theory in which each player does on this round what the other player did on the previous round.

Tort

A tort, in common law jurisdictions, is a civil wrong. Tort law deals with situations where a person's behaviour has unfairly caused someone else to suffer loss or harm. A tort is not necessarily an illegal act but causes harm. The law allows anyone who is harmed to recover their loss. Tort law is different from criminal law, which deals with situations where a person's actions cause harm to society in general. A claim in tort may be brought by anyone who has suffered loss after suing a civil law suit. Criminal cases tend to be brought by the state, although private prosecutions are possible. Tort law is also differentiated from equity, in which a petitioner complains of a violation of some right. One who commits a tortious act is called a tortfeasor. The equivalent of tort in civil law jurisdictions is delict. Tort may be defined as a personal injury; or as "a civil action other than a breach of contract."

Total Cost

In economics, and cost accounting, total cost (TC) describes the total economic cost of production and is made up of variable costs, which vary according to the quantity of a good produced and include inputs such as labour and raw materials, plus fixed costs, which are independent of the quantity of a good produced and include inputs (capital) that cannot be varied in the short term, such as buildings and machinery. Total cost in economics includes the total opportunity cost of each factor of production as part of its fixed or variable costs. The rate at which total cost changes as the amount produced changes is called marginal cost. This is also known as the marginal unit variable cost. If one assumes that the unit variable cost is constant, as in cost-volume-profit analysis developed and used in cost accounting by the accountants, then total cost is linear in volume, and given by:

total cost = fixed costs + unit variable cost * amount.

Total Cost Function

Relationship between a firm's total cost and its output.

Total Factor Productivity

The growth of real output beyond what can be attributed to increases in the quantities of labour and capital employed.

Total Fixed Cost

In economics, fixed costs are business expenses that are not dependent on the level of goods or services produced by the business. They tend to be time-related, such as salaries or rents being paid per month, and are often referred to as overhead costs. This is in contrast to variable costs, which are volume-related (and are paid per quantity produced).

Total Revenue

Total revenue is the total receipts of a firm from the sale of any given quantity of a product. It can be calculated as the selling price of the firm's product times the quantity sold, i.e. total revenue = price X quantity, or letting TR be the total revenue function:

$$TR(Q) = P(Q) \times Q$$

where Q is the quantity of output sold, and P(Q) is the inverse demand function (the demand function solved out for price in terms of quantity demanded).

Total Sum Of Squares (TSS)

The total sample variation in a dependent variable about its sample average.

Total Surplus

The sum of consumer and producer surpluses.

Total Utility

A number representing the level of satisfaction that a consumer derives from a particular market basket.

Total Variable Cost

A firm's total expenditure on variable inputs per period of time.

Trade Agreement

An international agreement on conditions of trade in goods and services.

Trade Pact

A trade pact (also known as trade agreement) is a wide ranging tax, tariff and trade pact that often includes investment guarantees. The most common trade pacts are of the preferential and free trade types are concluded in order to reduce (or eliminate) tariffs, quotas and other trade restrictions on items traded between the signatories.

Tradeable Permits

The government specifies an overall level of pollution we'll tolerate, then gives each polluter a "permit" for its portion of the total. Firms that keep emissions below their allotted level may sell or lease the surplus to other firms that can use the permits to exceed their original allotment. For example, The 1990 Clean Air Act which set up tradeable permits for sulphur dioxide emissions in an effort to reduce acid rain. Other cases where it can work include water pollution from both point and non-point sources and international trading in greenhouse gas permits. If the number of permit holders is very high, the programme can be expensive to operate. If the number is very small, some firms could monopolize the market.

Trade-Off

A trade-off (or tradeoff) is a situation that involves losing one quality or aspect of something in return for gaining another quality or aspect. It often implies a decision to be made with full comprehension of both the upside and downside of a particular choice; the term is also used in an evolutionary context, in which case the selection process acts as the "decision-maker". Trade-offs are important in engineering. For example, in electrical engineering, negative feedback is used in amplifiers to trade gain for other desirable properties, such as improved bandwidth, stability of the gain and/or bias point, noise immunity, and reduction of nonlinear distortion.

Traditional Economy

A traditional economy is any economic system involving extensive subsistence agriculture or one that otherwise falls outside the definitions of market or planned economies. Examples of traditional economies include those of the Inuit or those of the tea plantations in South India. Traditional economies are popularly conceived of as "primitive" or "undeveloped" economic systems, having tools or techniques seen as outdated. As with the notion of contemporary primitiveness and with modernity itself, the view that traditional economies are backwards is not shared by scholars in economics and anthropology.

Tragedy Of The Commons

The case of a communal pasture area where all individuals are free to graze their livestock. The 'tragedy' arises because these 'commons' were typically heavily over grazed.

Transaction Cost

In economics and related disciplines, a transaction cost is a cost incurred in making an economic exchange (restated: the cost of participating in a market). Transaction costs can be divided into three broad categories:

1. Search and information costs are costs such as those incurred in determining that the required good is available on the market, which has the lowest price, etc.
2. Bargaining costs are the costs required to come to an acceptable agreement with the other party to the transaction, drawing up an appropriate contract and so on. In game theory this is analyzed for instance in the game of chicken. On asset markets and in market microstructure, the transaction cost is some function of the distance between the bid and ask.
3. Policing and enforcement costs are the costs of making sure the other party sticks to the terms of the contract, and taking appropriate action (often through the legal system) if this turns out not to be the case.

Transfer Payments

In economics, a transfer payment (or government transfer or simply transfer) is a redistribution of income in the market system. These payments are considered to be exhaustive because they do not directly absorb resources or create output. In other words, the transfer is made without any exchange of goods or services. Examples of certain transfer payments include welfare (financial aid), social security, and government making subsidies for certain businesses (firms).

Transferable Emissions Permits

Permits to generate a certain amount of pollution, limited in number, that are allocated among firms and that can be bought or sold.

Transmission Elasticity (Or Exchange Rate Pass-Through)

Because markets are imperfect and there are barriers to trade, a change in international prices or exchange rates does not necessarily translate perfectly into a change in domestic prices. The transmission elasticity measures the rate of transmission and varies between 0 and 1. A transmission elasticity of 1 indicates that international price changes and exchange rate changes are perfectly transmitted to the domestic economy. A transmission elasticity of 0 implies no change in domestic prices from a change in international prices or exchange rates. Countries with highly imperfect markets and significant trade barriers have low transmission elasticities, while countries with open international markets have high transmission elasticities.

Travel Cost Method

Derives values by evaluating expenditures of recreators. Travel costs are used s a proxy for price in deriving demand curves for the recreation site.

Treasury Bill

A short-term debt issued by a national government with a maximum maturity of one year. Treasury bills are sold at discount, such that the difference between purchase price and the value at maturity is the amount of interest.

Trough

A point in the business cycle corresponding to the end of the slowdown and the beginning of expansion.

True Model

The actual population model relating the dependent variable to the relevant independent variables, plus a disturbance, where the zero conditional mean assumption holds.

Twin Deficits

Deficits that include both the government budget deficit and trade deficit.

Twin Deficits Hypothesis

The twin deficits hypothesis, also called the double deficit hypothesis or twin deficits anomaly, is a concept from macroeconomics that contends that there is a strong link between a national economy's current account balance and its government budget balance.

Two-Part Tariff

A pricing technique whereby the consumer pays an initial fee for the right to buy the product as well as a usage fee for each unit of the product that he or she buys.

Two-Sided Alternative

An alternative where the population parameter can be either less than or greater than the value stated under the null hypothesis.

Two-Tailed Test

The two-tailed test is a statistical test used in inference, in which a given statistical hypothesis, H0 (the null hypothesis), will be rejected when the value of the test statistic is either sufficiently small or sufficiently large. This contrasts with a one-tailed test, in which only one of the rejection regions "sufficiently small" or "sufficiently large" is preselected according to the alternative hypothesis being selected, and the hypothesis is rejected only if the test statistic satisfies that criterion. Alternative names are one-sided and two-sided tests.

Tying

A marketing technique whereby a firm producing a product that will function only if used in conjunction with another product requires its customers to buy the latter product from it, rather than from alternative suppliers.

Type I Error

A rejection of the null hypothesis when it is true.

Type II Error

The failure to reject the null hypothesis when it is false.

U

Unbiased Estimator
An estimator whose expected value (or mean of its sampling distribution) equals the population value (regardless of the population value).

Unconditional Forecast
A forecast that does not rely on knowing, or assuming values for, future explanatory variables.

Uncorrelated Random Variables
Random variables that are not linearly related.

Unemployment
Unemployment (or joblessness) occurs when people are without work and actively seeking work. The unemployment rate is a measure of the prevalence of unemployment and it is calculated as a percentage by dividing the number of unemployed individuals by all individuals currently in the labour force. During periods of recession, an economy usually experiences a relatively high unemployment rate. In a 2011 news story, Business Week reported, "More than 200 million people globally are out of work, a record high, as almost two-thirds of advanced economies and half of developing countries are experiencing a slowdown in employment growth".

Unemployment Benefit
Unemployment insurance are payments made by the state or other authorized bodies to unemployed people. Benefits may be based on a compulsory para-governmental insurance system. Depending on the jurisdiction and the status of the person, those sums may be small, covering only basic needs, or may compensate the lost time proportionally to the previous earned salary. They often are part of a larger social security scheme.

Unemployment Rate
The percentage of the total work force of people actively seeking employment who are currently unemployed. The nonaccelerating inflationary rate of unemployment (NAIRU) is the rate of unemployment that will not lead to increasing inflation in the economy. In the United States, that rate has been estimated to be approximately 5 percent.

Unitary Elasticity
An elasticity equal to 1.

Unrestricted Model
In hypothesis testing, the model that has no restrictions placed on its parameters.

Upward Bias

The expected value of an estimator is greater than the population parameter value.

User Benefits

Benefits deriving from the actual use of the environment. Anglers, hunters, boaters, nature walkers, bird watchers, etc. use the environment and derive benefits.

User Values

If we lose a species in the wild, such as the Bengal tiger, very few of us will have our welfare directly affected by not being able to see it, photograph it or hear it. That "use value" is very small. But many people will lose the option to do that in the future, should they care to. Economists call that "option value." Further, many people around the world derive some benefit just from knowing that Bengal tigers exist in the wild. That is "existence value.".

Utilitarian

Refers to a school of philosophy based on the ideas of Jeremy Bentham (1748-1832). The main principle involved was that private morality and government policy should be based on the concept of "general utility,"-the greatest good for the greatest number.

Utility

A number that represents the level of satisfaction that the consumer derives from a particular market basket.

Utility Possibilities Curve

A curve showing the maximum utility that one person can achieve, given the utility achieved by another person.

V

Value Added Tax (VAT)
A value added tax (VAT) is a form of consumption tax. From the perspective of the buyer, it is a tax on the purchase price. From that of the seller, it is a tax only on the value added to a product, material, or service, from an accounting point of view, by this stage of its manufacture or distribution. The manufacturer remits to the government the difference between these two amounts, and retains the rest for themselves to offset the taxes they had previously paid on the inputs. The value added to a product by or with a business is the sale price charged to its customer, minus the cost of materials and other taxable inputs. A VAT is like a sales tax in that ultimately only the end consumer is taxed. It differs from the sales tax in that, with the latter, the tax is collected and remitted to the government only once, at the point of purchase by the end consumer. With the VAT, collections, remittances to the government, and credits for taxes already paid occur each time a business in the supply chain purchases products.

Value Of Information
The increase in economic well being that can be achieved by taking advantage of new information that changes the degree of uncertainty (and perhaps eliminates uncertainty altogether). For risk-neutral decision makers, it is the difference in the expected monetary outcome that can be achieved with and without using the information. For risk-averse decision makers, it is the difference in the risk premiums that they would pay to eliminate uncertainty with and without using the information. In either case, it is the maximum amount that people would pay to obtain the new information.

Value Of Marginal Product
The marginal product of an input (that is, the extra output resulting from an extra unit of the input) multiplied by the product's price.

Variable Cost
Costs of a production process that increase or decrease along with changes in level of production, as opposed to fixed costs.

Variable Input
A resource used in the production process whose quantity can be changed during the particular period under consideration.

Variance
A measure of spread in the distribution of a random variable.

VAT
A form of indirect sales tax paid on products and services at each stage of

production or distribution, based on the value added at that stage and included in the cost to the ultimate customer.

Vehicle Bias

Difference in actual willingness to pay and willingness to pay revealed in a survey arising from the choice of a payment instrument for a survey. Vehicles include changes in local taxes, entrance fees, surcharges on bills, higher prices, etc.

Voluntary Export Restraint

Identical to an import quota except that the foreign market agrees voluntarily to limit exports from its county to a market.

Von Neumann-Morgenstern Utility Function

A function showing the utility that a decision maker attaches to each possible outcome of a gamble; it shows the decision maker's preferences with regard to risk.

W

Wage Labour

Wage labour (or wage labour) is the socioeconomic relationship between a worker and an employer, where the worker sells their labour under a formal or informal employment contract. These transactions usually occur in a labour market where wages are market determined. In exchange for the wages paid, the work product generally becomes the undifferentiated property of the employer, except for special cases such as the vesting of intellectual property patents in the United States where patent rights are usually vested in the original personal inventor. A wage labourer is a person whose primary means of income is from the selling of his or her labour in this way.

Wages

The general term applied to the earnings of the factor of production, labour.

Wants

The apparently limitless desires or wishes people have for particular goods or services.

Waste

When the relative value of a good is different from that goods marginal cost of production, waste occurs. Goods or resources are wasted when they are allocated to uses which are not the most valuable.

Wealth

The value of the existing stock of goods; those goods may be tangible or intangible.

Weighted Least Squares (WIS) Estimator

An estimator used to adjust for a known form of heteroskedasticity, where each squared residual is weighted by the inverse of the (estimated) variance of the error.

Wholesale Price Index

A measure of changes in the prices of goods at the wholesale level, particularly those goods sold between businesses.

Willingness To Accept (WTA)

Minimum amount of money one would accept to forgo some good or to bear some harm.

Willingness To Pay (WTP)

Maximum amount of money one would give up to buy some good.

Winner's Curse

If a number of bids are made for a particular piece of land (or other good or asset) and if the bidders' estimates of the land's value are approximately correct, on average, the highest bidder is likely to pay more for the land than it is worth if each bidder bids what he or she thinks the land is worth.

Work

Employment of people in jobs to make goods or services.

Working Poor

Workers earning inadequate income as judged by government-established standards of poverty.

World Bank

An international financial institution owned by its 181 member countries and based in Washington, D.C. Its main objective is to provide development funds to the Third World nations in the form of interest-bearing loans and technical assistance. The World Bank operates with borrowed funds.

WTO

The World Trade Organization is a global international organization dealing with the rules of trade between nations. It was set up in 1995 at the conclusion of GATT negotiations for administering multilateral trade negotiations.

X

X-Inefficiency

X-inefficiency is the difference between efficient behaviour of firms assumed or implied by economic theory and their observed behaviour in practice. It occurs when technical-efficiency is not being achieved due to a lack of competitive pressure. The concepts of X-inefficiency were introduced by Harvey Leibenstein. Economic theory assumes that the management of firms act to maximize economic profits -- which is accomplished by adjusting the inputs used or the output produced. In perfect competition, the free entry and exit of firms tends toward firms producing at the point where price equals long run average costs and long run average costs are minimized. Thus firms earn zero economic profits and consumers pay a price equal to the marginal cost of producing the good. This result defines economic efficiency or, more precisely, allocative economic efficiency.

Y

Year Dummy Variables

For data sets with a time series component, dummy (binary) variables equal to one in the relevant year and zero in all other years.

Youth Dependency Ratio

The proportion of young people under age 15 to the working population aged 16-64 in a country.

Z

Zero Based Budgeting (ZBB)

The practice of justifying the utility in cost benefit terms of each government expenditure on projects. The ZBB technique involves a critical review of every scheme before a budgetary provision is made in its favour. If ZBB is properly implemented it could help to reverse the trend of large deficits on the revenue account of the Union Government.

Zero Conditional Mean Assumption

A key assumption used in multiple regression analysis which states that, given any values of the explanatory variables, the expected value of the error equals zero.

APPENDIX – I
ECONOMIC SURVEY 2011-12

Categories and components	Units	2006-07	2007-08	2008-09	2009-10	2011-12	2010-112
1 GDP and Related Indicators							
GDP (current market prices)	₹crore	4294706	4987090	5630063	6457352[c]	7674148[d-c]	8912178AE
Growth Rate	%	16.3	16.1	12.9	14.7	18.8	16.1
GDP (factor cost 2004-05 prices)	₹ crore	3564364	3896636	4158676	4507637[c]	4885954[d-c]	5222027AE
Growth Rate Savings Rate Capital	%	9.6	9.3	6.7	8.4	8.4	6.9
Formation (rate) Per Capita Net	% of GDP	34.6	36.8	32.0	33.8	32.3	na
National Income	% of GDP	35.7	38.1	34.3	36.6	35.1	na
(factor cost at current prices)	₹	31206	35825	40775	46117	53331	60972
2 Production							
Foodgrains	Mn tonnes	217.3	230.8	234.5	218.1	244.8	250.4
Index of Industrial Production[b] (growth)	Per cent	12.9	15.5	2.5	5.3	8.2	3.6[c]
Electricity Generation (growth)	Per cent	7.3	6.3	2.7	6.1	5.5	9.4[c]
3 Prices							
Inflation (WPI) (52-week average)	%change	6.6	4.7	8.1	3.8	9.6	9.1[d]
Inflation CPI (IW) (average)	%change	6.7	6.2	9.1	12.4	10.4	8.4[d]
4 External Sector							
Export Growth (US$)	%change	22.6	29.0	13.6	-3.5	40.5	23.5[f]
Import Growth (US$)	%change	24.5	35.5	20.7	-5.0	28.2	29.4[f]
Current Account Balance (CAB)/GDP	Per cent	-1.0	-1.3	-2.3	-2.8	-2.7	-3.6[e]
Foreign Exchange Reserves	US$ Bn.	199.2	309.7	252.0	279.1	304.8	292.8[f]
Average Exchange Rate	?/US$	45.25	40.26	45.99	47.44	45.56	47.70g
5 Money and Credit							
Broad Money (M3) (annual) Scheduled	%change	21.3	21.4	19.3	16.8	16.0	14.4[h]
Commercial Bank Credit (growth)	%change	28.1	22.3	17.5	16.9	21.5	16.4[h]
6 Fiscal Indicators (Centre)							
Gross Fiscal Deficit	% of GDP	3.3	2.5	6.0	6.5	4.8[i]	4.6j
Revenue Deficit	% of GDP	1.9	1.1	4.5	5.2	3.2[i]	3.4j
Primary Deficit	% of GDP	-0.2	-0.9	2.6	3.2	1.8[i]	1.6j
7 Population	Million	1122	1138	1154	1170	1210[k]	na

APPENDIX – II

RATE OF GROWTH OF GDP AT FACTOR COST AT 2004-2005 PRICES

Table 1.1 : Rate of Growth of GDP at Factor Cost at 2004-2005 Prices (per cent)

	2005-06	2006-07	2007-08	2008-09	2009-10[PE]	2010-11[QE]	2011-12[AE]
Agriculture, forestry & fishing	5.1	4.2	5.8	0.1	1.0	7.0	2.5
Mining & quarrying	1.3	7.5	3.7	2.1	6.3	5.0	-2.2
Manufacturing	10.1	14.3	10.3	4.3	9.7	7.6	3.9
Electricity, gas & water supply	7.1	9.3	8.3	4.6	6.3	3.0	8.3
Construction	12.8	10.3	10.8	5.3	7.0	8.0	4.8
Trade, hotels, transport & communication	12.1	11.7	10.7	7.6	10.3	11.1	11.2
Financing, insurance, real estate & business services	12.6	14.0	12.0	12.0	9.4	10.4	9.1
Community, social & personal services	7.1	2.8	6.9	12.5	12.0	4.5	5.9
GDP at factor cost	**9.5**	**9.6**	**9.3**	**6.7**	**8.4**	**8.4**	**6.9**

Source : CSO.
Notes: PE : Provisional Estimate, QE: Quick Estimate,   AE: Advance Estimate.

APPENDIX – III
ENERGY GENERATED (GROSS)

	Utilities				Non-	Total
Year	Hydro	Thermal+Res*	Nuclear	Total	Utilities	(5)+(6)
1	2	3	4	5	6	7
1950-51[a]	2.5	2.6		5	1.5	6.6
1960-61	7.8	9.1		1	3.2	20.1
1970-71	25.2	28.2	2.4	5	5.4	61.2
1977-78	38.00	51.1	2.3	9	7.6	99.0
1978-79	47.1	52.6	2.8	1	7.6	110.1
1979-80	45.5	56.3	2.9	1	8.2	112.9
1980-81	56.5	61.3	3	1	8.4	129.2
1981-82	49.6	69.5	3	1	9	131.1
1982-83	48.4	79.9	2	1	10	140.3
1983-84	50.0	86.7	3.5	1	10.	151.0
1984-85	53.9	98.8	4.1	1	12.	169.1
1985-86	51.0	114.4	5	1	13	183.4
1986-87	53.8	128.9	5	1	13.	201.3
1987-88	47.5	149.6	5	2	16.	219.0
1988-89	57.9	157.7	5.8	2	19.	241.3
1989-90	62.1	178.7	4.6	2	23	268.4
1990-91	71.7	186.5	6.1	2	25.	289.4
1991-92	72.8	208.7	5.5	2	28.	315.6
1992-93	69.9	224.8	6.7	3	31.	332.7
1993-94	70.4	248.2	5.4	3	32.	356.3
1994-95	82.7	262.1	5.6	3	35.	385.5
1995-96	72.6	299.3	8.0	3	38.	418.1
1996-97	68.9	317.9	9.1	3	40.	436.7
1997-98	74.6	337.0	10.1	4	44.	465.8
1998-99	82.9	353.7	11.9	4	48.	496.9
1999-00	80.6	386.8	13.3	4	51.	532.2
2000-01	74.5	408.1	16.9	4	55.	554.5
2001-02	73.5	424.4	19.5	5	61.	579.1
2002-03	64.0	449.3	19.4	5	63.	596.5
2003-04	75.2	472.1	17.8	5	68.	633.3
2004-05	84.6	492.8	17.0	5	71.	665.8
2005-06	101.5	506.0	17.3	6	73.	697.4
2006-07	113.5	538.4	18.8	6	81.	752.5
2007-08	120.4	585.3	16.9	7	90.	813.1
2008-09[a]	110.1	616.2	14.9	7	99.	840.9
2009-10	104.1	677.1	18.6	7	10	906.0
2010-11P	114.2	704.3	26.3	8	11	959.0

Source: Ministry of Power.
p Provisional a Calendar year *Res: Renewable Energy Sources includes Small Hydro Projects, Wind Power, Biomass Power, Biomass Gasifier, Urban & Industrial Waste & Solar Power.

(Bilion KwH)

APPENDIX – IV
PATTERN OF ELECTRICITY
CONSUMPATION (UTILITIES)

Year	Domestic	Commercial	Industry	Traction	Agriculture	Others
1	2	3	4	5	6	7
1950-51	12.6	7.5	62.6	7.4	3.9	6.0
1960-61	10.7	6.1	69.4	3.3	6.0	4.5
1970-71	8.8	5.9	67.6	3.2	10.2	4.3
1980-81	11.2	5.7	58.4	2.7	17.6	4.4
1982-83	12.7	6.1	55.4	2.8	18.6	4.4
1983-84	12.9	6.4	55.8	2.6	17.8	4.5
1984-85	13.6	6.1	55.2	2.5	18.4	4.2
1985-86	14.0	5.9	54.5	2.5	19.1	4.0
1986-87	14.2	5.7	51.7	2.4	21.7	4.3
1987-88	15.2	6.1	47.5	2.5	24.2	4.5
1988-89	15.5	6.2	47.1	2.3	24.3	4.6
1989-90	16.9	5.4	46	2.3	25.1	4.3
1990-91	16.8	5.9	44.2	2.2	26.4	4.5
1991-92	17.3	5.8	42.0	2.2	28.2	4.5
1992-93	18.0	5.7	40.9	2.3	28.7	4.4
1993-94	18.2	5.9	39.6	2.3	29.7	4.3
1994-95	18.5	6.1	38.6	2.3	30.5	4.0
1995-96	18.7	6.1	37.8	2.3	30.9	4.2
1996-97	19.7	6.2	37.2	2.4	30.0	4.5
1997-98	20.3	6.5	35.4	2.3	30.8	4.7
1998-99	21.0	6.4	33.9	2.4	31.4	4.9
1999-00	22.2	6.3	34.8	2.6	29.2	4.9
2000-01	23.9	7.1	34.0	2.6	26.8	5.6
2001-02	24.7	7.5	33.3	2.5	25.3	6.7
2002-03	24.6	7.5	33.9	2.6	24.9	6.5
2003-04	24.9	7.8	34.5	2.6	24.1	6.1
2004-05	24.8	8.1	35.6	2.5	22.9	6.1
2005-06	24.3	8.7	36.8	2.4	21.9	5.9
2006-07	24.4	8.8	37.6	2.4	21.7	5.1
2007-08	24.0	9.2	37.5	2.2	20.6	6.5
2008-09	24.7	10.2	37.1	2.2	20.4	5.4
2009-10	24.9	10.4	36.7	2.2	21.0	4.8

Source : Ministry of Power/Central Electricity Authority

APPENDIX – V
OPERATIONS OF INDIAN RAILWAYS

OPERATIONS OF INDIAN RAILWAYS

	1950-51	1960-61	1970-71	1980-81	1990-91	2000-01	2006-07	2007-08	2008-09	2009-10	2010-11[p]
1	2	3	4	5	6	7	8	9	10	11	12
1. Route Kilometres (000's)											
Electrified	0.4	0.8	3.7	5.4	10.0	14.9	17.8	18.3	18.6	18.9	19.6
Total	53.6	56.2	59.8	61.2	62.4	63.0	63.3	63.3	64.0	64.0	64.4
2. Originating traffic (million tonnes)											
Revenue Earning	73.2	119.8	167.9	195.9	318.4	473.5	727.8[a]	793.9[a]	833.4[a]	887.8[a]	921.7[a]
Total Traffic	93.0	156.2	196.5	220.0	341.4	504.2	744.6[a]	804.1[a]	836.6[a]	892.2[a]	926.4[a]
3. Goods carried (billion tonne km.)											
Revenue Earning	37.6	72.3	110.7	147.7	235.8	312.4	481.0[a]	521.4[a]	551.4[a]	600.6[a]	625.7[a]
Total Traffic	44.1	87.7	127.4	158.5	242.7	315.5	483.4[a]	523.2[a]	552.0[a]	601.3[a]	626.5[a]
4. Earnings from goods carried (₹ crore)	139.3	280.5	600.7	1550.9	8247.0	23045.4	41073.2[a]	46425.5[a]	51749.3[a]	56937.3[a]	60687.1[a]
5. Average Lead all goods traffic (km)	470.0	561.0	648.0	720.0	711.0	626.0	649.0	651.0	660.0	674.0	676.0
6. Average rate/tonne km. (paise)	3.2	3.9	5.4	10.5	35.0	73.8	85.4	89.0	93.8	94.8	97.0
7. Passengers Originating (million)[b]	1284.0	1594.0	2431.0	3613.0	3858.0	4833.0	6219.0	6524.0	6920.4	7245.8	7651.1
8. Passengers kilometers (billion)	66.5	111	118.1	208.6	295.6	457.0	695.0	770.0	838.0	903.5	978.5
9. Passengers Earnings (₹ crore)	98.2	131.6	295.5	827.5	3144.7	10515.1[c]	17224.6[c]	19844.2[c]	21931.32[c]	23488.2[c]	25792.6[c]
10. Average lead: passenger traffic (km)	51.8	48.7	48.6	57.7	76.6	94.6	111.7	118.0	121.1	124.7	127.9
11. Average rate per passenger-kilometre (paise)	1.5	1.7	2.5	4.0	10.6	22.9	24.7	25.7	26.1	25.9	26.3

Source : Ministry of Railways
[p] Provisional [a] Excluding Konkan Railways Corporation Limited loading. [b] Excluding Metro Kolkata. [c] Includes Metro Railway/Kolkata's earnings.

APPENDIX – VI
INDEX NUMBERS OF AGRICULTURAL PRODUCTION

(Base : Triennium ending 1981-82 = 100)

1	eight	1970-71	1980-81	1990-91	2000-01	2005-06	2006-07	2007-08	2008-09	2009-10	2010-11[a]
	2	3	4	5	6	7	8	9	10	11	12
A. Foodgrains	62.9	87.9	104.9	143.7	158.4	169.2	175.9	186.8	189.8	176.5	195.5
(a) Cereals	55.0	84.1	105.0	144.2	165.5	174.7	181.2	192.7	196.2	181.5	199.3
Rice	29.7	84.4	107.8	149.4	170.9	184.6	187.7	194.4	199.4	179.1	191.7
Wheat	14.5	67.7	103.2	156.6	198.0	197.0	215.4	223.2	229.2	229.6	244.1
Coarse Cereals	10.8	105.4	99.8	113.1	107.2	117.7	117.3	140.9	138.4	116.0	146.0
(b) Pulses	7.9	113.6	104.1	140.5	109.3	131.1	139.1	144.6	142.7	143.7	177.3
Gram	3.1	126.3	105.4	130.2	93.7	135.6	154.0	139.8	171.7	181.8	200.5
B. Non-foodgrains	37.1	82.6	97.1	156.3	178.2	230.3	242.9	247.3	223.0	226.2	256.3
(a) Oilseeds Total[b]	12.6	97.1	95.1	179.5	176.5	262.9	238.7	266.1	249.8	243.5	274.6
Groundnut	5.6	101.8	83.4	125.3	106.8	133.3	81.1	153.1	119.5	90.5	125.7
Rapeseed and Mustard	2.4	97.2	113.0	256.3	205.2	398.5	364.5	285.9	352.9	323.8	375.8
(b) Fibres	5.1	65.6	94.2	128.2	126.6	229.5	277.4	303.4	267.3	293.4	360.2
Cotton	4.4	63.4	93.2	130.9	126.6	246.0	300.9	344.1	296.2	319.4	444.4
Jute	0.6	76.5	100.8	122.6	144.2	154.3	159.7	158.2	149.1	173.8	154.7
Mesta	0.1	77.3	96.7	76.7	72.5	50.9	55.9	58.0	42.8	34.4	34.4
(c) Plantation Crops	2.3	73.2	76.0	144.9	208.8	236.3	243.3	236.1	240.7	240.0	241.1
Tea	1.5	74.7	101.6	132.3	151.0	168.7	175.1	168.4	168.4	168.4	168.4
Coffee	0.4	79.0	85.1	121.7	216.8	200.8	186.2	188.5	188.8	208.4	215.2
Rubber	0.4	60.8	101.1	217.2	416.1	529.8	563.0	544.7	570.6	548.8	548.8
(d) Others											
Sugarcane	8.1	81.2	98.8	154.3	189.4	179.9	227.5	222.8	182.4	187.1	217.1
Tobacco	1.1	75.5	100.2	115.8	71.8	115.0	108.2	102.7	129.9	155.3	155.3
Potato	2.1	50.2	103.9	163.3	241.5	256.7	238.2	305.8	369.3	392.8	392.8
C. ALL COMMODITIES	100.0	85.9	102.1	148.4	165.7	191.9	200.7	207.1	194.1	191.4	215.3

Source : Directorate of Economics and Statistics, Department of Agriculture and Cooperation.
[a] On the basis of Fourth Advance Estimates as on 19.07.2011.
[b] Includes groundnut, rapeseed & mustard, sesamum, linseed, nigerseed, castorseed, safflower, sunflower and soyabean.

APPENDIX – VII
OPERATIONS OF ROAD TRANSPORT

1	2	3	4	5	6	7	8	9	10	11	12
	Unit	1950-51	1960-61	1970-71	1980-81	1990-91	2000-01	2006-07	2007-08	2008-09	2009-10
1. Length of roads	(Thousand km)										
Total		399.9	524.5	914.9	1485.4	2331.1	3373.5	4016.4	4109.6	na	na
Surfaced		157.0	263.0	398.0	684.0	1091.0	1601.7	1944.8	2036.1	na	na
2. Length of national highways	(Thousand km)										
Total		19.8	23.8	23.8	31.7	33.7	57.7	66.6	66.8	na	na
Surfaced		na	21.0	23.3	31.5	33.4	57.7	66.6	66.8	na	na
3. Length of state highways	(Thousand km)										
Total		na	na	56.8	94.4	127.3	132.1	152.2	154.5	na	na
Surfaced		na	na	51.7	90.3	124.8	129.9	150.7	152.7	na	na
4. Number of registered vehicles (Thousand)											
All vehicles		306.0	665.0	1865.0	5391.0	21374.0	54991.0	96707	105353	114951	na
Goods vehicles		82.0	168.0	343.0	554.0	1356.0	2948.0	5119	5601	6041	na
Buses		34.0	57.0	94.0	162.0	331.0	634.0	1350	1427	1486	na
5. Revenue from road transport (₹ crore)											
Central		34.8	111.7	451.8	930.9	4596.0	23861.0	54580.0	56758.2	53098.0	59345.3
States		12.6	55.2	231.4	750.4	3259.6	12901.7	21770.0	24025.8	34241.0	37733.5

Source : Department of Road Transport & Highways.
Includes roads constructed under the Pradhan Mantri Gram SadakYojana (PMGSY) since December 2000 and erstwhile Jawahar Rozgar Yojana (JRY) of the 1990s.
na: Not Available.

Sources:
National Highways - Roads Wing, Ministry of Road Transport & Highways
State Highways - State Public Works Departments
Registered Vehicles - Office of the State Transport Commissioners
Revenue from Road Transport (Central) - Directorate of Data Management, Central Excise and Customs.
Revenue from Road Transport (States) - State Finances- A Study of Budgets 2007-08 by RBI and its earlier issues.

APPENDIX – VIII
GROWTH OF CIVIL AVIATION

	Unit	1960-61	1970-71	1980-81	1990-91	1999-00	2004-05	2005-06	2006-07	2007-08	2008-09	2009-2010	2010-11
1	2	3	4	5	6	7	8	9	10	11	12	13	14
1. Total fleet strength													
(i) Air India		13	10	17	24	26	36	34	36				
(ii) Indian Airlines		88	73	49	56	53	61	64	70				
(iii) National Aviation Company of India Limited										122	108	113	104
2. Revenue tonne-Kilometers	(₹ crore)												
(i) Air India		7.56	27.52	98.01	138.10	145.65	221.80	236.40	221.96				
(ii) Indian Airlines		10.0	20.00	40.03	69.92	74.03	101.73	114.09	23.63				
(iii) National Aviation Company of India Limited										372.90	328.40	353.30	367.70
3. Number of passengers carried	(Lakh)												
(i) Air India		1.25	4.87	14.18	21.61	33.50	44.40	44.40	43.00				
(ii) Indian Airlines		7.90	21.30	54.29	78.66	59.30	71.32	78.61	85.70				
(iii) National Aviation Company of India Limited										133.20	117.80	117.50	127.80
4. Passengers handled at	(Lakh)												
AAI Airports		na	na	107.38	177.23	390.35	592.84	733.42	938.4	637.05	442.54	508.71	596.43
Joint Venture Int'l Airports									25.63	531.81	646.16	728.84	837.87
Total at Indian Airports									964.03	1168.86	1088.7	1237.55	1434.3
5. Cargo handled at	(Thousand tonnes)												
AAI Airports		na	na	178.70	377.33	797.41	1278.47	1397.30	1529.52	723.46	561.42	592.95	726.52
Joint Venture Int'l Airports									21.39	991.52	1140.57	1366.76	1621.92
Total at Indian Airports										1714.98	1701.99	1959.71	2348.44

APPENDIX – IX
COMMODITY BALANCE OF PETROLEUM AND PETROLEUM PRODUCTS

Item	1950-51[a]	1960-61[a]	1970-71[a]	1980-81	1990-91	2000-01	2006-07	2007-08	2008-09	2009-2010	2010-11	2011-12 (Apr.-Nov.)
1	2	3	4	5	6	7	8	9	10	11	12	13
I. Crude Oil												
1. Refinery throughput	0.3	6.6	18.4	25.8	51.8	103.4	146.6	156.1	160.8	192.8	206.2	139.9
2. Domestic production	0.3	0.5	6.8	10.5	32.2	32.4	34.0	34.1	33.5	33.7	37.7	25.5
(a) On-shore	0.3	0.5	6.8	5.5	11.8	11.8	11.3	11.2	11.3	11.8	16.4	11.9
(b) Off-shore	:	:	:	5.0	20.4	20.6	22.7	22.9	22.2	21.9	21.3	13.6
3. Imports	na	6.0	11.7	16.2	20.7	74.1	111.5	121.7	132.8	159.0	163.6	112.1
4. Exports	:	:	:	:	:	:	:	:	:	:	:	:
5. Net imports (3-4)	na	6.0	11.7	16.2	20.7	74.1	111.5	121.7	132.8	159.0	163.6	112.1
II. Petroleum Products												
1. Domestic consumption [b]	3.3	7.7	17.9	30.9	55.0	100.1	120.7	128.9	133.4	138.2	141.8	96.6
of which												
(a) Naphtha	:	:	0.9	2.3	3.4	11.7	13.9	13.3	13.9	10.2	10.7	7.7
(b) Kerosene	:	2.0	3.3	4.2	8.4	11.3	9.5	9.4	9.3	9.3	8.9	5.5
(c) High speed diesel oil	0.9	1.2	3.8	10.3	21.1	37.9	42.9	47.7	51.7	56.3	60.0	42.0
(d) Fuel oils	0.2	1.7	4.7	7.5	9.0	12.7	12.6	12.7	12.4	11.6	10.9	6.1
2. Domestic production [c]	0.2	5.7	17.1	24.1	48.6	95.6	135.3	144.9	150.5	179.8	190.4	130.2
of which												
(a) Naphtha	na	:	1.2	2.1	4.9	9.9	16.7	16.4	14.8	17.1	17.5	13.3
(b) Kerosene	na	0.9	2.9	2.4	5.5	8.7	8.5	7.8	8.2	8.5	7.7	4.9
(c) High speed diesel oil	na	1.1	3.8	7.4	17.2	39.1	53.5	58.4	62.9	73.3	78.1	54.0
(d) Fuel oils	na	1.6	4.1	6.1	9.4	11.4	15.7	15.8	17.7	18.3	20.1	13.3
3. Imports	3.1	2.5	1.1	7.3	8.7	9.3	17.7	22.5	18.5	51.0	12.0	10.0
4. Exports	na	na	0.3	:	2.7	8.4	33.6	40.8	38.9	46.0	59.0	40.6
5. Net Imports (3-4)	na	na	0.8	7.3	6.0	0.9	-15.9	-18.3	-20.4	-36.3	-47.0	-30.6

APPENDIX – X
INDEX OF INDUSTRIAL PRODUCTION

Industry Group	Industry	Weight	2005-06	2006-07	2007-08	2008-09	2009-10	2010-11
1	2	3	4	5	6	7	8	9
	General Index	100.00	108.6	122.6	141.7	145.2	152.9	165.5
10	Mining	14.16	102.3	107.5	112.5	115.4	124.5	131.0
15-36	Manufacturing	75.53	110.3	126.8	150.1	153.8	161.3	175.7
15	Food products and beverages	7.28	113.2	131.2	147.5	135.4	133.5	142.9
16	Tobacco products	1.57	101.0	102.9	98.4	102.7	102.0	104.1
17	Textiles	6.16	108.3	116.8	124.6	120.1	127.4	135.9
18	Wearing apparel; dressing and dyeing of fur	2.78	114.1	137.2	149.9	134.6	137.1	142.2
19	Luggage, handbags, saddlery, harness & footwear; tanning and dressing of leather products	0.58	90.9	104.0	110.0	104.4	105.8	114.3
20	Wood and products of wood & cork except furniture; articles of straw & plating materials	1.05	106.8	126.0	148.0	155.3	160.1	156.5
21	Paper and paper products	1.00	106.3	111.0	112.6	118.0	121.1	131.4
22	Publishing, printing & reproduction of recorded media	1.08	113.7	122.8	140.2	142.4	133.8	148.8
23	Coke, refined petroleum products & nuclear fuel	6.72	100.6	112.6	119.6	123.4	121.8	121.5
24	Chemicals and chemical products	10.06	101.0	110.4	118.4	115.0	120.7	123.1
25	Rubber and plastics products	2.02	112.3	119.6	135.7	142.6	167.4	185.2
26	Other non-metallic mineral products	4.31	107.8	119.5	130.6	134.9	145.4	151.4
27	Basic metals	11.34	115.5	132.6	156.3	159.0	162.4	176.7
28	Fabricated metal products, except machinery & equipment	3.08	111.1	133.3	143.8	144.0	158.6	182.8
29	Machinery and equipment n.e.c.	3.76	126.1	150.9	185.0	171.0	198.0	256.3
30	Office, accounting & computing machinery	0.31	145.3	155.5	164.8	148.8	154.4	146.3
31	Electrical machinery & apparatus n.e.c.	1.98	116.8	131.6	373.0	530.8	459.2	472.1
32	Radio, TV and communication equipment & apparatus	0.99	122.7	312.8	604.2	726.7	809.1	911.5
33	Medical, precision & optical instruments, watches and clocks	0.57	95.4	104.8	111.4	119.8	100.9	107.8
34	Motor vehicles, trailers & semi-trailers	4.06	110.1	138.0	151.2	138.0	179.1	233.3
35	Other transport equipment	1.82	115.3	132.9	129.0	134.0	171.1	210.7
36	Furniture; manufacturing n.e.c.	3.00	116.2	111.7	132.7	142.5	152.7	141.2
40	Electricity	10.32	105.2	112.8	120.0	123.3	130.8	138.0

APPENDIX – XI

GROSS CAPITAL FORMATION FROM BUDGETARY RESOUCES OF THE CENTRAL GOVERNMENT

	Gross capital formation by the Central Government				Gross financial assistance for capital formation to				Total (5+9)
	Fixed assets	Works stores	Increase in stocks of foodgrains & fertilisers	Total (2+3+4)	State govern-ments	Non-departmental commercial undertakings[b]	Others[a]	Total (6+7+8)	
1	2	3	4	5	6	7	8	9	10
First Plan (1951-52 to 1955-56)	594	10	9	612	816	81	96	993	1605
Second Plan (1956-57 to 1960-61)	1362	8	74	1445	1373	932	155	2460	3905
Third Plan (1961-62 to 1965-66)	2355	100	-10	2445	2837	1659	210	4707	7152
Annual Plans (1966-67 to 1968-69)	1411	12	-180	1243	2127	1594	164	3884	5128
Fourth Plan (1969-70 to 1973-74)	2858	104	7	2969	4570	2751	621	7942	10911
Fifth Plan(1974-75 to 1978-79)	5222	68	661	5951	9669	9381	921	19980	25932
Sixth Plan (1980-81 to 1984-85)	14148	675	na	14823	25693	21289	2663	49645	64468
Seventh Plan (1985-86 to 1989-90)	30729	888	na	31616	61469	31643	8829	101941	133557
Eighth Plan (1992-93 to 1996-97)	74043	-443	na	73599	130780	26950	21796	179526	253125
Ninth Plan (1997-98 to 2001-02)	95934	4634	na	100566	143451	43504	36547	223502	324070
Tenth Plan (2002-03 to 2006-07)	138379	5648	na	144027	180157	26055	74600	280813	424839
Eleventh Plan (2007-08 to 2011-12)	295535	9958	na	305493	307056	110552	304369	721975	1027468
1950-51	80	10	-9	80	41	5	2	49	129
1955-56	177	5	-30	153	275	22	33	331	483
1960-61	302	-38	44	307	319	211	25	555	862
1965-66	549	1	-30	520	739	493	53	1285	1805
1970-71	485	8	26	519	740	531	98	1369	1889
1975-76	950	18	237	1204	1433	1838	187	3459	4663
1976-77	1090	-30	53	1112	1524	2183	172	3879	4991
1977-78	1119	-11	na	1107	2221	2156	203	4580	5688
1978-79	1242	59	na	1301	3302	2105	205	5612	6913
1979-80	1443	84	na	1528	3244	2235	223	5701	7229
1980-81	1751	156	na	1908	3666	3166	273	7105	9012
1981-82	2411	141	na	2552	3928	3881	439	8247	10799
1982-83	2814	71	na	2884	4931	4074	514	9520	12404
1983-84	3219	137	na	3356	5974	4679	694	11346	14702

	Gross capital formation by the Central Government				Gross financial assistance for capital formation to				Total (5+9)
	Fixed assets	Works stores	Increase in stocks of foodgrains & fertilisers	Total (2+3+4)	State governments	Non-departmental commercial undertakings[b]	Others[a]	Total (6+7+8)	Total (5+9)
1	2	3	4	5	6	7	8	9	10
1984-85	3953	171	na	4123	7195	5489	744	13428	17551
1985-86	4452	106	na	4558	10054	6082	784	16920	21477
1986-87	5817	88	na	5905	10800	6523	1091	18415	24320
1987-88	5683	278	na	5961	12723	5667	1419	19810	25770
1988-89	6977	80	na	7056	13956	6317	1648	21921	28977
1989-90	7800	337	na	8137	13935	7054	3887	24876	33013
1990-91	8193	409	na	8602	20009	5541	905	26456	35057
1991-92	9056	203	na	9259	19377	4764	1765	25906	35165
1992-93	11643	232	na	11875	19651	4730	1392	25774	37649
1993-94 c	13106	-341	na	12765	23196	6632	2457	32285	45051
1994-95	14804	-476	na	14328	27416	7191	5265	39872	54200
1995-96	16858	-173	na	16685	27571	4222	6798	38591	55276
1996-97	17632	315	na	17946	32945	4174	5884	43004	60950
1997-98 d	18693	262	na	18955	23578	5849	6433	35860	54815
1998-99	20324	323	na	20647	25613	6401	5147	37160	57807
1999-2000	24983	1092	na	26075	29077	6944	5507	41527	67602
2000-01	20953	1305	na	22258	30653	7297	6752	44702	66959
2001-02	10982	1652	na	12634	34531	17014	12709	64254	76888
2002-03	20963	734	na	21697	37254	4686	13146	55085	76782
2003-04	22828	1169	na	23997	40908	4581	13074	58564	82561
2004-05	26508	888	na	27396	43320	7720	14419	65459	92855
2005-06	33182	1268	na	34450	27206	5304	17797	50307	84757
2006-07	34897	1589	na	36487	31469	3764	16164	51398	87885
2007-08	42381	1270	na	43651	43029	41825	15386	100240	143891
2008-09	50069	1396	na	51465	51697	10298	23477	85472	136937
2009-10	56410	2589	na	58999	53483	9698	62322	125502	184501
2010-11(RE)	66194	2253	na	68447	72724	33058	100594	206376	274823
2011-12(BE)	80481	2450	na	82931	86123	15673	102590	204385	287316

244

APPENDIX – XII
TOTAL EXPENDITURE OF THE CENTRAL GOVERNMENT

| | Final outlays | | | Transfer payments to the rest of the economy | | | Financial investments | Total expen- |
	Government consumption expenditure	Gross capital formation	Total (2+3)	Current	Capital	Total (5+6)	& loans to the rest of the economy (gross)	diture (4+7+8)
1	2	3	4	5	6	7	8	9
1980-81	5174	1908	7082	6912	1302	8214	7200	22495
1981-82	6096	2552	8648	7728	1525	9253	7500	25401
1982-83	7057	2884	9941	9590	1788	11378	9175	30494
1983-84	8130	3356	11486	11436	2337	13773	10729	35988
1984-85	9428	4123	13552	14938	2958	17896	12432	43879
1985-86	11210	4558	15768	18347	3825	22173	15172	53112
1986-87	14665	5905	20570	21243	4408	25651	17803	64023
1987-88	16551	5961	22512	25380	5474	30854	16938	70305
1988-89	18764	7056	25820	31399	5750	37148	18434	81402
1989-90	20784	8137	28920	37877	6835	44712	21417	95049
1990-91	22359	8602	30961	45134	7117	52251	21760	104973
1991-92	24466	9259	33725	51378	8449	59827	19179	112731
1992-93	26865	11875	38739	58518	9092	67610	19578	125927
1993-94[b]	31815	12765	44580	66750	11811	78560	22648	145788
1994-95	34878	14328	49206	76368	13974	90342	27450	166998
1995-96	41881	16685	58566	85304	15263	100566	26101	185233
1996-97	44238	17946	62184	100807	16294	117101	31975	211260
1997-98[c]	53090	18955	72046	111577	17360	128937	23884	224866
1998-99	59920	20647	80567	137811	18671	156282	26907	263755
1999-2000	68831	26075	94906	161549	20482	182031	30572	307509
2000-01	71977	22258	94235	183696	22404	206100	27929	328265
2001-02	77324	12634	89958	201188	28009	229197	41462	360616
2002-03	85389	21697	107086	228501	29406	257907	33886	398879
2003-04	87170	23997	111167	248436	32038	280474	34491	426132
2004-05	105692	27396	133088	259529	36822	296351	34393	463831
2005-06	116305	34450	150755	297267	41681	338948	11380	501083
2006-07	121609	36487	158095	356560	45758	402318	9771	570185
2007-08	131396	43652	175048	408676	53758	462434	51427	688909
2008-09	174345	51464	225809	543347	70287	613634	25087	864530
2009-10	210625	58999	269623	580898	113345	694243	28575	992440
2010-11(RE)	234395	68447	302842	652873	161616	814489	61685	1179016
2011-12(BE)	**248546**	**82931**	**331477**	**673712**	**186890**	**860602**	**41359**	**1233437**

APPENDIX – XIII
FINANCIAL PERFORMANCE OF THE DEPARTMENT OF POSTS

(₹ crore)

	1980-81	1990-91	2000-01	2007-08	2008-09	2009-10	2010-11	2011-12 (BE)
1	2	3	4	5	6	7	8	9
1. Gross receipts	278	840	3298	5495	5862	6267	6962	7518
2. Net working expenses	346	1033	4848	7006	9455	12908	13308	12827
3. Net receipts (1-2)	-68	-193	-1550	-1511	-3593	-6641	-6346	-5310
4. Dividend to general revenues	4	0	0	0	0	0	0	0
5. Surplus(+)/deficit (-) (3-4)	-72	-193	-1550	-1511	-3593	-6641	-6346	-5310

APPENDIX – XIV

EMPLOYMENT IN ORGANISED SECTORS – PUBLIC AND PRIVATE

(Lakh persons as on 31 March)

1	1991	1995	2000	2003	2004	2005	2006	2007	2008	2009	2010
	2	3	4	5	6	7	8	9	10	11	12
PUBLIC SECTOR											
A. By branch											
1 Central Government	34.11	33.95	32.73	31.33	30.27	29.38	28.60	28.00	27.39	26.60	25.52
2 State Governments	71.12	73.55	74.60	73.67	72.22	72.02	73.00	72.09	71.71	72.38	73.53
3 Quasi-Governments	62.22	65.20	63.26	59.01	58.22	57.48	59.09	58.61	57.96	58.44	58.68
4 Local bodies	23.13	21.97	22.55	21.79	21.26	21.18	21.18	21.32	19.68	20.73	20.89
Total	**190.58**	**194.66**	**193.14**	**185.8**	**181.97**	**180.07**	**181.88**	**180.02**	**176.74**	**177.95**	**178.62**
B. By Industry											
1 Agriculture, hunting etc.	5.56	5.39	5.14	5.06	4.93	4.96	4.69	4.75	4.71	4.77	4.78
2 Mining and quarrying	9.99	10.16	9.24	8.47	10.30	10.14	11.46	11.37	11.21	11.12	11.03
3 Manufacturing	18.52	17.56	15.31	12.60	11.89	11.30	10.92	10.87	10.44	10.60	10.66
4 Electricity, gas and water	9.05	9.35	9.46	9.13	8.74	8.60	8.49	8.49	7.96	8.39	8.35
5 Construction	11.49	11.64	10.92	9.48	9.32	9.11	8.94	8.66	8.52	8.45	8.59
6 Wholesale and retail trade	1.50	1.62	1.63	1.82	1.81	1.84	1.82	1.78	1.65	1.74	1.71
7 Transport, storage & communications	30.26	31.06	30.77	29.39	28.15	27.51	26.75	26.37	26.34	26.01	25.29
8 Finance, insurance, real estate etc.	11.94	12.83	12.96	13.77	14.08	14.08	13.90	13.69	13.47	13.56	14.13
9 Community, Social & personal services	92.27	95.04	97.71	96.09	92.76	92.52	91.76	90.90	88.54	90.11	90.51
Total	**190.58**	**194.66**	**193.14**	**185.80**	**181.97**	**180.07**	**178.73**	**176.88**	**172.84**	**174.75**	**175.05**
PRIVATE SECTOR											
1 Argiculture, hunting etc.	8.91	8.94	9.04	8.95	9.17	9.83	10.28	9.50	9.92	8.96	9.23
2 Mining and quarrying	1.00	1.03	0.81	0.66	0.65	0.79	0.95	1.00	1.11	1.15	1.61
3 Manufacturing	44.81	47.06	50.85	47.44	44.89	44.89	45.49	47.50	49.7	51.98	51.84

(Lakh persons as on 31 March)

1	1991	1995	2000	2003	2004	2005	2006	2007	2008	2009	2010
	2	3	4	5	6	7	8	9	10	11	12
4 Electricity, gas and water	0.40	0.40	0.41	0.50	0.47	0.49	0.40	0.50	0.51	0.64	0.64
5 Construction	0.73	0.53	0.57	0.44	0.45	0.49	0.55	0.70	0.69	0.80	0.91
6 Wholesale and retail trade	3.00	3.08	3.30	3.60	3.51	3.75	3.87	4.10	2.72	4.72	5.06
7 Transport, storgage & communications	0.53	0.58	0.70	0.79	0.81	0.85	0.87	1.00	1.04	1.32	1.66
8 Finance, insurance,real estate etc.	2.54	2.93	3.58	4.26	4.58	5.23	6.52	8.80	10.96	13.11	15.52
9 Community, social & personal services	14.85	16.03	17.23	17.56	17.92	18.20	18.78	19.50	21.73	20.23	21.4
Total	76.77	80.59	86.46	84.21	82.46	84.52	87.71	92.40	98.38	102.91	107.87
BY SEX											
PUBLIC SECTOR											
Male	167.10	168.66	164.57	156.75	153.07	150.86	151.85	149.84	146.34	147.04	146.66
Female	23.47	26.00	28.57	29.05	28.90	29.21	30.03	30.18	30.4	30.91	31.96
Total	190.57	194.66	193.14	185.80	181.97	180.07	181.88	180.02	176.74	177.95	178.62
PRIVATE SECTOR											
Male	62.42	64.31	65.80	63.57	62.02	63.57	66.87	69.80	74.03	78.88	81.83
Female	14.34	16.28	20.66	20.64	20.44	20.95	21.18	22.94	24.72	24.98	26.63
Total	76.76	80.59	86.46	84.21	82.46	84.52	88.05	92.74	98.75	103.77	108.46
PUBLIC AND PRIVATE SECTOR											
Male	229.52	232.97	230.37	220.32	215.09	214.42	218.72	219.64	220.37	225.92	228.49
Female	37.81	42.28	49.23	49.68	49.34	50.16	51.21	53.12	55.12	55.80	58.59
Total	267.33	275.25	279.60	270.00	264.43	264.58	269.93	272.76	275.49	281.72	287.08

Source : Ministry of Labour & Employment, Director General of Employment and Training.
Note : 1.Coverage in construction, particularly on private account, is known to be inadequate.
2. Employment in private sector relates to non-agriculture establishments in private sector employing 10 or more persons. Employment in public sector relate to all estalishments irrespective of size.
3. Excludes Sikkim, Arunachal Pradesh, Dadra & Nagar Haveli and Lakshadweep as these are not yet covered under the programme.
4. Due to non-availability of data as per NIC 1998, information in respect of J&K , Manipur, puducherry, Mizoram, Daman & Diu not included in totals.

APPENDIX – XV
TOTAL EXPENDITURE OF THE CENTRAL GOVERNMENT

Year	Employee (in lakh) Excl. casual & Daily rated workers)	Emoluments (₹ crore)	Per capita emoluments (₹)	Increase over 1971-72 in per capita (per cent)	Average index	Increase over 1971-72 (per cent)
1	2	3	4	5	6	7
1989-90	22.36	9742	43665	637.58	855	345.31
1990-91	22.19	10912	49179	730.73	951	395.31
1991-92	21.79	12311	56508	854.52	1079	461.98
1992-93	21.52	13983	64983	997.69	1185	517.10
1993-94	20.70	14913	72043	1116.94	1272	562.50
1994-95	20.62	17015	82517	1293.87	1402	630.21
1995-96	20.52	21931	106876	1705.34	1542	703.13
1996-97	20.08	22219	110662	1769.29	1687	778.65
1997-98	19.52	25385	129582	2088.89	1803	839.06
1998-99	19.00	26254	138179	2234.10	2039	961.98
1999-00	18.06	30402	168339	2743.56	2109	998.44
2000-01	17.40	38223	219672	3610.67	2190	1440.62
2001-02	19.92	38556	193554	3169.49	2284	1089.58
2002-03	18.66	42169	225986	3717.33	2375	1136.98
2003-04	17.62	43919	248481	4097.31	2467	1184.89
2004-05	17.00	48629	286053	4731.97	2561	1236.98
2005-06	16.49	46841	284057	4698.26	2674	1292.71
2006-07	16.14	52586	325869	5404.54	2853	1385.94
2007-08	15.65	64306	410898	6840.84	3030	1478.12
2008-09	15.33	83045	541716	9050.61	3306	1621.88
2009-10	14.90	87792	589210	9852.87	3715	1834.89
2010-11	14.44	96210	666276	11154.66	4103	2036.77

Source : Department of Public Enterprises.

APPENDIX – XVI
List Of Nobel Laureates In Economics

Year	Laureate	Country	Rationale
1969	Ragnar Frisch Jan Tinbergen	Norway Netherlands	"for having developed and applied dynamic models for the analysis of economic processes"
1970	Paul Samuelson	United States	"for the scientific work through which he has developed static and dynamic economic theory and actively contributed to raising the level of analysis in economic science"
1971	Simon Kuznets John Hicks	United States United Kingdom	"for his empirically founded interpretation of economic growth which has led to new and deepened insight into the economic and social structure and process of development"
1972	Kenneth Arrow	United States	"for their pioneering contributions to general economic equilibrium theory and welfare theory"
1973	Wassily Leontief	United States	"for the development of the input-output method and for its application to important economic problems"
1974	Gunnar Myrdal Friedrich Hayek	Sweden United Kingdom/ Austria	"for their pioneering work in the theory of money and economic fluctuations and for their penetrating analysis of the interdependence of economic, social and institutional phenomena."
1975	Leonid Kantorovich Tjalling Koopmans	Soviet Union United States	"for their contributions to the theory of optimum allocation of resources"
1976	Milton Friedman	United States	"for his achievements in the fields of consumption analysis, monetary history and theory and for his demonstration of the complexity of stabilisation policy"

1977	Bertil Ohlin James Meade	Sweden United Kingdom	"for their pathbreaking contribution to the theory of international trade and international capital movements"
1978	Herbert A. Simon Theodore Schultz	United States United States	"for his pioneering research into the decision-making process within economic organizations"
1979	Arthur Lewis	United Kingdom	"for their pioneering research into economic development research with particular consideration of the problems of developing countries."
1980	Lawrence Klein	United States	"for the creation of econometric models and the application to the analysis of economic fluctuations and economic policies"
1981	James Tobin	United States	"for his analysis of financial markets and their relations to expenditure decisions, employment, production and prices"
1982	George Stigler	United States	"for his seminal studies of industrial structures, functioning of markets and causes and effects of public regulation"
1983	Gérard Debreu	France	"for having incorporated new analytical methods into economic theory and for his rigorous reformulation of the theory of general equilibrium"
1984	Richard Stone	United Kingdom	"for having made fundamental contributions to the development of systems of national accounts and hence greatly improved the basis for empirical economic analysis"
1985	Franco Modigliani	Italy	"for his pioneering analyses of saving and of financial markets"
1986	James M. Buchanan	United States	"for his development of the contractual and constitutional bases for the theory of economic and political decision-making"

1987	Robert Solow	United States	"for his contributions to the theory of economic growth"
1988	Maurice Allais	France	"for his pioneering contributions to the theory of markets and efficient utilization of resources"
1989	Trygve Haavelmo	Norway	"for his clarification of the probability theory foundations of econometrics and his analyses of simultaneous economic structures"
1990	Harry Markowitz Merton Miller William Forsyth Sharpe	United States United States United States	"for their pioneering work in the theory of financial economics"
1991	Ronald Coase	United Kingdom	"for his discovery and clarification of the significance of transaction costs and property rights for the institutional structure and functioning of the economy"
1992	Gary Becker	United States	"for having extended the domain of microeconomic analysis to a wide range of human behaviour and interaction, including non-market behaviour"
1993	Robert Fogel Douglass North John Harsanyi	United States United States United States	"for having renewed research in economic history by applying economic theory and quantitative methods in order to explain economic and institutional change"
1994	John Forbes Nash Reinhard Selten	United States Germany	"for their pioneering analysis of equilibria in the theory of non-cooperative games"
1995	Robert Lucas, Jr.	United States	"for having developed and applied the hypothesis of rational expectations, and thereby having transformed macroeconomic analysis and deepened our understanding of economic policy"
1996	James Mirrlees William Vickrey	United Kingdom United States/ Canada	"for their fundamental contributions to the economic theory of incentives under asymmetric information"

1997	Robert C. Merton	United States	"for a new method to determine the value of derivatives"
	Myron Scholes	Canada/United States	
1998	Amartya Sen	India	"for his contributions to welfare economics"
1999	Robert Mundell	Canada	"for his analysis of monetary and fiscal policy under different exchange rate regimes and his analysis of optimum currency areas"
	James Heckman	United States	"for his development of theory and methods for analyzing selective samples"
2000	Daniel McFadden	United States	"for his development of theory and methods for analyzing discrete choice"
2001	George Akerlof	United States	"for their analyses of markets with asymmetric information"
	Michael Spence	United States	
	Joseph E. Stiglitz	United States	
2002	Daniel Kahneman	Israel/United States	"for having integrated insights from psychological research into economic science, especially concerning human judgment and decision-making under uncertainty"
	Vernon L. Smith	United States	"for having established laboratory experiments as a tool in empirical economic analysis, especially in the study of alternative market mechanisms"
2003	Robert F. Engle	United States	"for methods of analyzing economic time series with time-varying volatility (ARCH)"
	Clive Granger	United Kingdom	"for methods of analyzing economic time series with common trends (co-integration)"
	Finn E. Kydland	Norway	
2004	Edward C. Prescott	United States	"for their contributions to dynamic macroeconomics: the time consistency of economic policy and the driving forces behind business cycles."

2005	Robert Aumann	Israel/United States	"for having enhanced our understanding of conflict and cooperation through game-theory analysis"
	Thomas Schelling	United States	
2006	Edmund Phelps	United States	"for his analysis of inter temporal tradeoffs in macroeconomic policy"
	Leonid Hurwicz	Poland/United States	
2007	Eric Maskin	United States	"for having laid the foundations of mechanism design theory"
	Roger Myerson	United States	
2008	Paul Krugman	United States	"for his analysis of trade patterns and location of economic activity"
	Elinor Ostrom	United States	"for his analysis of trade patterns and location of economic activity" "for her analysis of economic governance, especially the commons"
2009	Oliver Williamson	United States	"for his analysis of economic governance, especially the boundaries of the firm"
	Peter A. Diamond	United States	
2010	Dale T. Mortensen	United States	
	Christopher A. Pissarides	Cyprus	"for their analysis of markets with search frictions"
	Thomas J. Sargent	United States	
2011	Christopher A. Sims	United States	"for their empirical research on cause and effect in the macroeconomy"
	Alvin E. Roth	United States	
2012	Lloyd S. Shapley	United States	"for the theory of stable allocations and the practice of market design"